TRIAL BY FIRE

TRIAL BY FIRE

A DEVASTATING TRAGEDY, 100 LIVES LOST, AND A 15-YEAR SEARCH FOR TRUTH

SCOTT JAMES

THOMAS DUNNE BOOKS
NEW YORK

First published in the United States by Thomas Dunne Books, an imprint of St. Martin's
Publishing Group

TRIAL BY FIRE. Copyright © 2020 by Scott James. All rights reserved. Printed in the
United States of America. For information, address St. Martin's Publishing Group,
120 Broadway, New York, NY 10271.

www.thomasdunnebooks.com

Designed by Jonathan Bennett

The Library of Congress Cataloging-in-Publication Data is available upon request.

ISBN 978-1-250-13126-3 (hardcover)
ISBN 978-1-250-13127-0 (ebook)

Our books may be purchased in bulk for promotional, educational, or business use.
Please contact your local bookseller or the Macmillan Corporate and Premium
Sales Department at 1-800-221-7945, extension 5442, or by email at
MacmillanSpecialMarkets@macmillan.com.

First Edition: 2020

10 9 8 7 6 5 4 3 2 1

For Helen and Owen

Paper may burn but words will escape.

—LAWRENCE FERLINGHETTI

AUTHOR'S NOTE

Most of this book is from first-person interviews, conducted over the course of years. For the main subjects I used a multistep process for accuracy. After an initial interview, I would write up a scene told from that person's point of view, then return later with a printed draft to review each word. These additional sessions would often prompt vivid memories and became a key part of my reporting process.

Anything in quotation marks came from these interviews, or was captured on audio or video by other journalists. Other quotes are from official documents, including thousands of pages of transcripts from once-secret grand jury testimony. In rare cases I used quotes from conversations that my subjects remembered others saying with a high degree of certainty, but it is clear on the page that these are recollections from the subject's point of view. If someone was less certain about the exact wording of what was said, I summarized the comment, or used italics. Italics are also used to denote the internal dialog some remembered. No dialog was invented by me, and quotes were not altered or corrected for grammatical purposes.

News coverage of the fire is quoted or referenced if from a credible journalist or reputable news organization. Occasionally I will mention something reported that was journalistically questionable, but in those instances, it is clear that's the point.

Some people depicted in these pages could not be interviewed or given the opportunity to review pages for accuracy. References to how a deceased person acted, felt, or spoke are based on firsthand witness accounts, direct quotes, documents, or photos. I corroborated this information when possible, and if minor details were in dispute, they were omitted.

I have used occasional footnotes for the sake of transparency, such as showing the math that was used to calculate a fact, or to note when I have a personal connection to people or situations. I have several, since the events in these pages represent the worst thing to happen in the place where I grew up.

FEBRUARY 20, 2003, 11:07 P.M.

It takes ninety seconds to sing "The Star-Spangled Banner." Human beings, on average, can hold their breath for up to ninety seconds. A typical person needs ninety seconds to read one page of this book.

Ninety seconds marked the moment between life and death on the night of February 20, 2003, at The Station, a scruffy, low-slung roadhouse nightclub in the old New England mill town of West Warwick, Rhode Island.

Tragedy started with a song.

Shortly after eleven the rock group Jack Russell's Great White took to the club's stage with screeching guitars in the dark. On cue the band's tour manager Daniel Biechele set off four gerbs—giant sparklers set on the floor behind the lead singer, two blasting bolts of sparks to the sides and two in the middle directed up toward the club's low, dark, glittered ceiling. The fireworks lasted seventeen seconds and were meant to evoke the aging metal band's former stadium glory days in the nineties, creating an ethereal glow behind the performers. The audience went wild.

The sparks ignited a small fire on the wall to the left of the stage. Nine seconds later a second trickle of flames appeared on the wall to the right of the stage.

Jeffrey Derderian, a local television news reporter and the club's co-owner, his clean-cut appearance at odds in a sea of rockers, saw the flames from the corner of his eye. As usual, he'd been too busy working the bar to watch the show, so his first thought was that something in the morass of sound equipment had caused an electrical fire. Jeffrey ducked under the counter and darted toward the stage and spotted soundboard operator Paul Vanner with a fire extinguisher in hand, also en route. Jeffrey pointed and barked, "Get up there!" Neither man could. The crowd was too thick, and as a deafening guitar riff raged, frenzied fans jumped up and down with their arms raised in the classic heavy metal tribute, a fist in the air with pinkie and forefinger extended. "Rock on!"

Great White's forty-two-year-old lead singer, Jack Russell, belted out the opening lyrics of "Desert Moon" from the band's 1991 album *Hooked*. His microphone was upcut at first, set too low to be heard over the guitars, but then his voice filled the club, his tenor still powerful a dozen years after the band's prime. "*Let's shake this town, baby, come with me! I need a little loving company!*"

Sixteen seconds after the first flames appeared on the walls, the fire expanded and reached the ceiling.

The crowd in front of the stage kept raving, many believing the growing pyre was theatrics, a planned part of the show. They howled in appreciation. Some patrons in the back of the audience, however, sensed trouble and began to orderly evacuate.

Singer Jack Russell was unaware he was surrounded by danger, so he hit the next lyric, "*Come on, now, I know where we can go!*" Then he noticed the burning wall, stopped singing, and the band quieted. "Wow. That's not good," Russell said, deadpan, and picked up bottled water to toss at the wall to no effect. He'd halted just short of the verse, "*I've got a fire like a heavenly light.*"

Thirty seconds had passed since the first flames appeared.

Two seconds later, like a lit match dropped into a pool of gasoline, the fire surged across the walls and ceiling.

As band members escaped through the stage door exit—forty-one seconds after the fire started—the nightclub's alarm blared, emitting an intense, piercing wail. Emergency strobe lights pulsated around the club. The siren signaled that the blaze was not part of the performance, and there was a sudden shift in the room. Panic. Patrons turned from the stage and raced toward the club's main entrance, the door they had arrived through. Few headed for any of the three other exits. In the melee, the casual camaraderie of fellow concertgoers was replaced by a fight for survival. "Get out of my way!" a man shouted, shoving others aside.

Sixty seconds after the first trickle of flame, the stage was fully engulfed and then disappeared from sight, replaced by choking pitch-black smoke that plunged the club into darkness. A survivor later described the smoke as a "thick, menacing blanket" dropped over everyone's heads.

With too many people trying to escape through one door, the stampede became a pile that made the exit impassable.

Ninety seconds after the fire started, the black haze reached the floor, smothering all inside. The building burst into a raging inferno and the night sky filled with jolts of flames and the sounds of explosions and terrified screams.

In ninety seconds nearly everyone still inside The Station nightclub was dead or dying. It was the deadliest single building fire in modern American history, and the nation's deadliest rock concert. In the United States, where billions have been spent on fire prevention and protection, there should have been time to escape, to be safe.

It would be years before anyone knew what really happened—and who was truly to blame.

EARLIER THAT SAME DAY

CHAPTER 1

"MY GOD, I don't have my cross on," Fred Crisostomi said after he pulled into the parking lot of The Station nightclub with fiancée Gina Russo. He'd patted his burly chest as he often did to touch his three-inch gold crucifix. It wasn't there. Then he remembered taking it off while cleaning up after work. It was probably back in the bedroom.

Fred never went anywhere without wearing that necklace, and he felt incomplete without it. That was silly, of course. It was something he cherished, but he wasn't the type who had fits about little things like jewelry. Smile, laugh, and go with the flow, that's how Freddy saw life. He wasn't going to let the missing cross interrupt their evening. He was excited to see Great White.

"Let's go home and get it," said Gina. The nightclub was only a few minutes' drive from Fred's house and they'd be back in plenty of time.

Fred smiled. Gina always looked out for him, one of the many reasons he loved her so much. She knew how much the cross meant to him, and wouldn't think twice of inconveniencing herself to please him. Great White wasn't one of Gina's favorites, and the only reason they were there was because Freddy was a fan.

The necklace snafu was just the latest in a series of little missteps that evening. It was one of those on again, off again, on again days. Fred was late getting home from work from his painting company for dinner at Gina's place, where her mom had slaved over the stove for most of the day, as she always did on Thursdays for pasta night. Mom, as he'd affectionately come to call her, made the best meatballs. Fred arrived in time to join a snowball fight with Gina's boys Nicholas and Alex, ages six and nine. He felt like a little kid again mixing it up like that, making such a ruckus that one of the neighbors waved and asked him how he was doing.

"What a great day to be alive," Fred told her.

He meant it. He adored Gina's sons, and their two families had quickly bonded. Fred's nine-year-old son Brandon and thirteen-year-old stepdaughter Nicole were both looking forward to everyone going up to New Hampshire that weekend, a preview of what life would be like when Fred and Gina were married and they officially became one big family.

It had been a whirlwind nine and a half months since he first met Gina. She was fresh from a nasty divorce and Fred could tell that she was being careful when she started dating again, not just to protect her sons, but also to guard her heart. Yet from the start the two had instantly clicked.

He owed it all to a local dating website, HipDates.com. Gina would later tell him that she was not impressed with the men she'd met through the site, and she was just about to close her account when she received Fred's message. They chatted through the service's instant messages for two hours, discovering they had so much in common: they loved the same TV shows, movies, music, and bands. They also both detested smoking, and it wasn't always easy to find a fellow nonsmoker in Rhode Island. When they felt the keyboards and typing were getting in the way of their conversation, they broke one of the cardinal rules of meeting strangers online and exchanged numbers to talk by phone. Fred was taken by Gina's voice the first time he heard it, with her familiar Rhode Island accent, a dialect that mixes New York, Boston, and sass. Within minutes of talking they realized they had mutual friends, not surprising in a state so small that it seemed like everyone knew everyone else. Fred had grown up in Silver Lake in Providence, the same neighborhood as Gina's ex-husband. Small world.

Rhode Island was such a tiny state. Fred loved to tell the story of when his parents, Nancy and Carmino, were first dating, and his dad was serving in the Coast Guard. One day he walked by a fellow Coastie's workspace on the base and noticed a picture of Nancy pinned up on the guy's wall.

"Why you got a picture of my girlfriend?" Carmino confronted the man.

"Girlfriend?" the man responded. "That's my sister!"

Inspired by his father's Coast Guard service, Fred went into the Navy right out of high school, and worked as a cook on a ship. The more Gina and Fred spoke on the phone that first night, May 2, 2002, the more it became clear how close their paths had already come to crossing. Fred's sister Crystal worked for Gina's doctor, and Gina had also met Fred's other sister Nancy through a friend. It was even possible that Gina attended a basketball game where Fred had played.

Before getting off the phone they made a plan to meet in person a couple days later, another no-no of the online dating service's rules. They were both grown-ups and it made no sense to move slowly. Fred was thirty-eight, six foot one, and a firm 285 pounds, with a mustache and a thick, salt-and-pepper curly mane some jokingly called "Elvis Hair"—a genuine bear of a man, not some insecure teenager, so he didn't need the guidance of a website to tell him how and when to date a woman.

When he finally met Gina in person he gave her a huge hug, like they'd already grown so close. She was pretty with her short-cropped dark hair and those intense hazel-colored eyes. And although she was somewhat shy and reserved at first, when Fred got her to relax she was actually lively, quick, and funny, and, as a guy who constantly made jokes, he loved that about Gina. In person they had even more chemistry than online or the phone. When he got home from that first date he immediately called his sister Nancy and told her he'd finally met the woman he'd spend the rest of his life with. It was like something out of a movie.

They'd spent nearly every day together since then. Why waste time? Fred had seen people he cherished pass away in the prime of their lives: his dad from a heart attack in his early fifties, and a beloved aunt who was killed when she fell off a horse. Maybe it was because his loved ones had died young, but Fred always needed to be doing something, needed to stay constantly busy. Friends called him the life of the party, but the truth was Fred couldn't sit still. If he wasn't working, he was playing. Similar to some other Italian Americans in Rhode Island, Fred spurned the Red Sox and was a rabid fan of the New York Yankees and took the bus to the Bronx for games several times a season. An avid collector of sports memorabilia, his two-bedroom apartment in a two-story house in Warwick was full of collectibles, including more than thirty boxes of trading cards.

Fred also loved live music, and he and Gina had seen Journey, Rick

James, REO Speedwagon, Alice in Chains, and Tesla. If not by going to a concert or a game, Fred was always looking for ways to have fun with Gina.

Earlier that evening, after the snowball fight with the boys and dinner, Fred and Gina took off to see the new Ray Liotta movie *Narc*, but when they arrived they discovered that the film had already started. Neither wanted to see a movie after missing the beginning, so they went home to Fred's apartment to regroup. There he checked his email and read about the Great White show. Gina wasn't thrilled, and pointed out that they didn't have tickets. They curled up in front of the TV instead, but after flipping through all the stations it became clear there was nothing good to watch.

"Great White?" Fred asked again.

Gina warmed to the idea—as long as they didn't stay out too late—so Fred called the club and was told there was still room. It was around 10 p.m., but other bands were on first, and Great White wouldn't take the stage until 11 p.m.

Fred called his young cousin Rene Valcourt to see if he wanted to join. Fred had given Rene the nickname "Ugly" because the man was so handsome. When he got Rene's voicemail Fred said, "Hey, Ugly. We're going to The Station tonight to see Great White if you want to come meet us. But we're not going to stay long." At ten thirty he and Gina were out the door and headed to the club in her '98 black Pontiac Grand Am.

Eight minutes later they were in the parking lot and Fred fretted about his missing necklace. It was so typically Gina to want to make him happy by going all the way home to get the cross. Fred saw people headed into the club, and with a national act like Great White he and Gina were lucky they found parking. It made no sense to leave and come back for the sake of jewelry.

"No," Fred said. "Let's go see the show."

CHAPTER 2

J ACK AND COKE," the young man ordered, and plunked a wrinkled
ten-dollar bill on the bar.

Jack Daniel's and Coke was probably the most popular cocktail at
The Station, club co-owner Jeffrey Derderian thought as he made the
man's drink, using a freehand pour of whiskey to fill the glass about
halfway, then topping it with soda. They didn't measure liquor with shot
glasses—customers hated that, figuring the precision meant less alcohol.
Most didn't order cocktails anyway. Beer was by far the drink of choice,
Bud, mostly, in longneck bottles.

Jeffrey didn't usually serve drinks, since he had bartenders who were
much better at it, and he'd have up to five working for a big show. It was
all hands tonight with Great White about to perform, the metal "hair
band" famous for its hit "Once Bitten, Twice Shy." That song came out in
1989, and the group had long ago lost its plumes of rocker hair and most
of its original members, but despite bitter cold weather a decent turnout
was expected. Julie Mellini was bartending, first at the large U-shaped
main bar near the front and then at the back bar when more patrons
arrived. Jeffrey had jumped in to help, running downstairs to the basement cooler to bring up cases of beer, or lugging around ice to refill the
bins. Now he'd get this kid his Jack and Coke.

It's going to be one of the last Jack and Cokes I make, Jeffrey thought.
After four taxing years of running The Station, he and his brother
Michael were finally getting rid of the nightclub. They'd sold it once before, but that deal had fallen through. Now there was a new buyer. The
purchase agreement had been signed the previous week, the deposit
check had cleared, and the money was in the bank. All they were waiting
for was approval from the West Warwick town council to transfer the

liquor and business licenses. Jeffrey might stay on to help with the tran-
sition, like the previous owner did for him, but nights like these would
soon be over, and he was eager to get back to his real life and the career
he truly loved. Co-owning a rock 'n' roll roadhouse had only ever been
a sideline, and at age thirty-six, he looked forward to focusing solely on
the new direction he had carefully plotted out for himself and his family.
It was all coming together, just as he'd planned.

Yet sometimes he had to smile to himself about these nights as a bar-
keep, and he suspected some of the regular patrons—those who knew who
he really was—were amused watching him do the donkey work of hauling
beer. In Rhode Island, Jeffrey was better known for carrying a microphone.

He'd risen to local fame several years earlier as a television news reporter for WLNE-TV ABC 6 in Providence, often fronting the station's
sensationalized "You Paid for It" reports that exposed government waste
and malfeasance, of which there seemed to be an endless supply. While
most TV news investigative units produced only a handful of reports
per year, timed to air during the crucial ratings "sweeps" periods when
advertising rates were set, Channel 6 aired new "You Paid for It" stories daily for months at a time. It was a grueling pace to maintain, but
not for lack of material. Rhode Island's notoriously corrupt politicians
constantly provided new scandals, and Jeffrey had exposés that helped
doom two of the state's highest-profile politicians. One report looked
at an attempt by Providence mayor Vincent A. "Buddy" Cianci Jr. to
blackmail Channel 6* into ceasing its reporting on City Hall corruption,
and another led to the removal of one of Rhode Island's most senior
Democratic Party leaders, John Hawkins, head of the state lottery, for
questionable use of taxpayer funds.

Those stories helped put Jeffrey out front in a business famous for
sharp elbows, yet it was in his live reporting where he truly shined:

---

* Author's note: As the TV station's news director, I was the recipient of Mayor Cianci's
blackmail threat. In a phone call Cianci said that if Channel 6 News did not stop its reporting on corruption at City Hall, he would accuse the television station of failing to pay
its taxes (the station was located in Providence and subject to property tax assessments).
When the station did not relent, Cianci fabricated a fake tax bill and went public with his
scheme. The TV station then aired a report about the blackmail plot. At the exact moment
the story was broadcast, my home on the East Side of Providence was broken into and ran-
sacked. When Cianci's Providence Police were called to the scene later, they walked in the
front door and without stopping to look at the destruction walked out the back door and
instantly declared the crime "unsolvable."

Jeffrey loved being on camera, and the camera loved him back just as much. Somehow he always found the interviews and pictures that would put him at the top of the newscasts, making him exceptionally reliable and a favorite of producers. He would block out his live shots like Hollywood productions and converse into the lens as if sharing a scoop with a neighbor over a backyard fence, walking and talking and treating the camera as an additional person on the scene. Videographers knew when they were assigned to work with Jeffrey Derderian that they might as well leave the tripod back in the news vehicle, because there was little chance they'd be standing still.

This grasp of the camera as an audience surrogate got Jeffrey noticed, and in 1997 he was hired for a prime reporting job in Boston at WHDH-TV 7, the largest NBC affiliate in the nation not owned by the network and one of the most successful and influential newsrooms in the country. Channel 7 set trends copied throughout the industry, and the station's newscasts, unparalleled for their technical perfection and high production values, featured preternaturally fast-paced story line-ups peppered with graphics and sound effects previously found only in top network sports programs. Flubs, studio errors, and miscued videos were the bane of most local TV newscasts, but not at 7 News. Industry lore said that one mistake was noted, a second was reprimanded, and a third could mean dismissal. Rather than crumbling under this pressure, the station thrived and put out flawless broadcasts that were the envy of other newsrooms. When asked if the high demands made 7 News an awful place to work, Jeffrey would quip, "They don't take beginners here."

The station dispatched its own journalists to national news stories, and Jeffrey was sent to report on the tragedies that defined the era, including the Columbine High School massacre in Colorado, and the September 11 terrorist attacks in Manhattan. It was a heady experience for Jeffrey, especially since he didn't fit the mold of the six-foot Ken Doll national correspondents he stood beside on live shot row, in either appearance or provenance. Jeffrey stood five foot five inches, his features dark and ruggedly appealing from his Armenian lineage, and he was always meticulously dressed and groomed for the camera, topped by a thick dark mane with enough hair gel to withstand hurricanes. What he lacked in physical stature or chiseled looks he made up for in an outsized, uninhibited personality, eager to dive into the fray and ask tough questions, an in-your-face approach that created drama. Yet many who faced Jeffrey's reportorial ire saw him as a likeable, approachable "regular guy," one who could give a ribbing and take one too. Because of his height, some colleagues referred to Jeffrey as "the pocket newsman," a jibe he'd brush off with a grin.

After all, he was grateful to work in television, a universe far removed from his working-class roots, one generation from poverty. Jeffrey's grandfather, Arshag, a refugee of the Armenian genocide, and then his father, Arshag Junior, ran a small grocery in a crime-ridden neighborhood on Providence's South Side. Everyone in the family worked at the store, even Jeffrey as a child, but running a business surrounded by a community beset with despair and violence came with a price: both his father and brother Robert were shot at the store. They survived, but the attack would remain a source of trauma for the rest of their lives.

Jeffrey's hardscrabble childhood became more difficult when he witnessed his mother's death from heart failure when he was eleven years old, leaving his rough-edged dad to raise three boys. Arshag tried to instill in his sons a demanding work ethic, figuring this would serve them well in life, but Arshag's long hours at the store kept him from home, and his inability to express emotions meant the boys received little affection. "There was no hugging in our house," Jeffrey would say, although he loved and respected his father, accepting "Archie" for his limitations.

Jeffrey wasn't enthusiastic about academics, but made it through high school as a B student and attended Providence College for a year. While there he took an internship at WJAR-TV 10, the NBC affiliate in Providence, and became hooked by the adrenaline rush of covering the news. Decades later he still gushed when remembering those first days in television studio when he met anchors he'd grown up watching, was amazed that such a profession could possibly be his. "They pay to do this?" he would say. He transferred to Rhode Island College and joined the school's radio station WXIN as a reporter and anchor. And the microphone he was elevated from his humble beginnings and bathed in the undivided attention he received from listeners. He talked his way into reporting assignments at nearby commercial radio stations and fill-in work at the local television stations, honing his skills and smoothing out the harshest aspects of his Rhode Island accent, until he landed his first full-time reporting job at Channel 6 in 1993.* His career had been in high gear ever since—a race for bigger stories, better assignments, more face-time on air, and larger paychecks.

By the time he reached Boston he was confident, even cocky, and would often think about what it would be like to take the next jump in his career, to join one of the national television networks as a correspondent. Jeffrey felt he could out-report any of his colleagues in pursuit of the day's news, brazenly skirting police barricades and other obstacles to get exclusive information and pictures. Each day he would review recordings of his work, analyzing each slight inflection in his voice to determine if it could have been better.

But after a couple of years at Channel 7 Jeffrey realized how few of his colleagues lasted very long in the profession. Television news had a habit of devouring journalists, leading to shattered personal lives and burnout, and Jeffrey noted that many were divorced, drank too much, and lived in fear that their contracts wouldn't be renewed. They had good reason. TV news was never known for career longevity, and with increased competition from the Internet, local television wasn't as lucrative as it once was, forcing stations to find ways to save. It became commonplace for stations to replace veteran reporters with comparative beginners, and pay them a fraction of the salary. Nobody threatened Jeffrey's job, but it seemed wise to consider other options.

Jeffrey's experience at Channel 7 had altered his ambitions in other ways as well. Chasing an embattled Rhode Island politician down the street to get a quote was relatively exhilarating work, but covering Columbine was about children killing children. It didn't make any sense. He also couldn't shake the memories of reporting from Ground Zero during 9/11, when people desperate to find missing loved ones would see Jeffrey with his camera crew and beg for him to accept a photo and put it on air in the hope that broadcasting the image would lead to a reunion. He knew there would be no such miracles, that the victims were in the dust and rubble of lower Manhattan. At first he tried to explain that his broadcasts were viewed only in New England, and that no one in New York would see any photos he put on air, but he realized that such

---

* Author's note: this is when I first met Jeffrey Derderian. I was news director at WLNE-TV and approved Jeffrey's hiring.

conversations would only add to the cruelty of those days. So he would somberly take the photos and let people believe what they needed.

Maybe he was just getting soft, Jeffrey thought, or perhaps those stories hit home because he now had a family of his own. His wife Linda had given birth to fraternal twin boys, Max and Jake, just after Jeffrey started at Channel 7, and he wasn't about to let them grow up in an emotional void without their father around, the way Jeffrey did. Even after getting the big job in Boston he'd kept his family in their modest white colonial in a family-oriented neighborhood in Cranston, Rhode Island, near supportive relatives and Linda's job with the records department of a local hospital. But that decision created a long commute, and Jeffrey always seemed to be working, or could be assigned to report out of town on a moment's notice. He worried that he was following the same path as his father, and he had no intention of missing Max and Jake's childhood.

Then there was the nightclub, which was supposed to help support the family, but instead turned out to be a distraction. Jeffrey was the one who'd pestered his oldest brother Michael into pursuing a business venture together, part of Jeffrey's plan to have a back-up revenue stream going if his days in television news abruptly ended. Jeffrey had always admired his brother's gregarious entrepreneurial spirit—Michael had left Merrill Lynch to go off on his own as a financial advisor and had been successful, earning enough to buy a second home near the beach and own an aircraft leasing company. Michael's affluent trappings, especially compared to their modest childhoods growing up next to the airport in Warwick, led Jeffrey to jokingly nickname his brother "Rolex." When Michael finally agreed to go into business together, they named their company Derco LLC, and selected a small laundromat as their first investment. When that deal fell through, Michael spotted a classified listing in the *Providence Journal* for The Station nightclub in West Warwick, described in the ad as "a successful Rock 'n' Roll club."

Running a roadside bar and live music venue was the antithesis of Jeffrey's work in television news. Broadcasting was regimented and demanding to the fraction of a second, but the nightclub was like a large extended family. As a place where many locals performed, The Station was the center of a community, a beloved haven for its working-class patrons. The line between customers and employees was blurry, with someone having a beer at the bar one night, and then earning fifty dollars the next to check tickets at the door. There were men who'd excitedly show up to help run the lights or babysit the stage door in exchange for having their beer paid. There was innate goodwill and genuine affection for the place, and Jeffrey had never seen a business run like that, especially compared to television news where employees kept meticulous track of every second on the clock.

Most of the staff and regulars at The Station worked blue-collar jobs during the day as mechanics, furniture movers, or waitresses, the-salt-of-the-earth types Jeffrey had grown up with, forging a familial bond between them. There were times when the club was undeniably fun, like when they hosted tribute bands that mimicked current hit-makers, like "Human Clay" with its impersonation of the rock group Creed. Even the occasional rock prima donna drama would provide memories and laughs that would last years, like when the lead singer of The Fixx refused to perform until a specific Marshall brand amplifier was provided. One of the club's regulars raced home and brought back the exact speaker, plugging it in with minutes to spare.

As a business venture, however, the nightclub was an investment, not a profit maker. On nights when there were no performances the bar attracted only a handful of customers, and attendance on show nights could be slim too. Jeffrey realized that many of his clientele lived paycheck to paycheck, so there were certain times when they simply lacked money, no matter what was booked—tax time, the end of the month, when Christmas bills came due, and around Mother's Day were tough weeks for fielding an audience. Bad weather could kill turnout, too. In all the time the brothers had owned The Station, Jeffrey remembered selling out only twice. Even the night of The Fixx lead singer's tantrum was a modest crowd.

An insurance inspection report estimated food and drink sales in 2001 at $220,000, with 70 percent of the revenue coming from alcohol. The rent for the building was about $45,000 and proceeds from shows were marginal, so after the staff and bills were paid, whatever was left over was reinvested into the club for improvements. Many months the brothers dipped into their own pockets to pay bills, and they'd never taken anything close to a paycheck.

Michael oversaw club operations, and Jeffrey managed the marketing, forging partnerships with local radio stations to promote the shows and building on relationships from his past years working in the Rhode Island media. The brothers also added eye-catching color to the exterior by hiring local artist Anthony Baldino to paint a mural featuring exaggerated images of classic rock performers against an enormous American flag. Improvements inside included adding soundproofing foam to help mollify neighbors' complaints that the music was too loud.

Jeffrey and Michael divided up the nights for supervising the club, each taking turns to troubleshoot and make sure the bands and staff were paid. Jeffrey often drove directly to the club after finishing a live shot for the news up in Boston, and his wife Linda brought the twins to the club so they could briefly see their dad before bedtime. The Station siphoned a precious limited resource: time with his family. It was true what people said—kids change everything. Toward the end of 2002 Jeffrey concluded that he had to make some significant changes, with both the club and his career in television news.

It struck him that TV news anchors tended to have better job security than reporters, and anchors certainly had more predictable work hours, since they had to be on air for scheduled broadcasts and were rarely sent out on breaking news stories. Getting an anchor chair in Boston would take several years, and it might never happen, so Jeffrey turned back to Providence. The old guard was changing, with several longtime anchors retiring, creating opportunity, and Jeffrey was already well known there, which should have given him an advantage. He agonized over the decision— was he really willing to give up all he had achieved in Boston? Working at Channel 7 was like playing for the NFL, and going back to Providence would be akin to scrimmaging on a high school team. That was discouraging, but it had been gnawing at him that his priorities were misplaced.

Jeffrey reached out to his contacts in news management at the Providence stations, and eventually agreed to take a job at WPRI-TV 12, the CBS affiliate. The pay cut was significant, from $150,000 to $80,000 per year, but the plan would eventually have him co-anchor the morning news with Pamela Watts, a former colleague from his days at Channel 6. Jeffrey would finally get an anchor chair, and once the nightclub was sold he'd get his life back. With his brother Michael, Derco LLC was already involved in another venture, a Shell gas station in nearby North Kingstown, so the company should produce some decent income.

The Thursday night of the Great White show at The Station was Jeffrey's fourth official day on the job at Channel 12, although it was actually his fifth day working—he'd volunteered to go into the newsroom a day earlier on Sunday to help with coverage of a large snowstorm. He always loved live reporting, and as a native New Englander there was ingrained excitement about bad weather, but he also wanted to send a message to his new employer and colleagues: even though he'd arrived from Channel 7, arguably a large step down in the ladder of television news success, he was on their team now. The snowfall had turned out to be significant, depositing a couple feet in some places that crippled the Northeast travel corridor to New York, and five days later there were still large piles in the parking lot of the nightclub.

Jeffrey had stopped home after appearing live on the 6 p.m. news and changed from his TV news uniform, a suit, into his nightclub apparel, a blue button-down shirt emblazoned with The Station's logo. He'd reached the club in time to watch one of the warm-up bands, a local group called Fathead featuring Steve Mancini, a club regular who with his wife Andrea had become friends with Jeffrey and his wife Linda. The Derderians had recently attended the couple's wedding. While Steve played onstage, Andrea collected tickets and checked IDs inside the club entrance, right at the point where the hallway narrowed to make sure no one slipped by unnoticed. The price to attend was fifteen dollars in advance, seventeen at the door.

Shortly after Jeffrey arrived at the nightclub he welcomed Brian Butler, a photojournalist from Channel 12, one of his new colleagues. Since it was the February ratings sweeps, Jeffrey had been assigned a series about safety at public venues. A few days earlier, on February 17, twenty-one people died in a stampede at Chicago's E2 nightclub after security guards reportedly used pepper spray to break up a fight. Channel 12 asked Jeffrey to report on whether the same type of tragedy could happen in Rhode Island, and if there were any precautions taken locally to prevent deadly crowd panics. Jeffrey had already recorded footage for the story at the Dunkin' Donuts Center arena and the Rhode Island Convention Center and needed video from a live music venue, something notoriously difficult to get because of the myriad permissions needed. As co-owner of The Station he could get around that red tape. When Jeffrey told the club's manager Kevin Beese about the photographer and the story on public venue safety, Beese laughed and joked, "Are you trying to jinx us?"

Jeffrey introduced Butler to bouncer Tracy King, who escorted the brawny forty-two-year-old, two-hundred-pound photographer with a thirty-five-pound camera perched on his shoulder around to capture nightclub and crowd footage they'd need for the story, so-called b-roll images that would help visualize the story during Jeffrey's reporter soundtrack. Butler was under orders to shoot only "generic" footage. "Don't identify the place. Nothing with the nightclub's name on it," he was told by the assignment desk and Jeffrey. Butler circled the floor and recorded scenes of friends drinking and socializing, careful to avoid the club's logo.

"Got everything you need?" Jeffrey asked Butler at quarter to eleven. The photographer said yes and was ready to pack up his gear, but then heard the announcement that Great White would soon take the stage. The footage wasn't needed, and this was his fifth assignment in a long day, but Butler thought the guys back at the station might enjoy seeing some of the show, so he decided to stick around for the first song or two. *I'll get one more shot*, he said to himself.

From behind the large U-shaped bar Jeffrey watched Butler. Television news was Jeffrey's true calling, not owning a nightclub. He'd made the right decision to sell the club, leave Channel 7, and get back into Rhode Island journalism. Jeffrey enjoyed reporting here—he grew up here, knew the players, and loved covering the state's parochial swamp of shady politics and suspect governance. Or as local reporters would like to say, "In Rhode Island, on a *slow* day you can do a corruption story."

Here in Rhode Island, especially when he became an anchor, Jeffrey's plan was to achieve a level of success and fame that would make him a household name. It was just around the corner.

CHAPTER 3

THE SHOW WAS about to start when Bates College student Phil Barr's cell phone rang. His buddy Evan, finally, had shown up.

"Don't try to find me," Phil said. "I'll come and get you." Phil had secured a great view, just five people deep from the stage. It would be easier to bring Evan there, rather than try to direct him through. The crowd was cool and the big guy next to him said he'd save Phil's spot so he could buy his old friend a beer before Great White performed.

Phil had waited at The Station for Evan for two hours, killing time by chatting up locals and getting a kick out of the two warm-up bands. With Phil's perpetual smile, blue-green eyes, and tidy looks, the twenty-one-year-old had an easy way with people, and even though it was his first time in a club full of regulars, he'd had no problem socializing. He was excited to actually get into the place—he'd tried once before, hoping to see Quiet Riot, but was not old enough for that show and was turned away.

The Station was a long way from the idyllic campus of Bates in Lewiston, Maine, where he was a junior studying economics and history. Phil grew up in Rhode Island, but the blue-collar nightclub was a universe apart from his upbringing and where his life had taken him. Earlier that week he'd been in New York City for summer internship interviews at some of the world's top investment banks, including Credit Suisse, J.P. Morgan, and Lazard Frères. It had taken weeks to book those meetings, since Bates was too small for recruiting visits by the big firms. Phil had to cold-call alumni and use all his charms to get a foot in the door. It had been grueling, but he'd filled his calendar with ten interviews.

Then a blizzard crippled the New York metro area, and Phil realized he'd have to cut the visit short and return another time. He took

Amtrak, which remarkably was still running, to visit his parents in Lincoln, Rhode Island, before returning to Maine. Still, the few interviews he'd had before the storm went so incredibly well, and he allowed himself to daydream a bit about a future amid the skyscrapers and hustle of Midtown Manhattan. What a jump start for his career.

In the meantime, Phil was back home and happy that circumstances allowed him to reconnect with his buddy Evan Clabots. They'd been friends since high school when they both went to Moses Brown in Providence, one of the state's top and toughest private schools. Phil's parents wanted him to have competitive advantages in life and get into a good college, and even though he was only a 3.3 GPA student at Moses Brown, colleges recognized that as an accomplishment, which helped him get into Bates, one of the Little Ivies. Being a competitive swimmer in butterfly and long-distance freestyle didn't hurt either, since Bates had a team in the NCAA's New England Small College Athletic Conference with ambitions to someday bump longtime champion Williams College from its perch. At six feet and thick, Phil was built more like a linebacker, and he didn't have the monster arm span that would define the nation's top swimmers, but no one out-hustled him.

Evan went to the Rhode Island School of Design. A lacrosse player and math and science whiz, he could have gone to MIT, but Evan had ambitions to make things, so he opted to study industrial design at RISD. During their days at Moses Brown the two young men would leave the campus and cruise around Providence in Phil's black Mustang convertible, blasting rock. Evan thought the loud music and fast car were a way for teenage Phil to rebel against a strict, conservative upbringing, a struggle that played out in his attire—while others their age sported T-shirts and sneakers, Phil typically wore button-down shirts and leather loafers, "like what a lawyer would wear on weekends," Evan said.

Phil hadn't seen Evan in ages, so when he realized he'd be back in Rhode Island for the night, he called in hopes that they could catch up. RISD was on a break, so Evan was staying with his mother out in the rural town of Exeter. On the phone they flipped through the entertainment listings in the *Providence Phoenix* weekly paper to see if anything was happening close to them, rather than having to haul themselves to Providence. That's when they spotted the Great White show.

Perfect. Despite his Ivy education, investment banker ambitions, and the allure of places like Manhattan, Phil had been a rocker since childhood. It began when he was nine years old and three teenage neighbors started a band in their garage. Phil would ride his bike over to listen to the brothers jam out on covers of Aerosmith and Ozzy Osbourne. While the most popular songs on the radio at that time in the nineties were power diva ballads and boy band saccharine, the soundtrack of Phil's life was rock and metal. He'd blast rock radio station WHJY, and he'd lost count of the number of metal concerts he'd attended.

Phil even took his love of rock with him to Bates and deejayed a late night rock show on the campus radio station. If anyone thought there was an inherent contradiction between investment banker Phil and rocker Phil, he didn't. He saw himself as an individualist at his core, and had studied and embraced the works of Emerson and Thoreau while just a teenager, and idolized an uncle who eschewed technology and tended horses in nearby Attleboro. The concept of "the self-reliant man" appealed to Phil, and that type of person certainly didn't let pop culture dictate his musical tastes. Phil was a rocker in his soul and had no qualms about it.

His attorney father Philip, however, was more skeptical of the rock world. Whenever Phil would head out to a concert, his dad would have a quip like, "Don't get robbed. Don't get stabbed."

Phil didn't understand why his father worried so much. As he looked around the nightclub, he saw working-class folks blowing off steam. Many had made themselves up to look like Great White in its long-gone prime, complete with spandex and headbands. Phil had also dressed for the occasion, donning a T-shirt and baseball cap, both emblazoned with the logo of the late NASCAR great Dale Earnhardt, one of his favorites. Phil also put on his beloved brown waterproof leather boots, since there was still plenty of snow around from that storm.

Toward the nightclub's entrance Phil finally spotted Evan, who admitted he'd driven around for a while looking for parking and eventually ditched his car next to the front door, unsure if it was a legal space. The two men hit the bar for beer, with Phil grateful for a new drink. He'd nursed his first beer for hours, since he didn't have much cash left after the expensive trip to New York, and he'd been saving his remaining dollars to treat his old friend.

They'd barely had a sip and spoken a few words when the show was about to start, so they slipped back to the spot in front of the stage. Phil smiled when lead singer Jack Russell walked out wearing his trademark bandana, this one purple paisley. Phil raised his hand like so many others in the rock salute.

As the opening guitar riff wailed Phil was instantly a million miles away from Bates and its manicured campus for the well educated and well-to-do. For now, at least, this was his tribe. Huge plumes of fireworks shot out from the stage. *Amazing*, Phil thought. He'd never seen anything like it before in a club this small.

CHAPTER 4

"OKAY, BOYS, PLEASE stop," Linda Derderian said to her four-year-old twin sons in the back seat.

The twins, Max and Jake Derderian, played rough with each other more and more as they got older. Their mother didn't miss changing diapers and sleepless nights of feedings, but sometimes she longed for the days when they were infants. Back then she'd put the boys to bed in separate ends of the same cradle and somehow during the night they'd find each other and sleep holding each other's hands. These days those hands were used for pushing or hitting.

It amazed Linda to see how quickly each of their distinct personalities had emerged. Max was a natural showman, a big personality who loved the spotlight, much like his TV star father. Jake had a quieter soul, perhaps taking after her. Linda never sought attention, content with a quiet life centered on Jeffrey and the boys.

Her mother, June Berube, sat next to her in the passenger seat, breaking Linda's no-smoking-in-the-vehicle rule, as usual. June cracked the window and held the cigarette outside, arguing somehow that this did not actually constitute smoking in the car. It didn't matter that it was freezing—a huge snowstorm had hit only days earlier—and wisps of sooty air still got inside.

Linda only pushed her mother so far on this. June had been through too much, wasn't in great health, and smoking seemed to offer some comfort. June had divorced Linda's father, and then in 1977, had to tell little Linda, just ten years old, that her dad had died from a heart attack. That was one of the bonds Linda shared with her husband Jeffrey—he lost his mother when he was a child. That hole in their lives, the devastating disappearance of a parent, was one of the reasons they both told their sons "I love you" every day, without exception. Who knew when those might be their last words. When Jeffrey and Linda lost their parents nothing profound had been said, and then suddenly they were gone.

After her father's death, it was just Linda, her mother, and sister, Tracy, fending for themselves, and even now June lived only thirteen minutes away—they'd timed it—and nearly always joined Linda and the boys on their outings. Linda scaled back her hours managing the medical records department at a local hospital so she could be with the twins in their precious early years. Today they'd seen *Kangaroo Jack* at the Apple Valley Cinema a few towns away in Smithfield. It wasn't the worst family film Linda had been forced to sit through, but she wasn't keen about the mafia subplot. Which Hollywood executives thought that was appropriate for small children? They must be from Rhode Island.

"Stop the car!" June yelled. "Stop. The. Car."

"What's the matter?" Linda asked.

"My cigarette. I dropped my cigarette in the car. I don't see it. I can't find it. The car's going to catch on fire!"

"Oh, mom." Linda pulled over. They hadn't even left the parking lot.

"Okay, now, everyone needs to get out of the car," Linda said calmly as she put the white leased Lexus SUV into park.

The boys unbuckled themselves, having conquered the supposedly childproof safety seats long ago, and stood at a snow bank next to their grandmother. Linda got out and looked under the front seats. She didn't see anything smoldering. She moved the floor mats and felt under the seats, finding the typical detritus of a family car—toys, books, Cheerios, a stale peanut butter cracker—but no cigarette. *Where could it have gone?*

"What are you doing?" asked Max.

Trying not to panic, Linda checked the crevices of the back seats. Again, nothing. She had to find it. The thought of a roaring car fire flashed in her mind.

It wasn't a random fear. When Linda was just four she went with her mother and Tracy to shop at a local crafts store. Tracy was thirteen months younger and had fallen fast asleep during the drive, and for a moment June considered letting the toddler snooze in the car. After all, she'd be in and out in just a few minutes. But at the last moment she changed her mind and nudged Tracy from her slumber. Minutes later the car burst into an inferno. A helpful neighbor earlier that day had done an amateur repair to the vehicle and something had gone horribly wrong.

Two years later fire struck again when six-year-old Linda watched their family home burn, destroying all their belongings. The words "ten minutes" had been singed in her mind since. That's how little time it took for their house to become completely engulfed. *Everything gone in only ten minutes.*

"I can't find it," Linda said to her mother. There was no trace of the lit cigarette in the Lexus.

June looked flush, now tightly grasping the boys' hands. "If you don't find it the whole thing will go up in flames."

"Wouldn't you know if you dropped it in the car?" asked Jake.

Linda patted the floor and searched crevices for a third time. If a burning cigarette were there, *wouldn't there at least be a whiff of smoke?* "Mom, it's just not here," Linda finally conceded. "It's fine." The cigarette was probably in a mound of snow somewhere. Everyone piled back inside for a mostly silent ride back home. June did not light up again.

As they turned onto their street Linda noticed the house at the corner was still for sale. She wished Steven and Andrea Mancini would buy it, and she'd even told them so. She'd met the couple through Jeffrey's nightclub, and they'd become fast friends. Andrea gushed over the twins each time she saw them, perhaps because she wanted children of her own sometime soon—Steven was thirty-nine, but Andrea was just twenty-eight. The boys adored Andrea too, especially when they all went to the club and watched Shania Twin, the tribute band impersonator of country music pop star Shania Twain. They'd all had so many laughs.

Yes, the Mancinis would be perfect neighbors in their niche of modest three-bedroom bungalows in Cranston, Linda thought, a street where people looked out for each other in an almost old-fashioned way, doing little favors like bringing up trash cans and collecting mail during vacations. She'd mention again to the Mancinis that the house was still on the market.

Linda was on her own for the night, since Jeffrey would be working late. "Remember, I'm not coming home tonight," he said as he left that morning, "I have to work on a story." He explained that part of the reporting would be shot in the nightclub.

Double duty. Linda was glad the nightclub work was finally coming to an end with the impending sale. It was just in time, as far as she was concerned, since the boys would soon be old enough to stay up later with their dad, and it wouldn't be long before they'd be in school, with homework that Jeffrey would want to supervise.

After she put the boys down for the night Linda busied herself with chores. New furniture for the den had just arrived, so she arranged and rearranged the room until it seemed just right. At 11 p.m., when she went downstairs to the basement to get clothes from the dryer, a vision of flames came into her mind from nowhere.

The dryer. But fear of a dryer fire didn't make any sense, since the machine wasn't old and she regularly cleaned the lint trap. Linda felt silly at the irrational tricks her thoughts played.

The phone rang. Linda tried to get to it quickly, so the boys wouldn't be awoken. *Who's calling at this time of night on the house phone?* Then Linda remembered that she'd given her cell phone to Jeffrey because his wasn't working.

"Linda, where's Jeff?" It was Gary Silverman, a friend of Jeffrey's since childhood. Like so many of her husband's longtime friends, Gary was clean-cut, meticulously dressed, and hard-working. He was also tangentially connected to the world of show business. Starting as a teenager he'd been a disc jockey at parties, eventually creating his own business, G Force Entertainment, and these days he was a popular fixture on the Rhode Island wedding circuit.

Linda told Gary that Jeffrey was at the club. What's this about?

"There's a fire," Gary said. "We need to get there. You need to find where he is."

Fire. Flames had just been in her head, and in the car earlier with her mother's cigarette drama.

"Fire? What fire?" Linda stiffened.

It was all over the television news, Gary explained. The Station nightclub was on fire. They had to find Jeffrey.

Linda heard a noise behind her. It was Jake in his Buzz Lightyear pajamas.

"Mommy, who are you talking to on the phone?"

Linda didn't mention the fire, unaware herself of the enormity of the tragedy unfolding, and she would make sure the boys never learned of the disaster for years. Only when the twins reached fourth grade would they be told the truth.

CHAPTER 5

FRED CRISOSTOMI AND Gina Russo, the newly engaged couple who'd met on HipDates.com, had been to The Station several times, most recently to see Human Clay, the Creed tribute band. It was amazing how much those guys sounded like the originals, especially performing "With Arms Wide Open." Human Clay had announced they were breaking up, and The Station was their last concert in the area. Fred and Gina were thrilled to be there for that final show.

As they entered the nightclub to see Great White they walked through a vestibule and down a six-foot-wide corridor, passing through an additional interior door, and stopped to get tickets from Andrea Mancini. Once inside they noticed the place was busy, but not too packed. To their right was a large open space facing the stage, with fans gathered in front on the dance floor. To their right was the sunroom, with its tinted windows, and that area too would fill during a popular show. The ceiling was dark, with glitter, and black lights scattered around the club helped provide the aura of rock 'n' roll. As usual, Gina and Fred were greeted by the club's signature smell, a combination of stale beer, cigarette smoke, and some sort of cleaning product. To their left was the main bar, a large varnished-wood, horseshoe-shaped counter surrounded by stools with padded red seats with backs.

Beyond that, closer toward the stage, was a smaller second bar, only open during big events, like tonight. Gina and Fred ordered drinks and chatted up bartender Julie Mellini, a friend and one of their favorites at The Station. A sense of excitement grew in the room as showtime approached, with people counting down the minutes. A man asked Fred for the time.

"Quarter to eleven," Fred said after looking at his watch.

He and Gina wandered toward the stage, stopping to chat with another friend, Linda Fisher, who was working that night in exchange for $40 and a free T-shirt to sell the band's merchandise. Fred hit the men's room, which was down a dead-end hallway past a small kitchen behind the horseshoe bar, and by the time he returned Mike Gonsalves, the deejay known as Dr. Metal from WHJY radio, was tossing baseball caps and T-shirts with the rock station's logo into the crowd. Fred and Gina stood so close to the stage that Dr. Metal simply reached down and handed a cap to Fred and a shirt to Gina.

Great White was announced and elation in the room swelled when guitars screeched their first notes and large arcs of fireworks spewed from the stage. It seemed like the sparks would never stop.

Fred immediately saw that something was not right. "Look at that," he said to Gina, "there's something wrong. There's a fire. Something's on fire." He put his hands firmly on Gina's shoulders and directed her toward the side exit. She placed her drink on the stage, right next to the feet of lead singer Jack Russell. As the aging rocker belted out his opening lyrics the crowd yelled, danced, and sang along, but Fred was stone-faced. That's a real fire. They had to get out.

CHAPTER 6

BATES COLLEGE STUDENT Phil Barr watched as small flickers of flames crawled up the walls. He'd noticed earlier how so much of the club, including the ceiling, was covered in thick foam, painted dark with specks of glitter, unlike anything he'd seen in other live music venues, and he'd been to dozens. He'd studied it up close while waiting for his old high school buddy Evan to arrive.

The flames must be part of the show, Phil first thought, a special effect pretty cool for such a modest place. The crowd sure got into it, like they were reliving the days of those big arena shows.

Then it hit him. *Oh, shit, this isn't part of the act.*

Phil felt a shove as a club worker pushed by and headed toward the stage carrying a small fire extinguisher. Phil took note of how dinky the extinguisher looked.

The flames burst, instantly covering the wall, and the experience of years of concerts flipped through Phil's mind. No, this was not normal. This was an actual fire. *They've gone and done it with those fireworks.* Phil and Evan listened as the lead singer stopped the show and people calmly turned and headed back toward the entrance to evacuate. Damn, Phil thought, it's already late, and by the time they put this out and get everyone back inside to restart the show it's going to take forever. Maybe he should just go home.

As they turned and walked toward the club's entrance to leave, Phil noticed a backup as too many people tried to jam their way through the one door. "There's no way we're getting out there," he said to Evan.

Emergency lights flashed, followed by the piercing sound of an alarm. Then all light disappeared as thick smoke descended from the ceiling. The timing made no sense. The fire began only seconds ago, and there was already all this smoke. Where did it come from so fast? It was over-powering, foul, acrid, and choking. Phil and Evan crouched down and pulled their T-shirts over their mouths, trying to filter out the stench, but even getting low didn't help—the smoke was already almost to the floor.

They'd only made it to the middle of the room. Phil felt around try-ing to determine which way to go. Having spent so much time wan-dering the club earlier he had a fairly good sense of the floor plan. The horseshoe-shaped bar was close, and he remembered what looked like an exit near it. They could head that way.

But with the darkness came chaos. People screamed, followed by a stampede of panic. Evan was swept away from Phil in the surge. Phil was pushed the other direction toward the bar stools, falling over one and onto the floor, his legs entangled in the chair, trapped. He was stomped and trampled. The weight. The pressure. Phil couldn't breathe. He was suffocating. *Get off me!*

CHAPTER 7

F RED GUIDED GINA toward the exit at the side of the stage, only a few steps from where they'd watched the show. A man in a black T-shirt guarded the door. He wasn't as big as Fred, but with his arms folded and a firm look on his face, he was a resolute blockade.

"We need to get out right now," Fred said.

The bouncer, who had his back to the stage and was not positioned to see the flames, shook his head. Not this way.

Through the blaring guitars Fred tried to explain that there was a fire, but the bouncer apparently couldn't hear or understand the danger. Fred tried yelling louder, but it was no use. No one was getting past the bouncer and out that door.

Fred was incensed. "We can't stay here and argue with this guy," Fred said to Gina. "We have to get out of here."

Fred grabbed Gina by the wrists and pulled her toward the other side of the room, toward the entrance they'd come through only minutes earlier. They'd easily moved around then, so it should be just as simple to leave. Incredibly, people still danced, even though the stage alcove was nearly fully engulfed. Jack Russell and the band abruptly stopped playing, but many in the crowd were in a daze, so suddenly jolted out from the fun. Fred whisked Gina past them. Some in the crowd realized they needed to move away from the flames. They dropped their drinks on the floor and quickly headed to the exit, the same door Fred brought Gina toward.

In seconds, the audience was smothered in impenetrable, choking smoke, and people wailed in terror. What had been a somewhat orderly evacuation instantly turned into a riot, with Fred and Gina caught in the middle. In the pitch black the mass of humanity came to a near stop

29

Something blocked the way out. Fred and Gina couldn't see what held them back, but they felt crushed as people jammed in tighter and bodies squished them on all sides. There was no way to move in any direction. Trapped and unable to breathe, some violently shoved to try to break free from the suffocating horde.

Fred kept his hands on Gina's back, protecting and pushing and holding her upright whenever it felt like the crowd's surges would trample them. Somehow they'd inched their way to an inner set of swinging doors near the ticket booth, just inside the main entrance. Freedom was only feet away. "Go! Go!" Fred screamed at Gina.

The frenzied crowd, human beings now reduced to their most base survival instincts, pushed and pulled and fought to try to extricate themselves from the mob. All around the fire raged, the flames difficult to see in the dense smoke, but the heat reached beyond scorching, as if they were all trapped inside a raging oven. In the hysteria Fred and Gina felt themselves being torn apart from each other. Fred took all of his bear strength, his 285 pounds, and aimed it toward his fiancée, placing his hand on the square of Gina's back and shoving her toward the exit.

"Go!" he yelled.

Light bulbs exploded, windows shattered, and people bellowed in agony. The flames and heat surged in closer and from above a molten substance dropped onto the packed throng, a fiery goop that would later be called "black rain." The drips brutally seared flesh as they struck their victims, and hair spontaneously combusted. People stood with their heads on fire, some not seeming to even notice. All that mattered was reaching the door.

Fred struggled to breathe. The air seemed to have left the club, replaced instead by the relentless black of the acrid smoke. He could no longer see Gina, and was surrounded by others. The room went completely dark.

CHAPTER 8

THE CRUSH OF panicked patrons carried club owner Jeffrey Derderian like an ocean wave until he was pinned up against the right
vestibule wall near the narrowed entrance where tickets were collected.
Through the din of the fire alarm he heard screams.

Jeffrey reached into the murk and pulled people toward the exit. "Let's
go! Let's go!" he shouted. From the blackness he plucked out Charlene,
the diminutive midthirties hairdresser who was a club regular and wife
of Al Prudhomme, drummer for the hard rock band Fathead that had
performed before Great White. Charlene appeared more astonished
than frightened, having not yet realized the gravity. She would later tell
friends that at that point she was still considering going back into the
nightclub to get her coat.

Jeffrey grabbed Charlene by the shoulders and directed her into the
three-foot passageway that led outside, giving her a hard shove. "Get
out!" he yelled. Charlene was angry that Jeffrey had pushed her so hard.

This isn't good. Those words kept replaying in Jeffrey's mind over and
over as he was pushed out with the stampede. *This isn't good. This isn't
good.*

Outside Jeffrey found bartender Julie Mellini standing near the front
of the building. She'd been busy working the back bar and kept serving
drinks even after the fire started, thinking at first the flames were part of
the show, until sound engineer Paul Vanner told her, "Get out of here.
Get out of here now." Mellini escaped through the kitchen exit as the
black smoke followed her to the door. When she turned to look back
inside a plume of soot smacked her in the face.

In the confusion Mellini had grabbed the cash drawer and her tip jar, not realizing the magnitude of the crisis, and now stood watching the flames, terrified for friends inside.

"Help them!" Jeffrey yelled. He grabbed the cash drawer and tip jar and tossed them into the snow.

Jeffrey ran around the building to check the other exits. The doors were open, but few emerged through the piceous fumes. Enormous flames shot into the night sky as harrowing wails came from inside. When Jeffrey returned to the main entrance a stack of people jammed up to the top of the doorway, crammed so tight none could escape.

"Let me out!" a man hollered. A chorus of others shouted in desperate agony.

Men outside frantically pulled on those in the pile, yanking some free.

"Rip this thing off!" someone yelled, gesturing to a large banner tied to the metal railing in front of the club that was getting in the way. The sign read in a variety of large fonts "The Station presents Great White." Jeffrey and another man raced over to remove the banner as rescue crews arrived.

Firefighters scrambled to unfurl their hoses. Daniel Biechele, Great White's twenty-six-year-old tour manager who had ignited the fireworks, got down to the ground and tried to help manage a hose, then stood up and stared at the blaze. From a side door a person stumbled and fell to the ground, consumed in flames.

Firefighters told Jeffrey and the others to get back, even though people were still being saved. It's too dangerous, rescue workers said. The building could explode.

Jeffrey had been on the front lines of dozens of tragedies as a television news reporter, sometimes on the scene of a disaster when first responders arrived, routinely closer to more death and destruction than most people would ever see. Yet he'd never witnessed anything like this. The scale of it. The speed. The nightclub burst into a massive inferno and crews struggled to get it under control. Dozens of ambulances rapidly arrived, and just as quickly collected and departed with the injured.

Pushed away by the police, Jeffrey paced back and forth. He went around to look at the side exit, now also engulfed. There was nothing he could do. *I can't fix this*, he thought. Unable to find his own cell phone, Jeffrey borrowed one from a stranger and called his brother Michael, the club's other owner, who was on vacation in Florida.

"Michael, the club is on fire," Jeffrey blurted into the phone.

"Who the fuck is this?" Michael didn't recognize the phone number, one from Massachusetts area code 508, and the voice on the line did not sound like anyone he knew.

"Michael, this is your brother, Jeffrey," the frantic voice said. "The club is on fire."

"What do you mean the club's on fire? They put it out?" Michael asked.

Jeffrey could say little more. He couldn't explain or understand how in a matter of moments their nightclub had succumbed completely to flames. He'd have to call his brother back. As he hung up, all Jeffrey could do was stand with the others who escaped and watch in terrified awe.

This is like World War III, he thought. *The end of the world.*

CHAPTER 9

PAIN. EXCRUCIATING. INTENSE heat. College student Phil Barr heard explosions and tortured howls, and then an eerie silence.

Phil's eyes were wide open, but only registered blackness. He felt disoriented by the smoke, but a sudden agony near the base of his spine made him acutely alert. His brain instantly processed his reality: he remained inside the burning nightclub. *How much time has passed?* A superheated sensation like an iron pressed against his face. He couldn't see what it was, but then he realized he was facedown, and the floor was scorching.

He had to get out, but couldn't move. Paralyzed? No, something pinned him with incredible weight and he couldn't get his legs free. It was a person. Another human being was on top of him, but not moving. Unable to tell if the person was dead or alive, or a man or a woman, Phil knew he had to break free or die.

You have one shot at this, he told himself.

The instincts he'd developed for years as a competitive swimmer kicked in. He'd drilled thousands of times how to race the length of a pool inhaling just three times, or in dolphin kick practice to hold his breath for more than a minute, techniques that were now second nature. He inhaled deeply from the searing floor, singeing his tongue and lips. The molten air scalded his lungs. Summoning surprising strength, Phil crawled out from under the lifeless body, still holding his breath as he bolted in the direction he thought was an exit he'd spotted earlier.

As he ran, he picked his legs up high so he wouldn't trip over anything in the dark. His hand hit a wall. The door was either to the left or right of that spot. He patted his hands to the left, and there it was. He pushed the door with his left shoulder. It didn't open. Then he hit it again and felt himself tumbling outside and down concrete steps.

He faced a firefighter, who appeared astonished. Phil lay down onto a nearby snow bank, trying to cool the burning on his back.

More than six minutes had passed since the fireworks ignited the nightclub's walls.

"Get the hell out of here!" the fireman shouted as he worked to get his hose pointed at the building.

Free from the choking smoke, Phil's lungs greedily sucked in cold fresh air, and he became aware that he was hyperventilating. He got up and stumbled away to the parking lot until he reached a fire truck and collapsed onto the bumper. He slowed his breaths down by taking a few deep inhales.

What happened? Was he really just left for dead? *Focus*, he told himself. He was injured, that much he knew for sure. His face hurt.

CHAPTER 10

BRIAN LOFTUS, DAVE Fravala, and Jessica Studley huddled outside in the freezing parking lot when they heard mayhem from inside the club.

For a moment it sounded like a fight. "Let's go see," one of them said.

They had only been outside a few minutes. On many nights the parking lot of The Station was as active as the club, with a constant parade of patrons escaping outdoors to enjoy themselves in ways not allowed inside. People who didn't want to pay the full price of well drinks would stow bottles in their cars and take swigs to get drunk a bit quicker at a fraction of the price. Others would do drugs or couple, free from the prying eyes of the crowds and club management. Brian, a waiter across the street at the Cowesett Inn, loved smoking pot. He would sometimes go into a large broken-down walk-in refrigerator and smoke in there to keep warm, but he'd been warned earlier in the evening by one of the club's employees, "No smoking in there. The owner's here tonight."

Brian dropped by the club nearly every night after his shift at the restaurant to meet up with Dave, who worked at a bank. The Station was definitely not a gay bar, perhaps the total opposite, but Brian and Dave were a couple, and when that eventually became known they felt accepted by the staff and the other regulars. One of the bartenders nicknamed Brian "Cupcake," which the burly waiter got a kick out of, and he recalled with fondness the night he went with one of the very straight regulars to smoke in a car in the nightclub's lot. "If you had asked me a year ago if I would ever be in a car with a gay guy, just us two, hanging out smoking as friends, I would have said no fucking way," he remembered the man saying. "I never knew any gay people. You guys are my fags now. I love you guys." Brian knew the man didn't say "fags" in a hateful way, and in that small nook of Rhode Island it felt like he and Dave were breaking down barriers.

Earlier Brian, Dave, and Jessica had watched Fathead, their friends' band that was one of the warm-ups for Great White. Brian wanted to get high, but didn't have any pot. His friend Tommy Barnett didn't smoke, but he sometimes held for his girlfriend. "Hey, Tommy, I'm out of weed. You got any weed?" Brian asked.

"Yeah," Tommy said. "Just make sure you take my girl out."

"Of course, I love Jess. Why wouldn't I?" Brian replied.

"Just make sure," Tommy said. Brian would later remember how emphatic Tommy sounded.

As Brian, Dave, and Jess left the club Great White hit its first blaring notes. About ten minutes before the show Dave and Brian witnessed a flurry of activity, which they later concluded involved hastily arranging pyrotechnics in darkness. After hearing the commotion Brian quickly sucked hard on the joint to get it down to a roach and headed with Dave and Jess toward the entrance. As they walked over they saw flames peeking out of the roof. "Oh my God, the place is on fire," Brian said.

"Holy shit!"

A mass of people poured out the front door. Brian thought of Paula Gould, another server from the Cowesett Inn. He'd talked her into going to the show, even though she repeatedly said she didn't want to after a long day on her feet. "Come on, Johnny's working," Brian said. He'd introduced his friend John, a bouncer at the club, to Paula and Brian knew she liked him. There was no way to get back inside to find Paula or anyone else—too many people surged out, and in what seemed like only seconds, the whole building was ablaze. A woman covered in flames ran from the club. Brian was stunned. It happened so fast. *Where's the fire department? Why isn't anyone putting this out?*

Dave reached the front door and saw a ball of fire hurtling toward him. Nearby he spotted Joey Barber, another club regular, who had left through a side exit when the fire started and was lifting people out a broken window. "I ran up to where he was, and all you could hear was screaming and panic," Dave later remembered. Soon, however, no one came to the window. The two men ran to the club's entrance to find the pile of wailing patrons jammed in the doorway and the frantic effort to free them. Joey desperately pulled people out, but the fire raged. "We could visually see people melting. Like in front of my face," Dave said.

When Joey grasped the arms of one man stuck in the gruesome tumulus, the man's flesh peeled off, like removing a sweater, and fell to the ground. The flames consumed Joey's hands, causing second- and third-degree burns to his fingers.

"Next thing you know, everything was just silent. There wasn't a peep, like the screaming, it stopped all at one time," Dave said.

Chaos surrounded as ambulances and fire trucks arrived, and crews struggled to unfurl their hoses and haul them over parked cars to reach the flames. In the mayhem, Brian and Dave saw members of Great White apparently trying to conceal something near their tour bus and a dumpster. Brian grabbed a police officer and said, "They're hiding shit over there." Brian watched the officer retrieve items.

Brian found Paula. Someone had pulled her out a window, possibly Joey. Her arms and hands were badly burned, but emergency medical workers said her injuries were not as grave as those suffered by others, so Brian sat with Paula on the bumper of a rescue vehicle until it was her turn to go to the hospital. *What about everyone else? Where's Tommy?* Earlier that night Brian had seen his friends Andrea and Steve Mancini, with their cousin Keith Mancini, plus Dina DeMaio, the cocktail waitress who went around serving shots. Dina worked that night, even though it was her thirtieth birthday. She got the shift from someone else because she thought it would be fun to hear Great White perform on her special day. And what about Brian's friend Chris Arruda?

They were all dead. Ten friends of Brian, Dave, and Jessica were lost, they would later learn. Chris Arruda went back into the building twice and saved others, but when he returned a third time he never made it back out.

Had Brian and his friends not gone outside to smoke pot, they too could have been among the victims. Days later, Brian found the remnants of the joint from that night in the small coin pocket of his jeans. He thought of Tommy. The joint represented the last moment they shared on earth, when Tommy insisted that Brian bring Jess outside to smoke, a prophetic demand that saved her life. Brian came to see the joint as sacred and had it framed, along with the show's ticket stubs, creating a memorial to remind him of their close call with death.

"The roach that saved my life," he called it.

TRIAGE

CHAPTER 11

F IREFIGHTERS ARRIVED AT The Station five minutes after the fire
  had started, stunned to see that somehow the building was already
fully engulfed.

It should not have been possible in the United States in the twenty-
first century.

Horrific fires were remarkably common in America's earlier days, especially after the Industrial Revolution. Among the most infamous that
firefighters studied was the Triangle Shirtwaist Factory fire in New York
City in 1911, which killed 146 garment workers, many jumping to their
deaths from ten stories. Tragedies of that scale were not supposed to
happen anymore, especially since fire codes were upgraded nationwide
in the 1970s. Yet here it was happening again, in their small town. Firefighters watched as people emerged from the nightclub, some walking
while covered in flames. Later, many of the rescue workers would suffer from severe psychological trauma, and some would never talk about
what they witnessed.

Captain John Gregson of the North Providence Fire Department
stood ten feet from firefighters battling the flames. Like so many nearby
cities and towns, his department raced to West Warwick when the call
went out for help and arrived in an unfathomable sea of mayhem. Gregson's job was to wait by the front door of the club with another rescue worker and a stretcher, so any survivors could be moved to nearby
ambulances. The captain remembered the details of that night years
later for "The Station," a documentary by David Bettencourt.

Instead of survivors, there were bodies. Firefighters used ropes flung
into the entrance of the burning building to lasso victims from a pile
and pull them out. A protocol was established: if there was no movement

or breathing, the person was considered "not viable" and the corpse was taken to a makeshift morgue nearby, a tarp spread out on the icy ground. Concertgoers' cars were parked close to the building, so Gregson used the gurney to get victims to the hood of a car, pushed and pulled the bodies across, and then dragged them the rest of the way to the tarp. In the bitter cold, warm flesh steamed in night air.

"Is that a breath?" he said to his colleague. More than once Gregson momentarily wondered if a survivor had been placed on the tarp by mistake. Many looked nearly intact, not badly injured, at least on the outside. It was wishful thinking. It was only condensation, not a gasp of life.

As another victim was pulled out, a young man walked by and looked alarmed. "It moved," he said.

"No, it didn't," Gregson responded. Later he would realize that he had never before referred to a fellow human being as an "it." The person's injuries were so severe it was impossible to determine gender. One arm was badly burned, and a hand was missing. The fire had burned away all the hair, down to the skull, and the person's ears were gone.

As the two men argued over whether the body moved, the person's head raised up and let out a desperate shriek to let everyone know: I'm alive!

Oh, God, Gregson thought.

Gregson and the other rescuer got the survivor to their truck, and realized they couldn't get out. The massive response to the fire had them surrounded and trapped by other rescue vehicles. "We're not going anywhere," his colleague said.

The men went to work in the vehicle, injecting the patient with medications to stabilize. When they cut off the person's clothing, a hand went up, as if trying to cover oneself in modesty. A woman? Fingers grasped Gregson's hand, and he realized the person was conscious and aware of what was happening. Incredible, he thought, that the brain had survived the intense heat that had destroyed the body. Then there was the smoke that must have been inhaled, and the burns. This person should not be alive.

Gregson held the woman's hand. Her face was turned down and he knew that she couldn't see him, but he wanted her to know that he was with her. Gregson prayed, but not for the woman's survival. As heinous as it was to contemplate, the best thing for this soul was to leave this body.

"I was praying that someone wasn't going to make it," Gregson later said. "I remember that feeling of just looking at the totality of this young woman's injuries and the fact that modern medicine is where it's at, the potential of her surviving this was greater than I had wanted it to be. I know that sounds terrible but she needed to be comfortable. We needed to be there. She needed to be out of there ten or fifteen minutes sooner, or we needed to be there five minutes later."

Gregson's prayer was eventually answered. Linda Dee Suffoletto, forty-three years old from Glocester, Rhode Island, a revenue officer for the state Department of Labor and Training who had worked a full-time job and a part-time job in order to put herself through Johnson & Wales University, was pronounced dead at 5:17 a.m. on Friday, February 28, a week after the fire, at Massachusetts General Hospital in Boston. Linda was at first a "Jane Doe" in the hospital, since she was burned beyond recognition, and her identity was only confirmed with her jewelry and boot. Her husband Ben, an architect, also perished in the blaze, leaving behind their teenage son Zack, still in high school.

"I had never prayed like that before. It's a hard thing to swallow. It's not something that you usually do," Gregson later said about wishing that God would spare the woman agony and take her life. "My faith has wandered. I have a hard time now thinking of God and heaven."

CHAPTER 12

A S PHIL BARR, the college student, sat on the fire truck bumper, his buddy Evan appeared, covered in soot, his eyes huge, as if popping out of his head.

Even though the two young men had known each other since high school, neither were the touchy-feely types, so it startled Phil when Evan hugged him with the most intense embrace, a grip overflowing with exposed emotions.

"Oh, God, you're here," Evan said, loudly laughing a mixture of intense relief and joy.

When the crowd inside the nightclub stampeded, Evan was pushed away from Phil. Evan remembered carefully placing his beer on the floor, crouched next to a young woman as the acrid smoke smothered the room. "Get your head down," he told her. But the fumes were too harsh, and a thought flashed through Evan's mind: *I'm not going to survive.* There was movement to his side and Evan followed others to an open window and jumped down into the parking lot. Since his escape he'd been looking for Phil and feared the worst.

"I'm hurting," Phil said, his voice raspy. Phil could feel the pain of burns on his hands and face and worried he was disfigured. He spat black, chunky mucous into the white snow at this feet, and coughed specks of blood into his hand. Rescue crews, ambulances, and firefighters surrounded them and a firefighter ordered Phil and Evan to move back farther. After asking around Evan discovered that a triage center to help the injured was across the street at the Cowesett Inn and decided it was best to head there, since Phil struggled to both breathe and speak.

As they walked across the parking lot toward the inn they were passed by other survivors, some moaning in torment, the skin on their faces melted like wax on a candle. Others shouted the names of missing loved ones, but there were no replies. Those in spandex had the synthetic cloth dissolve into their flesh from the fire's heat. Phil's decision to wear a cotton T-shirt, hat, and jeans meant he was at least spared that agony.

They crossed the road and sat on a guardrail next to the inn and looked back toward the nightclub.

"The roof is collapsing!" someone yelled as the enflamed structure caved into itself.

"There are a lot of people that died tonight," Phil said.

"It's not that bad," Evan tried to assure, sensing a rising panic in his friend. "Most people got out. You're okay."

As the two men watched the fire rage, Phil touched and studied the guardrail. It was brand new, as if installed that same day, made of big thick timber, strong enough to save a life. In the daze of the trauma, he found himself marveling over an object so sturdy.

When Phil and Evan got to the inn, they found a disturbing whirlwind of gore. "Can you take a look at my friend?" Evan repeatedly asked, but crews were busy attending to those with much more severe injuries, so Phil and Evan sat patiently at one of the restaurant's tables. Evan tried to avert Phil's eyes from witnessing the surrounding carnage, as charred skin fell off victims. Phil was deteriorating, but still conscious and speaking, making him comparatively unharmed. He called his father by cell phone.

"Dad, the building's on fire. I'm hurt."

"Where are you?" his father asked. "Don't move."

His dad kept asking questions, but Phil struggled to answer. With each successive syllable the sounds evaporated as they left his lips, as if his voice was disappearing. Phil was losing the ability to talk.

CHAPTER 13

"D AD . . ."
Barry Warner was just drifting off when his son Brendon came into the bedroom. Warner turned to see his wife Barbara asleep by his side and noticed the room was filled with a strange glow. Outside he heard screams, loud despite the home's triple-pane windows.

Brendon told his father the nightclub next door was on fire, and then the beefy twenty-year-old was out the door and headed down the hill toward the flames. Warner got dressed, walked out into the icy yard, and looked toward The Station. The club was encased in flames and Warner heard cries of agony—no words, just pain.

The club had been nothing but trouble to the neighborhood, and now this.

The building at 211 Cowesett Avenue was constructed in 1946 as Casey's, featuring orchestra music with dancing and dining, and then the next year became The Wheel, a hangout for Navy sailors from the Quonset Point base in North Kingstown ten miles away. By the mid-1960s there was a revolving door of owners and name changes, and in 1974 Triton Industries, controlled by local businessman Raymond J. Villanova, purchased the property and turned it into an Italian restaurant, part of the Papa Brillo's regional chain. Warner decided to construct a house on Kulas Road, up the hill overlooking the property. At the time Warner thought there were nicer neighborhoods for his family, but his father-in-law had the land and since Warner didn't have experience building homes, he thought he'd do his first project there, a Colonial. Warner didn't see any issue with an eatery as his neighbor.

After a run as Brillo's the property became Glenn's Pub, a quiet local gathering spot. Then in 1991 neighbors were notified that a new business wanted the location, this time a sports pub.

Instead, it became a live music venue called CrackerJacks that blared hard rock. Warner and other neighbors immediately filed complaints with the town of West Warwick about the sudden noise, with Warner protesting that they had been victims of a bait and switch. Had neighbors been told about the potential change of use from a peaceful restaurant or pub to a raucous live music venue, they would have objected before it opened. Now that the place was in business and attracting crowds, Warner felt like his concerns fell on deaf ears at Town Hall. West Warwick was a poor community of thirty thousand people that had suffered hard times since its long ago heyday as a mill town, and it seemed to Warner like officials were desperate to see businesses succeed. It didn't matter that the neighbors' quality of life was ruined and their property values hurt. Warner's home was one of four clustered atop the hill like its own little idyllic community, and the boisterous nightclub below destroyed that tranquility.

Warner seethed. He always considered himself an easy-going, affable guy, a salesman, no less, someone trained to be likable by trade. He coached kids' soccer and was a contributor to the community who deserved at least a modicum of respect from the town, and it wasn't right that officials were so dismissive.

Warner was also a native Rhode Islander, who knew how things really worked in the state. Growing up in the adjacent town of Coventry, where his father had been in the restaurant business and dealt with the entertainment world through the liquor industry, Warner had overheard countless conversations and knew there were plenty of rules businesses had to abide. So he began a war against the nightclub by filing complaints for being a nuisance and disturbing the peace. Warner would later estimate that he filed complaints or called police about noise from the club as many as sixty times.

In 1993 the nightclub business was sold and changed its name to The Filling Station. The new owner was Raymond "Skip" Shogren, whom Warner described as someone who talked a lot but said nothing. The music roared unabated, and Warner's onslaught of complaints continued. Then the club sold again to Howard Julian, the first owner Warner considered an actual, professional businessperson. Still, no matter how many grievances were filed, the noise problem continued.

Then in March 2000 Michael and Jeffrey Derderian bought the business and shortened the name to just The Station. Warner's first encounter with the brothers came as a surprise when they showed up unannounced outside his screened-in porch one afternoon. At first glance he thought they were twins, since they looked alike and were both short in stature. They introduced themselves as the new owners of the nightclub business, and Warner invited them in to talk.

The two men excitedly chewed Warner's ear for the better part of an hour about their new venture and planned improvements. The Derderian brothers also wanted to address the noise. In all the years Warner had lived next door, with the numerous owners, it was the first time anyone had come to seek a resolution.

It was more than just the goodwill of being new neighbors that brought the Derderians to Warner's doorstep. Recently installed West Warwick police chief Peter Brousseau saw the club's change of ownership as an opening to finally fix The Station's long-running nuisance issues. In a conversation with Michael Derderian, the chief threatened to prevent future performances if the brothers failed to resolve complaints from neighbors. In an internal memo dated May 12, 2000, the chief summarized his discussion with Michael: "Spoke to Mike in reference to noise problems at the Station. Was strongly advised that his entertainment license would not be approved unless he corrects the noise problems. He is going to speak to the neighbors to work on issues."

The brothers offered to buy Warner an air conditioner, so he could shut his windows to block the noise. Warner rejected this idea, since he already had an air conditioner. As the conversation went on Warner talked about his experience playing saxophone, and that he'd been to venues with a series of thick curtains on the back walls of stages that were known to contain sound. He also suggested building false walls, which would create an empty space inside the walls to thwart sounds from getting out.

Warner also talked about foam. For decades he'd worked for American Foam, a local company. As a salesman he mostly worked with clients with large accounts, like the firearms manufacturer Smith & Wesson, but he knew that foam could also be used for soundproofing.

That first meeting made an impression, and Warner watched the brothers leave his home and walk over to visit another neighbor.

Now, as Warner stood outside his home on a bitter cold February night, he saw flames shoot into the sky from the excited brothers' venture. He walked down the hill, being careful not to slip in the snow. When he got closer a woman passed him, her hair frazzled and face blackened with soot. She stared into oblivion and spoke to herself, reminding Warner of a zombie from the movies.

"Whoa," Warner said. *That woman is in shock.*

Then a man jumped into a snow bank, and when he hit the mound a puff of steam came up, as if someone had poured hot water on ice. Firefighters and rescue vehicles converged on the scene. Two police officers pulled up near Warner and when they saw the destruction one said, "What the hell?" Then they both headed toward the blaze.

As Warner walked closer to the nightclub he saw that the structure was surrounded by dozens of parked cars, tightly packed in close to the flames. He yelled, "Look out! These cars are gonna catch on fire!"

A bright light hit his eyes. Behind a flashlight an officer ordered Warner to move back. Warner was fifty-three with thick dark hair that made him look younger, and he was fit enough, he thought, to help. Once again, he was being dismissed. Dozens of additional fire engines and ambulances arrived, and Warner felt the heat coming from the fire. It was a force like nothing he'd experienced before, and not a little one. It physically pushed him away.

Warner followed the officer's command and moved back.

CHAPTER 14

WITH HER FATHER-IN-LAW Archie Derderian driving his old Mercury, Linda Derderian and their friend Gary Silverman, the one who called her with the news of the fire, got as far as the Pep Boys auto repair shop down the road from the nightclub when a West Warwick police officer stopped them.

"You can't go down there," the young man said, his tone firm and serious.

"Is everyone all right?" Archie asked.

"There are fatalities," the officer replied.

"Fatalities?"

"Multiple fatalities."

They parked the car in the repair shop lot and Linda, Archie, and Gary headed toward the club on foot, walking quickly on the side to avoid the endless swarm of fire trucks, rescue vehicles, and ambulances. It was midnight, and in the distance flames from The Station reached into the night.

As they got closer Linda saw what appeared to be nightclub patrons wandering around the inferno, many wrapped in blankets. Several cried, while some seemed emotionally frozen. Others searched for loved ones, shouting names. It all seemed unreal to Linda, like she had succumbed to an otherworldly fog. Where was Jeffrey? Was her husband dead?

Archie was more grounded and took charge, as was his nature. As patriarch of the Derderian family and a descendent of Armenian immigrants who escaped the Turkish genocide in their homeland, Arshag Derderian was raised on stories of relatives so poor they would rinse off and reuse paper coffee filters. Waste was anathema, especially the squandering of time. When Archie lost his wife Joan to heart failure, and his sons were still children, he faced a daunting challenge. He didn't have an affectionate side like Joan, and his first response as sole parent was to be a firm taskmaster. A year after Joan died, he became involved with their family friend Karen Allen, in part to have the warmth of a family again. For Archie there was not a moment to waste, but to his sons the relationship caused strife—it happened too soon.

Still, the Derderian brothers loved their dad and looked to him for strength, guidance, and help.

At the fire, Archie assumed the role of family leader, asking questions to try to figure out what happened. Linda would always remember Archie's steady control during the crisis.

As the three got closer to the burning club they came to a car dealership. In between the vehicles in the parking lot they spotted Jeffrey. *He's alive.*

"Are you all okay?" Linda asked.

Jeffrey could barely speak. Later he would say that he didn't want to talk about himself. There was so much going on around them, so many people hurt, it was overwhelming. At that moment he could only watch the monstrous display of destruction.

Linda gaped too. At one point she found herself standing next to Jack Russell, the band's lead singer. As all the havoc swirled around them, Russell was flipping his hair. It was a detail Linda would never forget. She wondered: Who works on their hair at a time like this?

Archie continued to take command, trying to hunt down information from anyone who would talk, but there was total confusion. At first there was word that some of their friends, including Andrea and Steve Mancini, did not escape. Then someone said they spotted the couple being transported away to the hospital, and described Steve in the back of a truck. Still, it wasn't clear if that was really them, or just people who looked like them. No one had firm answers.

Linda realized she was freezing cold. In her haste to get out the door after receiving the phone call she had slipped out of her pajamas into the nearest sweatpants she could find, a pair of razor-thin material that offered no protection from the frigid air. She'd put on a winter jacket, but forgot gloves and a hat. A friend noticed she was shaking and took her to his truck a few blocks away and turned up the heat so she could try to warm up.

As he shut the door Linda momentarily separated from the terror outside and was left alone with her thoughts. Once again she felt the surreal fog descend, and wondered if this was really happening.

CHAPTER 15

A N HOUR AND a half after the fire started, the nightclub's structure
was nearly gone, burned to the ground with only the remnants of
walls remaining. There could be no one else alive, so firefighters continued the grim task of recovering bodies. At the area that had once been
the front entrance they'd found a macabre five-foot-tall pile of corpses.

One by one the crew removed the dead, with some firefighters overcome with grief. As they got close to the bottom of the heap, a firefighter
felt something grab his leg. He looked down and a hand held his boot.
Someone was alive under the pile. The firefighter reached down and
grasped the hand in his own, and with that touch, Raul "Mike" Vargas
knew he would live.

Like so many others, Mike was at first elated when he saw the fireworks. It was the seventh time he'd seen Great White, never before with
pyrotechnics. He initially thought, *You guys don't need to be doing that,
you already have a great stage presence*, but the place went nuts at the
spectacle. When it became clear that the wall had caught fire, Mike
yelled with others at Jack Russell, "Turn around!" Mike was only four
feet from the stage.

Mike tried to stay calm as he made his way back toward the main
entrance to exit the club, but when the room got dark everyone panicked. People yelled, "Get out! Get out! Get out!" as they tried to break
free of the mass. Mike was pushed from behind and fell onto the floor
up against a wall, and others piled on top of him. A former wrestler, he
knew to stay on his side, in a fetal position, with his hands up toward his
face—if pinned down on his chest or back he would suffocate.

The weight on top of him became heavier and the screams grew
louder. At first he heard anger, but the voices quickly changed to fear

and panic. As the pressure bore down harder, he thought, "*Oh my God, I don't want to die like this.*" Getting hysterical, however, would not free him or save his life, he told himself. He had to stay calm. The building was clearly on fire, and he felt small burns on his left leg, probably from embers, more irritating than agonizing, and he realized that the mass of people on top of him was probably protecting him from the flames. Soon the cries of agony from others began to tone down, and then stopped completely. They're dead, Mike thought.

He sucked in cool fresh air that had somehow reached the cocoon he had created for himself, and he used his hands near his mouth to keep his breathing area clear. In that tiny air pocket he prayed to the spirit of his deceased father, a heavy equipment operator who died in 1994 when he was crushed by a backhoe, a devastating loss that had Mike once consider taking his own life. Then he thought of his ten-year-old son. Mike had to make it through this for him. Don't fall asleep, he scolded himself. If you do, you'll die. He listened for signs of hope. Through the mass that surrounded him he heard sirens and rescue radios. Okay, I'm getting out of here.

He heard one firefighter say, "Oh my God, they're all dead." Mike wondered if rescuers would abandon the search for survivors and leave him under the pile. No, they can't assume that, he reasoned, they have to eventually find him.

The pressure lightened as bodies were removed from the top of the pile. Mike saw a sliver of light. Where there's light, he thought, there's got to be people. He thrust his hand toward the light and grabbed a firefighter's boot.

When a body was lifted off him, Mike sat straight up and looked in the eyes of a firefighter, who appeared stunned. Then Mike felt something behind him, a movement. He turned and saw it was another victim, a woman who was badly burned and didn't have on any clothes. She reached toward Mike.

"Just get her. Get her. I'm okay. Just get her," Mike said.

The firefighter, whom Mike later identified as Patrick Rollo, a twelve-year veteran of the West Warwick Fire Department, asked for his name.

"My name is Mike. I'm okay. My leg's just trapped underneath here, but I'm fine. I can walk out of here."

"All right, we're going to get you out of here," Mike remembered Rollo saying.

"Please take the girl behind me," Mike answered back, "she's worse off than I am."

It was 12:30 a.m. Mike had been trapped inside the inferno for nearly an hour and a half. He got up to head to his car, but was ushered instead to a nearby gurney and transported to the hospital. Mike was the last person to walk away from the fire. Wet, cold, and shivering, he had four small burns on his left leg, but was otherwise physically unharmed.

CHAPTER 16

I N THE AMBULANCE to Providence's Miriam Hospital Gina Russo talked nonstop, but not because of her injuries. "Someone call my sons," she insisted. She wanted to make sure they were okay. She also told the EMT that she had an ID card, twenty dollars, and keys to her house in her jeans pocket. Gina usually never carried her license or money with her, since her fiancé Fred, the big jovial bear, always insisted on driving and paying for everything, but for some reason she popped the ID and money in her pants that night.

She couldn't stop thinking about her sons. Images of Alex and Nick raced through her mind during her final moments of consciousness inside the burning nightclub. Fred's powerful push lunged her so close to the door, yet still she was trapped, wedged inside a mass of people all desperate to escape. Gina heard explosions and windows smashed, but the air that came inside as people escaped fueled the fire. She looked for Fred. He was gone. Instead she saw dozens of people, some on fire. The wails and cries for help became fewer, replaced by a terrifying silence, and Gina's own breaths became shorter until she could barely inhale.

This is it, she thought. *This is where I'm going to die.*

She prayed to God for her boys, that they would have good lives and forgive her for leaving them like this. The last thing she remembered as she blacked out was the impact of her head hitting the floor.

Somehow rescue workers got into the building and dragged Gina out. Triaged on the scene, she was given an injection of the powerful sedative Ativan. She was badly burned and disfigured, even under her clothes. Her skin wept from its wounds. The EMT in the ambulance remembered Gina's remark about having her ID card in her jeans, so when she arrived at Miriam Hospital in Providence she was identified. A worker in the emergency room noted on Gina's chart that she was in a state of "severe agitation."

Gina received more Ativan, plus morphine for pain, as the staff gave her a CAT scan to see if she suffered any neck, spine, or abdomen injuries in the stampede inside the club. After finding no obvious hemorrhages or injuries in the scan, doctors assessed and cataloged her burns. The flames and heat had ravaged nearly half of her body, with third-degree burns on her forearms, hands, and left shoulder, and fourth-degree burns on the left side of her face and scalp. Little of her left ear remained, and a respiratory exam revealed severe smoke and burn injuries in her airways. Death was imminent.

Gina needed to be stabilized just to survive the next few hours. She was intubated and put on a ventilator to keep her breathing, and administered doses of morphine and propofol to prevent pain. The swollen, oozing parts of her charred skin were treated with the topical antiseptic povidone iodine to destroy any microbes that might infect the open wounds.

In the following hours a surgeon performed a debridement of the burned skin from Gina's face and hands, removing the dead flesh as a way to foster healing. Her face was covered in an antibiotic ointment, and her hands and arms treated with Silvadene cream, another antibiotic, then loosely wrapped in bandages. Throughout the surgery and treatments she was heavily sedated to avoid feeling some of the most severe levels of pain a human being can endure.

By six in the morning the decision was made to transfer Gina to the burn unit at Shriners Hospital in Boston, one of twenty-two facilities nationwide that specialized in treating children. Under normal circumstances, Gina should have been transferred to Massachusetts General Hospital with its state-of-the-art burn unit, but the number of casualties from the nightclub fire had overwhelmed New England's top trauma centers and beds were full. For only the second time in the Shriners' eighty-year history, the hospital agreed to care for adult patients, and Gina was one of four. The only other time the Shriners hospital system opened its doors to adults was after the terrorist attacks on September 11 in New York.

Under more heavy sedation Gina was carefully prepared for the trip and driven by ambulance. When her mother Carol and sister Stephanie arrived in Boston they were startled by what they saw in the hospital bed. The swelling and bandages made Gina appear nearly three times her normal size, like a wrapped mummy, and her family questioned if it was really her. The disfiguring burns of the nightclub fire had made many of the survivors difficult to identify, causing agonized confusion for loved ones.

Gina's mother and sister remembered a small heart tattoo on Gina's right ankle, so the bandage was unwrapped there for a look. Once they saw it they all agreed that it really was Gina.

CHAPTER 17

W HEN BATES COLLEGE swimmer Phil Barr got out of the ambulance at Rhode Island Hospital a fiftyish nurse in scrubs yelled at him in her thick local accent: get on the gurney. I can walk just fine, Phil argued. But the nurse was having none of it. He was to get on the stretcher immediately—face down.

Phil brushed off the urgency. An EMT at the makeshift triage center at the Cowesett Inn had assessed Phil, and, yes, he needed to go to the hospital, but he didn't have the horrific burns that so many others suffered. Phil's face was blackened, but his lips were not visibly scorched, so during the triage examination it was determined that he probably hadn't suffered as much respiratory damage as others. Even in the ambulance ride, when Phil asked for oxygen, he was told that the severely burned woman on the stretcher needed it more. Phil was considered too healthy to even lie down during the ride up to Providence. Instead, he sat to the side, and it was getting progressively harder to breathe.

His face worried him most. It hurt, especially when he touched it, ten times worse than the most severe sunburn he'd ever had. In the ambulance he asked for ice for his face, but paramedics said no. Having seen the injuries of those who walked by at the fire, looking like a horror movie, Phil became increasingly aggravated, even angry—he needed some sort of relief from the pain on his face.

The nurse at the hospital didn't seem concerned about Phil's face. She was alarmed by the burn on his back. Phil had almost forgotten about it, too consumed with his face and the soot and blood he spat up. The wound on his back was severe enough that he was required to lie down on his chest.

They rolled him down the hallway through a sea of frenzy, with people running in every direction. In that position, floating prone on the gurney, it reminded him of swimming, his face slightly elevated by a pillow. The floor, everywhere for that matter, was strewn with black, bloody sheets, like a war zone.

Attendants cut off his clothes, but then moved on to others apparently in more dire need. For what felt like long periods of time Phil was left alone, stranded in a cordoned off part of the emergency room, surrounded by a white curtain. There seemed to be hundreds of people around, and at times he worried that he was forgotten. He had to urinate badly and begged to use the bathroom, but was told not to leave the stretcher for any reason, so he was eventually handed a bedpan. It became increasingly difficult to catch his breath. He complained aloud to anyone who passed that he needed help. At some point he was turned over onto his back, and that's when he saw something that made no sense.

Joe?

Phil saw a familiar face looking down on his. It was his classmate Joe Chan from Bates College. How was this possible? They'd known each other since freshman year, and had lived and dined together at Smith Hall, one of the dormitories. But that's way up in Maine, not here in Rhode Island.

"Phil," Joe said. It really was him.

Joe was on the last night of an internship at the hospital, part of a pre-med program, moments away from going home when news of the fire hit and the hospital was put on alert and told to expect a large number of casualties. All hands were needed, even students in training. Although Phil's face was covered in black soot, and he was one of hundreds of people in the emergency room, Joe had somehow recognized his friend through a small opening in the curtains.

Phil tried to tell Joe about his struggle to breathe, but he couldn't get all the words out. From that moment on Phil was swept up into a burst of attention and whisked off for a chest X-ray. Joe stayed by Phil's side as they learned the grim diagnosis: even though he was relatively uninjured on the outside, there was respiratory damage, but the doctors couldn't tell how bad it was until they conducted a more thorough, invasive investigation. To save Phil's life, they had to put him out, and it had to happen right now.

As the IV went into his arm, Phil looked up at Joe's face, searching for some sort of reassurance in his friend's eyes. Instead, the last thing Phil saw was fear. Joe Chan was as white as a ghost.

CHAPTER 18

"THERE'S A BAD fire," Kenny McKay, the governor's aide, said over the phone. Twenty people were feared dead.

It was eleven thirty and Rhode Island governor Donald Louis Carcieri and his family had moments earlier tucked in their grandchild after an evening at Disney World in Orlando. They'd just made the two-hour drive back from the theme park to the family's condominium on Hutchinson Island in Stuart, Florida, an area of beaches and nature preserves north of Palm Beach.

The vacation had started on an awkward note when a snowstorm hit Rhode Island earlier in the week. Blizzards and bad weather historically had an oversized impact on the political careers of governors in the tiny state, leading to fame or infamy, depending on how quickly roads were plowed. Luckily this latest storm wasn't severe, so Carcieri only had to put up with some ribbing for being hundreds of miles away soaking up rays in the Sunshine State while his constituents shoveled.

His colleagues had warned him that as a new governor some sort of disaster would likely test him within his first six months. Tonight was only six weeks. It was Carcieri's first job in politics, an entrée into government work starting at the top—his background was business, a career that brought him to the highest levels of management at Old Stone Bank and Cookson America, a manufacturing giant. Bespectacled with a gray mane and a soft-spoken, solid demeanor, at sixty years old he looked the part of a successful executive. His roots, however, were working-class Rhode Island, the son of a local high school teacher and coach. After graduating from Brown University, Carcieri was a math teacher before transitioning into the corporate world.

McKay told the governor he was on his way to West Warwick and would know more once there. When the aide described the location, Carcieri knew the place. He'd been there many times when it was a restaurant. "Brillo's? That's a nightclub?" McKay explained that the property had been a club for many years, but the governor remembered fondly bringing his children there when it was a restaurant with big bowls of spaghetti and pitchers of Coke. Carcieri always thought the joint was a bit of a dump, but the kids loved it. Then he recalled the battered wooden floors and all the grease and oil they must have absorbed over the years.

After midnight McKay called back. It looked like there could be thirty or even forty people dead.

"You've got to get me the hell out of here," the governor said.

By two in the morning the Florida State Police picked up Carcieri and raced him to the nearest airport in West Palm Beach for the first flight out at five thirty. Carcieri had always considered himself a problem solver in the business world, with a knack for analyzing a challenge and mapping out the steps necessary. That was his strong suit, he thought, and that reputation had brought him all the way to the governorship on his first try, beating out his own Republican Party's establishment that had sided with his opponent in the primary, and later winning the race against the state's deeply entrenched Democratic Party machine. Carcieri began thinking of ways he would apply his problem-solving techniques in this crisis. In business he made sure people got the resources they needed, and he wanted to set that same standard as governor. He ran and won on that vision, and now it would be tested.

When the governor changed planes in Charlotte every TV monitor played nonstop national cable news coverage of the nightclub inferno. At the gate the agent looked at Carcieri and motioned to one of the screens. The governor looked up to see a photograph. Reporters said they were waiting for the man in the picture—the person in charge—to arrive at the fire.

The man in the photo was Don Carcieri.

THE TOLL

CHAPTER 19

A T SHRINERS HOSPITAL Gina Russo's family was told to prepare for the worst.

Burn victims often die for three reasons: shock from a loss of fluids that perilously lowers blood pressure, infections, or lungs so damaged they no longer process enough oxygen.

Gina faced all three perils. Her burns were so severe that her skull was exposed. Doctors raced to replace lost fluids in a precarious balancing act—too much could cause more swelling or blood clots. She suffered a dangerous infection, and couldn't breathe on her own. By Sunday, three days after she was pulled from the fire, her oxygen-starved organs began failing.

Doctors suggested that the entire family should come to the hospital for Gina's final hours. A priest administered last rites. "May the Lord Jesus protect you and lead you to eternal life . . ."

Gina's brother-in-law Matt Reinsant, normally a driven type-A guy, explained to Nicholas and Alex, ages six and nine, that their mother was about to go to heaven. A social worker gave Matt a card to be opened when Gina died that would explain death to the boys in words that they could understand, written at the Dr. Seuss level.

Alex asked one of his aunts to take him to the hospital's chapel. He went in alone and prayed. When he emerged he was suddenly smiling, and explained that after his conversation with God he was confident his mother would not die.

The optimism of a child faced a grim reality. Gina continued to deteriorate.

Doctors threaded flexible fiber optic scopes into Gina's lungs and discovered that the inside was coated with a thick tar substance that crippled her ability to take in air. With a new type of ventilator they'd never before used on a patient in this condition, doctors applied a solution of nitric acid to try to break up the tar. Within hours her organs began to show improvement. For Gina's family it was a miracle. Doctors, however, cautioned that it was only a sign of hope, and very little at that.

TWO YEARS EARLIER Gina wondered if she'd ever have love in her life again. She'd spent her entire adult life with a man whom she determined had not loved her back, at least not enough.

She met Jim Odsen when they were in high school. After dating for four years, with a few breakups along the way, they married. Gina would look back later and wonder if those early splits were signs of trouble she should have heeded, but she was young and in love, and smitten with the idea of creating a happy wedded home. In her senior year of high school she was hired for part-time secretarial work at a local hospital, which eventually became full-time. Gina took on other jobs to help make ends meet, trying to build a life like the one she grew up with in her own family. Gina knew that marriage had its challenges. Her parents, Carol and James, endured their struggles, especially when it came to having children. They tried for ten years and had started the process of adoption when, unexpectedly, Gina's older brother Jim was born. Within four years there were three children, with Gina in the middle. Their family bliss would not last long. At age fifty-two, Dad was diagnosed with diabetes, and seven years later he died of a heart attack. Gina was eighteen.

She remembered her parents as a devoted team, and was delighted when her mother found affection again later in life and married Vincent Richards, whom Gina had grown to love as her stepfather. The happiness of her mother's new relationship drew more attention to the fact that Gina's married life was so different. While Gina had multiple jobs, she often felt Jim didn't work enough. They fought about money. Yet it was on another level that Gina thought she was getting the short end of the bargain: emotion. As years went by, Gina grew to believe that Jim couldn't reciprocate when it came to her level of love. The emptiness between them soon evolved into resentment, resulting in bitter arguments.

"To have and to hold, from this day forward, for better, for worse, for richer, for poorer, in sickness and in health, until death do us part."

Gina thought of her vow. She couldn't throw in the towel on her marriage—even if she wasn't sure about Jim, she was still committed to making the relationship work. Five years into the marriage their first son, Alex James Odsen, was born. Gina hoped the new baby would change everything, yet she and Jim continued fighting, and even separated a few times. After each breakup, though, they reconciled and life would go on without too much drama, for a little while. Three years after Alex came a little brother, Nicholas. Gina was hopeful when she saw Jim being fatherly with his sons, especially when they were old enough to go on walks and play ball.

The arrival of the boys didn't heal the couple's deep wounds, and if anything, the problems worsened. In 1999 Gina asked for a divorce, and eventually moved with the boys into her mother and stepfather's home. When attempts at reconciliation failed, the divorce proceedings devolved into acrimony that lasted two years. When the paperwork was finalized in July 2001, Gina felt an enormous burden lifted.

Despite the emotional exhaustion of her failed marriage, Gina wasn't about to completely give up on men. But by the beginning of 2002, at age thirty-four, it had been nearly two decades since she'd last dated anyone. Gina wondered, how do you find a guy these days? Probably not in a bar, her friends said. Besides, technology and the Internet had upended the whole idea of dating since the last time Gina looked for a boyfriend. With the help and encouragement of her friend Trish, Gina created a profile on HipDates.com.

It was hardly a panacea, and Gina soon learned the painful truth about online dating: the odds are good, but the goods are odd. Gina received inquiries almost immediately, but didn't click with any of the guys. On April 28, when a man arrived at their dinner date in Providence via public bus, Gina was done. What type of guy doesn't even own a car? She lived in the suburbs of Cranston, with kids no less. Was she going to give him rides every time they went somewhere? She was about to deactivate her account on May 2 when she saw the note from Fred Crisostomi, a big grizzly of a guy who owned his own painting business.

Moments later Fred happened to sign on live to the site at the same moment and sent Gina an instant message. "Did you copy my profile?" he jokingly asked as his opening line.

Gina grinned as she read Fred's description page. Sure enough, they had so much in common, sharing the same answers to so many of the website's get-to-know-you questions. Gina decided to take a chance and instant-messaged Fred back, and so began the chat session that would change her life.

IT WASN'T A fluke.

The new ventilator with the nitric acid had worked to break up the tar coating in Gina's lungs, and now doctors at Shriners wondered if they'd discovered a breakthrough treatment that could be used on other burn patients. For Gina the progress was slow, but within a week her organs, no longer oxygen-starved to the point of failure, were able to perform sufficiently on their own. The progress was remarkable, even though her lungs remained so damaged that she couldn't breathe on her own. She required ongoing intubation and the use of a ventilator.

Now relatively stable, there was chance of survival. That meant it was time to deal with the burns, and dead skin needed to be removed and replaced with healthy skin grafted from other parts of her body, an agonizing process. If not done soon the necrosis could spread, and Gina risked having her limbs amputated.

Doctors didn't want Gina to feel the pain of the gruesome and protracted procedures ahead, so they placed her in a medically induced coma, pushing her consciousness into a dark void from which she might never emerge.

CHAPTER 20

THE REMNANTS OF the nightclub still smoldered when Governor Donald Carcieri arrived Friday around noon. The chaos of EMTs treating the injured, the bloody mayhem of the makeshift triage center at the Cowesett Inn, and the howling sirens of ambulances racing survivors away to hospitals had been replaced by the solemn task of recovering bodies.

Heavy construction equipment carefully lifted small pieces of debris where the club's floor had collapsed, and workers feared a cluster of corpses below. The state of Connecticut loaned cadaver dogs for multiple sweeps of the site. As each person was retrieved, work paused for a moment of prayer.

Carcieri had seen death up close once before. Many years earlier he witnessed the collision of a small car with a large truck, and when he went to see if he could help he watched two trapped passengers in the car die while waiting for first responders. Those images stuck with him: seeing the car fly into the air as if lifted by some invisible force, and then the blood, and a little French Canadian woman in the back seat crying, "Help me! Help me!" He could never shake what he saw that day, but even that horror could not prepare him for The Station.

The number of dead was ninety-six.

Families had come forward to report the names of missing loved ones who were at the show, but could not be located at hospitals. The state developed a list of those possibly deceased, although identifying bodies and matching remains to someone on the list would be difficult. Many of the bodies were disfigured or destroyed beyond recognition.

Adding to the confusion were false reports of missing people. One local landlady said her tenant told her he was going to the show and had not come home. After a multistate manhunt, the man was located. He had changed his mind and went to visit a friend out of state. There was also an attempt at fraud. Within hours of the fire someone filed a false report in an apparent attempt to fake someone's death. "You want to strangle them," the governor later said. Precious time and resources had been wasted investigating the hoax while families suffered.

The state opened a center for victims' families four miles away from the nightclub at the Crowne Plaza hotel in Warwick, with the Red Cross and local clergy there to console and deliver the news when a loved one was identified. The governor and his team felt these professionals were more experienced and better suited for managing such a shattering trauma.

The hotel also provided families a place to grieve in private and offered protection from aggressive members of the press corps, which had grown into a huge international scrum. The scope of the tragedy had grabbed worldwide attention: no single fire had claimed so many lives in America in decades.

Adding to the drama was the video shot by Jeffrey Derderian's Channel 12 news photographer, Brian Butler.

Butler was recording as Great White took the stage, burst into song, and ignited the fireworks, and the news photographer continued videotaping inside as the nightclub walls turned into sheets of flames. After he escaped Butler kept recording outside as the building succumbed to inferno in mere seconds. Moment by terrifying moment, including the agonizing doomed faces and screams of patrons, was captured on video in horrific detail. "I saw what happened. I have it all on tape from inside," Butler said as he called back to the newsroom from the scene. Professional news crews rarely captured catastrophes of this scale, the footage comparable to the *Hindenburg* airship explosion in 1937 and the collapse of the Twin Towers on September 11, and the video quickly became a media sensation and obsession, picked up by countless news organizations, both on television and the Internet. Tens of millions watched the disturbing images, broadcast in nearly every corner of the planet.

Then there was the added news that Butler's reason for being in the nightclub was to videotape for an upcoming story on safety in public venues, an irony that added a vicious, irresistible twist. News organizations from across the nation, and some from foreign countries, raced reporters to West Warwick, with each team competing for its own unique angle or scoop. As was often the case in covering major breaking news stories, the rush to be first led to reporting laden with errors.

The Crowne Plaza was where relatives of the missing could get reliable news about the investigation and recovery efforts. Many had been antagonized and whipped into anger at news coverage that the governor later described as "all bad information." Rumors were reported that the state had identified victims and withheld the information, which tortured loved ones. To squelch this upsetting gossip, the governor gathered the families at the hotel and told them to stop believing what they'd read in the paper and seen on TV. Going forward, he would be their source.

"Look, here's my promise to you," Carcieri told the families. "I'm going to be here twice a day and if you don't hear it from me, don't believe it. I'm going to tell you exactly what's happening during the night and during the day. I'm going to tell you everything I know and if you don't get it from me, forget it. It's people talking that don't have the knowledge."

The hard truth was the enormous number of victims was beyond anything the state medical examiner's office could process quickly. Carcieri's first encounter with Dr. Elizabeth Laposata, the chief of the Office of the State Medical Examiner, was frustrating. The governor immediately sized Laposata up as capable, but officious. The doctor told Carcieri she had experience with identifying the dead from disasters involving a large number of casualties, pointing to her work on the Egypt Air crash off the coast in 1999 that killed 217 people and involved 6,000 pieces of human remains—no victims were found intact.

"Doctor, no offense, but if I recall, that took a year," the governor said. "We've got a week."

Carcieri could not fathom making families at the Crowne Plaza wait for more than a week to learn the fate of loved ones. He asked Laposata about how many hours it took to process each victim, and then said he wanted shifts staffed twenty-four hours a day to complete the process. Carcieri had his businessman hat on again: the problem solver. This was a matter of determining the amount of resources needed, and then supplying the personnel. Neighboring states offered their best forensic specialists to Rhode Island, and that's how the work would be done quickly.

Still, the process was excruciatingly slow. By Saturday afternoon, two days after the fire, only nine of the ninety-six bodies found at the site had been identified, and that number increased to just fifteen by that night. As the names trickled in, the crowd at the hotel became smaller. The victims identified in those first rounds were those whose remains were still recognizable, or could be determined by the jewelry they wore or tattoos. After that, the governor had to go to the families with a difficult request.

"We need more information," the governor told the remaining families. "One of the things we need is the name of the dentists."

As he looked into the aghast faces of the crowd, Carcieri could tell the families knew what this meant. Their loved ones' remains were so burned beyond recognition that it would take dental records to positively identify them. Family members wept as they envisioned horrific, agonizing deaths. The governor assured them that their relatives did not suffer the way they imagined—most had perished due to the lack of oxygen and the smoke. "They were dead before their bodies were burned," he told them. It was an upsetting detail, but knowing that someone was likely unconscious when they died brought some measure of comfort.

Carcieri also consoled survivors. While making the rounds at hospitals to check on the status of those injured, the governor discovered that some who escaped were overcome with survivor's guilt. At a hospital in Worcester, Massachusetts, Carcieri was struck by one young man's grief.

"Governor, why did I survive?" the man cried. "My friends didn't. Why did I? I don't understand why."

"Nobody knows that," Carcieri replied. "Only God knows that. But you survived for a reason. You'll find that reason at some point and some time, but you know you survived."

Despite being a weekend, and with the help of a local insurer, dental records were located and the number of victim identifications grew. Carcieri returned to the medical examiner's office to keep up the pressure to work as quickly as possible, one time hovering over the coroner as she signed a stack of reports. The number of families waiting for news at the Crowne Plaza continued to shrink.

One week after the fire the bodies of four victims remained unidentified, not recognizable even with dental records. The governor had to confirm the families' worst fears with his latest request for their help.

He needed DNA samples.

CHAPTER 21

W HEN MICHAEL DERDERIAN, The Station nightclub's other co-owner, left the plane with his son Alec at T. F. Green Airport in Warwick on Friday afternoon he was confronted by a coterie of police and prosecutors, including William J. Ferland, one of the top lawyers from the office of Patrick Lynch, Rhode Island's attorney general.

Michael looked at the men warily. There must have been at least ten of them.

"Would you talk to us?" one asked.

Michael was stunned. He never expected to be accosted at the airport. It wasn't supposed to happen, he thought. *These guys were specifically told not to talk to me.*

When he received Jeffrey's frenzied phone call from the fire, Michael and his son were leaving Emeril Lagasse's restaurant at Universal Studios in Orlando, with plans to board a cruise the next day with Michael's girlfriend Kristina Link. Hearing his little brother's anguished voice had made the adrenaline pump through Michael's veins and scatter his thoughts, and upon reaching the parking lot he could not remember where he left the rental car.

Panic was not his style. Michael was the cool one of the brothers, the money guy who had long ago left the family's grocery business to become a financial advisor, first with Merrill Lynch and then on his own. He wore nicely tailored suits over his fit five-foot-four frame, had two homes, one near the beach, and knew how to get along with people, all types, from blue collar to wealthy clients. Michael was a charmer to some, a smooth operator to others, and admittedly sometimes a bit too full of himself, and even though he'd just gone through a bitter divorce— and after nearly twenty years of marriage Judi really knew how to push his buttons—he still exuded confidence, crucial in his line of work. Michael did not show weakness. He was Archie Derderian's son.

When Michael and son Alec arrived at their Florida hotel room the fire was on CNN with wall-to-wall coverage. *Holy shit*, Michael thought, it was worse than he imagined. They were reporting there might be people dead. He repeatedly called Jeffrey to find out more, and at one point his brother handed the phone to a police officer who peppered Michael with questions. Did you give the band permission to do this? No. "Did you arrest them?" Michael asked in return. He told the officer that he and his family were scheduled to leave on a cruise the next day. It's best you come back to Rhode Island, the officer said.

At six in the morning Michael received a call from his attorney, Kathleen M. Hagerty, who had seen the fire on the news. Hagerty had handled Michael's divorce, and her office was working on the sale of the nightclub. Kathy, as Michael called her, was steely and smart, with a youthful visage that defied being in her forties, and she was intimately familiar with the Rhode Island criminal justice system as a former special assistant attorney general for eight years, when James O'Neil and Jeffrey Pine were in charge. Hagerty knew the players and their agendas, and she told Michael not to talk to investigators. Michael explained that he'd already spoken to the police over the phone, and Jeffrey had talked to police and prosecutors from the attorney general's office at the scene. The brothers had nothing to hide.

No more, Hagerty said. Later she told Michael that she called Ferland, the prosecutor, and informed him that her client had legal representation and that police and the attorney general's office did not have permission to question Michael.

So after the flight, where he watched on a tiny seatback monitor the nonstop news coverage of the growing number of deaths in his club, Michael was floored when he departed the plane and a lineup of officers and attorneys confronted him. They'd been explicitly told that he had a lawyer and they were not allowed to question him, and yet they showed up to create a scene in the middle of the airport, in front of a crowd of onlookers.

So that's how this is going to work, Michael said to himself.

"You've got to talk to Kathy," Michael said to the men as he walked away, referring them to his attorney.

Michael was unaware that the focus of the investigation had already shifted.

Despite Brian Butler's Channel 12 video that showed Great White igniting the fireworks—explosives that were outlawed in Rhode Island except under strict conditions—the finger of blame had turned from the band toward the club owners. West Warwick police chief Peter Brousseau told the Associated Press that the Derderians "most definitely" would face criminal charges. Only hours had passed since the blaze started, no investigation had been completed, and, in fact, the quest for answers had barely begun—the nightclub site still smoldered. No grand jury had considered any evidence, and it would take a team of federal experts more than two years to piece together exactly what went wrong and issue its findings.

None of that mattered. There had already been a rush to judgment. The police chief had publicly pronounced guilt, and his statement was carried by the news media, both locally and around the world.

CHAPTER 22

THE DERDERIANS AND their lawyers had good reason to be wary of local officials. Corruption in Rhode Island, especially its legal system and government, was legendary. At a time when many Americans increasingly harbored doubts about the workings of their institutions, Rhode Island was well ahead of the nation in providing reasons for distrusting authorities.

Geographically it's the nation's smallest state, just thirty-seven by forty-eight miles in size, but actually has the longest official name: Rhode Island and the Providence Plantations. When some thought the slavery-era word "plantation" was racially insensitive, an amendment to shorten the state's name to just "Rhode Island" was put on the ballot. It failed miserably by a four to one margin. Defiance has been part of the state's essence from its beginnings, earning it the nickname Rogues' Island during the era of the pilgrims.

Rhode Island was founded in 1636 by Roger Williams after he was convicted of heresy and sedition and banished by the Massachusetts Bay Colony, the Puritan settlement in Boston, for spreading dangerous ideas, such as the separation of church and state and freedom of religion. Having learned the languages of the Native Americans, upon his arrival Williams greeted members of the Narragansett Indian tribe in their own tongue, saying, "What cheer, netop (friend)." Tribes granted Williams land at the top of Narragansett Bay, an idyllic perch of stunning natural beauty, and he founded a settlement called Providence, "having a sense of God's merciful providence unto me in my distress." Williams established the First Baptist Church there, but unlike most of the colonies at that time, his settlement made no religious demands on its inhabitants, did not force natives to convert to Christianity, and welcomed people of all faiths, including Jews as early as 1658. The first synagogue in America was built in Newport, and remains open.

Williams's ideology for his colony was "a lively experiment," and from its earliest days Rhode Island was ahead of others in spurning authority and conventions. In 1652, more than two hundred years before the Civil War, it was the first of the thirteen colonies to pass an abolition law against African slavery. Rhode Islanders were among the first to rebel against the crown when they set fire to the British naval vessel *Gaspee* in 1772, sixteen months before the Boston Tea Party. Two months ahead of the Fourth of July and the Declaration of Independence, Rhode Island was the first colony to renounce its allegiance to King George, and in 1790 was the last to ratify the Constitution and become part of the United States—and that only happened by a narrow vote after the founding fathers agreed to create the Bill of Rights. The Industrial Revolution started in America in Pawtucket, Rhode Island, when Samuel Slater built a water-powered cotton-spinning mill in 1793, basing his plans on a mill he'd apprenticed at in England. Slater had absconded with the most sophisticated technological knowledge of the day, and helped launch a fledgling nation into becoming an economic powerhouse, one not subservient to Europe. The British called him "Slater the Traitor."

Brash, rebellious thinking like this would serve the state well for decades, making it a leader in manufacturing, commerce, and finance. By the late 1800s and into the turn of the century Providence was one of the richest cities in America, and Newport became a favorite playground of the nation's high society, with mansions for the wealthiest families of the era, including the Vanderbilts, Astors, and Morgans. The culmination of this age of opulence and success was construction of the Rhode Island State House, completed in 1904, composed of 327,000 cubic feet of white Georgian marble with the third-largest self-supporting marble dome in the world, after St. Peter's Basilica and the Taj Mahal, and atop it stands a symbol meant to capture the spirit of the state, sculptor George Brewster's eleven-foot-tall gilded statue of "The Independent Man."

Starting in the late 1800s a wave of immigrants arrived, primarily from Italy and Ireland, attracted by innumerable jobs at local factories and mills, and by the 1920s and 1930s they began to assert their own political will, altering the fabric of Rhode Island. Roger Williams's Protestant outpost became the state with the highest per capita percentage of Roman Catholics in the nation, with the church wielding considerable influence. Organized crime gained a foothold with the Patriarca family reportedly controlling the entire New England mob from its headquarters on Providence's Atwells Avenue, the city's Little Italy neighborhood. Historians have debated whether the Mafia was the cause of widespread corruption that enveloped the state, or if organized crime simply took advantage of the situation, but from the 1940s onward the state's rebel-*with*-a-cause spirit was replaced by pay-to-play.

To a large extent, Rhode Islanders accepted this change. In working-class neighborhoods it was a badge of honor to figure out how to manipulate the system to one's advantage, epitomized by the phrases "one hand washes the other" and "I know a guy." No-show government jobs were de rigueur, and getting paid "under the table" in cash, to avoid payroll taxes, was widely accepted. If you didn't know someone on the inside, whether in government or business, you wouldn't get the best deal, and it took little effort to find those connections since the state's population had stagnated at around one million for decades, and everyone seemed to know everyone else, or at least could find someone who did. This familiarity made for a close-knit community, with only one or two degrees of separation between many people. As a result, Rhode Islanders tend to be remarkably comfortable engaging strangers, figuring they're probably already connected in some way.

In this atmosphere it was not surprising that the populace shrugged when their leaders acted less than honorably, and corruption flourished at nearly every level of state and local government. Residents had low expectations for their authorities, and their politicians lived up to those expectations. In 1983 the *Wall Street Journal* described Providence as "a smudge on the road from New York to Cape Cod."

It would often take outsiders, like the news media or federal prosecutors, to weed out the worst corruption, with some of the most egregious cases beginning to surface in the 1980s. In 1986, Chief Justice of the Rhode Island Supreme Court Joseph A. Bevilacqua resigned during impeachment proceedings over his alleged ties to organized crime. The next chief justice, Thomas Fay, was convicted of illegally directing lucrative court contracts to his own real estate firm. Governor Edward DiPrete pleaded guilty and went to prison for accepting $250,000 in bribes during his tenure from 1985 to 1991. At one point DiPrete allegedly bungled a handoff and mistakenly threw away a bag of cash and ended up dumpster diving at a Walt's Roast Beef to retrieve it. Pawtucket mayor Brian J. Sarault was arrested in City Hall in 1991 and later pleaded guilty to racketeering. Officials from the cities of Central Falls and North Providence, plus the speaker of the Rhode Island House of Representatives, all pleaded guilty in bribery and extortion cases.

Corruption was so widespread that it impacted the lives of ordinary citizens. The economy stagnated in this atmosphere of graft, leading to one of the highest unemployment rates in the nation. The state's banking system collapsed when the president of a credit and loan embezzled his customers' money, and it was discovered that the statewide insurance system created to protect deposits at dozens of local financial institutions was not properly funded, causing a banking crisis not seen since the Great Depression. Accounts were frozen and banks were surrounded by state police and closed to prevent runs, and more than three hundred thousand people were cut off from their savings for up to a year.

Despite episodes like these, Rhode Island voters defiantly continued to return politicians of dubious character to office again and again.

No single politician personified Rhode Island's embrace of corruption more than Vincent A. "Buddy" Cianci, a mob-busting state prosecutor who became mayor of Providence. Cianci was a master at whip-smart one-liners who was engaging and entertaining, but also suffered deep character flaws that would overshadow his achievements and further stain the state's reputation. He envisioned Providence as an unpolished gem and catalyzed a renaissance that led to an economic and cultural rebirth, but Cianci was forced to resign and received a suspended sentence in 1984 after pleading nolo contendere to assaulting his estranged wife's alleged boyfriend with a lit cigarette, ashtray, and fireplace log, and then urinating on the man.

Cianci would later deny the details of this incident and claim that he merely threatened the man. "No one urinated on anyone," he told the *New York Times*, but he turned his infamy into a popular career in talk radio and as a local television news commentator. After his sentence expired he was eligible to run for mayor again and was reelected in 1991, only to be convicted of racketeering corruption in 2002 and sentenced to five years in federal prison. When released he went back into radio and television and ran again for mayor as an independent in 2014, then seventy-three years old, but lost in a three-way race after the Republican Party candidate essentially quit the contest and asked his supporters to vote for the Democratic Party candidate to prevent Cianci from prevailing.

The disgrace Cianci brought to Providence, and the state as a whole, mattered little to many locals. While in other jurisdictions he would be stripped of his pension for a corruption conviction, in Providence he was honored with an official portrait at City Hall in 2015. Sensing the irony, Cianci joked at the unveiling ceremony, "This is not the first time I've been framed." When he died of colon cancer in 2016, Cianci was hailed as a hero. Flags were lowered to half-staff statewide, his body was on display in repose in City Hall for two days while thousands lined up to pay their respects, and a black carriage drawn by two white horses led a funeral cortège across the city in a snowstorm. Cianci was a rogue, to be sure, but that also made him the quintessential Rhode Islander.

Despite all of the state's travails, or perhaps because of them, Rhode Island's official motto is one simple word: *Hope.*

CHAPTER 23

O N FRIDAY MORNING, like most everyone in Rhode Island, Rene
Valcourt woke to the news of the nightclub fire. A house painter
by day and a drummer for local bands his entire adult life, The Station
wasn't a place where Rene performed or attended shows, but he knew
people who went often, including his son, also named Rene, and his
nephew Freddy Crisostomi. As the senior Rene watched coverage of the
inferno on TV, he prayed they weren't there. The news said many people
were dead, and they were still counting.

Rene was surprised to discover that someone had filmed inside the
nightclub when the fire started. He watched the images with dread, and
at the beginning of the clip he felt his heart pound as he recognized two
people he knew. In the video, right at the front of the stage, were Freddy
and his fiancée, Gina Russo.

Rene raced over to the home of his niece, Freddy's sister Nancy De-
Pasquale.

"He was right in front the stage," he told her, describing what he'd
seen on the video.

He called Freddy's cell phone. No answer. He kept calling over and
over.

Nothing. Nothing. Nothing.

Rene felt fear and panic building inside, but that wasn't going to help
anyone. He'd always been a solid, steady guy, one who wasn't given to
complaining, so Rene instinctively switched into work mode. The news
said victims were taken to local hospitals, so he got on the phone and
called one after another and asked if they had Freddy.

"We're not sure if he's here," he was told at one local emergency room, but they'd check. When Rene called back he was told Freddy was at an-other hospital and told him to call there.

He's alive! Thank God. Rene shared the news with his niece Nancy, and Freddy's mother, also named Nancy, who was at the house. They hadn't seen him yet, but Freddy was in a hospital. That meant he had survived. Everyone breathed a sigh of relief.

Rene called the other hospital, but they didn't have Freddy's name on their list either. Instead, they directed him to another emergency room where they had information that Freddy had been admitted. Rene called that hospital, and again he couldn't get a firm answer. It became clear that with so many people hurt there was a great deal of confusion, and the names of the injured were not all known. Rene called every hospital he could think of, and his niece Nancy got in her car and went in person as they received tips about where Freddy might be. Between the two of them, on the phone and in person, they'd find Freddy. With each call Rene realized just how huge the fire had been. On the television they kept increasing the death toll. He felt terrible for those people who'd lost loved ones.

As the search for the correct hospital continued, Rene was flooded with memories of Freddy. Even though Freddy was his nephew, his sis-ter's son, they were remarkably close. When Freddy was born, Rene was fifteen years old, still a kid himself. At first he was Freddy's babysitter, but over the years they became buddies and then friends. It was Rene who introduced Freddy to the world of live rock music, since Rene was a musician. He wanted Freddy to play drums too, but Freddy just didn't have the knack.

Rene, of French Canadian ancestry—but his name doesn't include the accent, so it's pronounced "rainy"—had better luck teaching Freddy the house-painting business. After his stint in the Navy, Freddy worked for Rene at first, and eventually went off on his own and started F.C. Painting, with decent success. Rene wasn't surprised. Freddy was such an upbeat, charming guy that customers couldn't help but love him, and they would eagerly refer him to others—all of his new clients came in by word of mouth.

In the decades he'd known Freddy, Rene had never seen him down in the dumps. When Freddy's relationship with his girlfriend Denise ended, he shook it off and saw the bright side—they had a son together,

Brandon, and Freddy loved his stepdaughter Nicole, Denise's child from a previous relationship. Those kids meant the world to Freddy, and they wouldn't be in his life if he hadn't met Denise. Why would he not be cheerful? He just didn't see things in negative terms.

Since Gina entered the picture they'd gone on so many double dates with Rene and his wife, Eileen. They saw rock shows down at the Foxwoods casino in Connecticut, great acts like Three Dog Night and The Guess Who.

Gina.

Gina had survived too. He'd heard she was gravely burned and in a hospital in Boston, but alive. Rene hoped Freddy wasn't also badly hurt. The couple stood next to each other in that video, and they were inseparable—Rene thought of how they'd always snuggle when they sat together—there's no way Freddy would have left Gina inside in that fire.

It was agonizing not knowing which hospital had Freddy. Friday turned into Saturday and they still couldn't locate him.

Nancy's visits to the hospitals became more and more distraught, but at each place there was an explanation for the chaos. Hospitals admitted they weren't 100 percent sure of the identities of the victims because some were so badly burned they weren't recognizable. Survivors were being identified by the remnants of clothing they wore, or tattoos.

Nancy finally got good news at one local hospital. They'd located Freddy. She was brought to his bedside and there he was, so completely wrapped in gauze that hid his face and body that he looked like a mummy.

Then a hospital worker took her aside. It's not Freddy.

They were sorry to get her hopes up. In fact, the person in that bed wasn't even a man. The victim was so disfigured that no one was sure of the gender at first, but they had now determined it was a woman.

As news got back to Rene and the family that Freddy could not be found in any of the hospitals, Rene mentally prepared for the worst. The television news said the number of dead was now getting close to one hundred. Maybe Freddy didn't make it out.

Rene knew a guy. He feared making the phone call, but if anyone had the truth it was probably this guy who worked for the coroner's office up in Providence. They were the ones counting the dead, and the guy was a friend of both Rene and Freddy. Three excruciating days had gone by since the fire and the hospitals were still no help. They just kept saying go here, go there. No answers. Rene could feel the family's nerves at their limits for being kept in limbo so long.

Rene made the call.

The man answered. After a pause he said, "We've got Freddy here."

CHAPTER 24

WHILE FAMILIES GRIEVED their losses, and public anger swelled that a tragedy of such magnitude was even possible, stories also circulated of incredible heroics at The Station. As flames consumed the nightclub and hundreds struggled to escape, others ran toward the danger in an attempt to save lives.

Tracy King, thirty-nine years old, was a larger-than-life native Rhode Islander. Standing six feet two inches tall and more than three hundred pounds, he had an outsized personality to match. Never known for being shy, and always up for a good time, Tracy had become somewhat famous as a guest on *The Late Show with David Letterman* in the 1990s on the program's "Stupid Human Tricks" segment.

After a childhood of ear infections, Tracy had a mastoidectomy when he was in his early teens, an ear surgery that removed damaged cells from the skull, likely caused by the infections. Following the operation Tracy had a preternatural sense of balance, as if a gyroscope had suddenly been transplanted into his body. He could ride a unicycle, even up stairs, and was able to balance just about any object on his chin.

On the David Letterman show Tracy mounted a fifteen-foot canoe on his chin. He could actually manage two canoes at once, but was limited due to the height restrictions in New York's Ed Sullivan Theater where the show was taped. Tracy parlayed his celebrity and showed off his unusual talent at fairs and schools, balancing a fifteen-foot ladder, a refrigerator, a motor scooter, and picnic tables, and he often donated proceeds from his performances to Providence's Hasbro Children's Hospital. Tracy supported his wife Evelyn and three children with his day job for the city of Warwick's public works, but with his seemingly limitless energy he also did side gigs, including working as a bouncer at The Station. He was on duty the night of the Great White concert.

Tracy's brother Jody King, a local quahog fisherman in nearby Warwick, received a call from Evelyn, who'd heard about the fire on the news and was worried when she couldn't reach her husband. Jody drove to the club with his dog Princess, a shepherd-collie-Lab mix, and noticed fire trucks headed in the same direction, but it didn't immediately click then that this was a sign of danger ahead. "Tracy's gonna be at the front door," Jody King later recalled thinking during the drive, "making light of whatever just happened."

Jody arrived while the tragedy was still unfolding and parked in the lot of the Cowesett Inn. He walked to the front entrance of the nightclub, stunned to see bodies piled in the doorway. Jody took Princess and continuously circled the burning club throughout the night, searching for Tracy. As locals, the King brothers had known many of the first responders, especially police. After high school Tracy had served as a military police officer in the Army for four years.

None of the officers had seen Tracy. His remains were later found in the club.

Survivors said that Tracy pulled them out of the burning building. He was credited with breaking a window and lifting people outside to safety. Over the years, Jody King said, nine survivors have said that his brother saved their lives. Tracy kept running into the burning club to retrieve people, and sacrificed himself.

Jody wasn't surprised by his brother's heroism. They were the children of a mixed-race couple in the 1950s, a black father and a white mother, and his parents faced oppressive discrimination. Theirs was a life built on endurance and sacrifice.

"My parents always told us, 'Never say die. Never give up. Turn the other cheek to live another day.' Those are some of the mantras because of skin color that we had to live with," Jody said. "And Tracy lived it fullest. Never say die. Never give up."

Jody faced racism in the Warwick schools as one of only a handful of black students. One of his best friends during those tough years was a young man who never made an issue of someone's skin color: Michael Derderian, the future co-owner of The Station nightclub. The two men shared a special bond since childhood, one that would be tested in the aftermath of the fire.

In close-knit Rhode Island, there were countless connections like that with the nightclub and its victims.

Also trapped inside the burning club was one of Tracy's first loves. They'd met when they were young teens at the Riverdale Roller Rink in Warwick. Tracy was her first kiss, and she was his first kiss. They were all grown up with families of their own by the time of the nightclub disaster, but that early teenage romance was fondly remembered.

Tracy's first kiss was shared with Gina Russo.

CHAPTER 25

MICHAEL DERDERIAN HAD never experienced anything like it. His little brother had been on television for years, but that was Jeff's world, not Mike's. He was from another profession, a financial advisor, so when Michael walked into the ballroom at the Sheraton Hotel in Warwick at six o'clock on Saturday evening, two days after the fire, he was astonished.

News media from all around the world packed the room—dozens of photographers, television cameras, and reporters from newspapers, television, radio, and cable—assembled for a press conference. A bank of microphones sat in front of a small desk with chairs. As Jeffrey, his wife Linda, Michael, and the brothers' father Archie walked from a side door across the room to take their place, the room was silent. No one yelled a question. No one made a noise. They were there to listen. It was the first time the Derderians, the nightclub's owners, would speak publicly about the fire.

The silence struck Jeffrey. He'd been part of media hoards countless times, and never recalled a press corps so devoid of sound. Even though some in the crowd were his journalism peers, people he'd worked alongside for most of his professional career, no pleasantries were exchanged. He would remember later, "No one came up to me and said, 'Oh hey, how are you doing? How are you holding up?' And I didn't go up to anybody."

Their legal advisors opposed the brothers talking to anyone in the press or making any sort of statement. Anything the Derderians said could and would be used against them, but Michael and Jeffrey had nothing to hide. They never gave the band permission for fireworks, and they were waiting for answers like everyone else to find out why the fire spread and killed so quickly.

Jeffrey was especially adamant about talking. "I covered people for twenty years and people who didn't come forward and didn't say anything or ran from cameras, they were guilty. And I wasn't guilty," he said.

Michael agreed. "We weren't dodging and hiding," he said. "That's just not what we do."

It stunned the Derderians how quickly officials in Rhode Island turned on them. They remembered how only a few weeks earlier, during preparations to sell the club, West Warwick's affable homegrown police chief, Peter Brousseau, wrote a letter that praised the brothers. "Over the last couple of years the Police Department has received great cooperation from the current owners whenever there was a problem. I would assume that the new owner would also work with the Police Department to be a good neighbor."

Great cooperation. Good neighbor. Yet now they were treated with suspicion, with remarks from town officials to the media that made it seem like the brothers had been notoriously bad businessmen.

It wasn't true, and the Derderians wanted their side of the story heard. They would keep it brief. The plan was for Jeffrey to read a prepared statement, and that would be all. Michael would not speak, and they would not take questions.

As the Derderians sat at the table, their attorney Kathleen Hagerty stood behind them. Linda gently placed her hand on Jeffrey's leg, a touch to remind him she was there and she loved him. Linda had made sure that no one had seen her cry since the tragedy, not the boys and especially not her husband or his family. She felt she needed to be a steady force during the crisis, for everyone else's sake. When she couldn't hold it in any longer she wept in private in her car or behind closed doors. Now her touch would remind Jeffrey of her strength.

It was not enough.

Jeffrey openly sobbed almost as soon as he started to read the statement. Images of the fire bombarded his mind with every choked word. Why did he live when so many died? The guilt and trauma crushed him, and not just mentally—his body was in rebellion too. In the days since the fire he could not stop trembling, and Linda kept holding him to try to absorb the tremors.

"It's very difficult to express what I experienced at the club that evening trying to get people out safely," Jeffrey said. "Please know I tried, as

SCOTT JAMES • 94

hard as I could. Many people didn't make it out, and that is a horror that will haunt me and my family for the rest of our lives."

He couldn't stop the tears, but needed people to hear the truth about the fireworks. "It was a total shock to me to see the pyrotechnics going off when Great White took the stage," Jeffrey continued, thinking of the video. "No permission was ever requested by the band or any of its agents to use pyrotechnics and no permission was given."

When he finished reading the statement the press corps reacted with more silence. As the Derderians walked across the room to the exit, not a single reporter shouted a question, the way Jeffrey would have if he'd been among them. The only reporter to be aggressive was one from his old TV station, Channel 7 in Boston, who showed up at Archie's house to corner Jeffrey as he walked out to his car. Jeffrey gave a brief comment about how he too was searching for answers. "Obviously we're devastated by what happened here. We want to cooperate." He'd been advised by attorneys to not grant interviews, but later he would explain that it was "in my DNA" to speak when the reporter showed up, so he wouldn't look like he was concealing anything. It would be the last time Jeffrey was interviewed by anyone in the news media about the fire.

Michael, for his part, felt relieved. It was unnerving to face that onslaught of cameras, but the information had to be said. At least they were doing *something*.

The *New York Times* and other news outlets had already jumped on the question of whether Great White had permission to use fireworks. Within the first full day's news cycle, reporters tried to verify Great White's claim that it only used pyrotechnics when the band received prior permission from venues.

"We had permission," Great White's lead singer Jack Russell said in an interview at the Crowne Plaza, where the families of the dead gathered. "We never have not had permission."

Nightclub owners across the country immediately said this was not true.

Domenic Santana, the owner of the famed Stone Pony club in Asbury Park, New Jersey, where Bruce Springsteen got his start, said Great White used fireworks similar to those that caused the fire during its show on February 14, less than a week before The Station tragedy, and the band never mentioned its plans ahead of time. If they had asked, they would have been denied, Santana said, since fireworks were not allowed at that club. To prove the point, the club provided reporters with copies of Great White's contract for the show, which was so detailed that it mentioned the specific make and brand of amplifier required, and even the size of a bag of potato chips for the band to eat. There was nothing in the contract about pyrotechnics.

"After the show, we read them the riot act and told them that was totally uncool and they put us in a precarious position and put the safety of our patrons on the line without telling us," Santana said. "They told us 'no big deal,' that these are just sparklers and they don't hurt anybody."

Jack Russell disputed Santana's comments and maintained that Great White had permission to use fireworks at the Stone Pony. Russell also said that he regularly used pyrotechnics at his shows, and that he was "standing in the sparklers like I always do."

John LaChance, general manager of the Pinellas Expo Center in Pinellas Park, Florida, said that Great White's promoter and tour manager said there would be no fireworks when the band performed there on February 7, two weeks before The Station fire, but just as the show started the pyrotechnics came out. The burst of sparks looked just like the display captured on video in Rhode Island.

"We were shocked that it happened, very upset," LaChance said.

The *Times* reported that club owners in Maine and elsewhere also said the band set off fireworks without prior permission. But some in the music industry came to Great White's defense and said the band followed the rules. Tom Fletcher, a frequent sound technician for Great White who was not at the Rhode Island performance said, "There is not a chance" that the band's tour manager, Daniel Biechele, would have used pyrotechnics unless he had permission.

The state of Rhode Island, for its part, had already moved beyond solely blaming Great White. Band members were allowed to return home to California, even though the criminal investigation had just started.

Instead, prosecutors began to focus on the Derderians, under the direction of Rhode Island's new attorney general, Patrick Lynch.

At age thirty-seven, Lynch was one of the nation's youngest attorneys general, sworn into office only forty-four days earlier. Youthful, six foot five, and lean, with handsome looks and an accent reminiscent of a

lower-tier member of the Kennedy clan, Lynch was the product of a political dynasty—his brother was a leader of the state's Democratic Party,
and his father was once mayor of Pawtucket, famous for going to the US
Supreme Court to fight to display a crèche at City Hall. Although newly
elected and politically unpolished, Lynch was not a newbie to litigating
serious crimes, having worked for years as a state prosecutor handling
murders and other violent cases. "Blood and guts" crimes, he called them.

When the fire happened Lynch had just gone to bed in a condo in
Ashland, New Hampshire, during the winter school vacation with his
wife and two young children, the first family break they'd had together
since the campaign and his installation as the state's top law enforcer.

"What's up, Kels?" he said as his daughter told him his pager and cell
phone were both going off at the same time in the kitchen. Moments later
Lynch sped along the snowy roads in the state-issued Crown Victoria,
losing a hubcap along the way, until he reached West Warwick.

Lynch walked into a nightmare, a "mass of bodies and body parts," he
said. "The one thing that that you just cannot prepare for, and you don't
get over, is the smell." The stench of burned flesh would stay with him
for a month.

"Visually, it's so overwhelming you're kind of stunned, but I just kept
saying, all right. You've seen crime scenes. This is a crime scene. You've
got to go to work, you know?"

Rhode Island was one of only a few states where the attorney general manages all serious crimes—there are no independent district attorneys to prosecute felonies, as there are nearly everywhere else in
America. At the same time, the attorney general was also responsible
for defending the state and "represents all agencies, departments and
commissions in litigation and initiates legal action where necessary to
protect the interests of Rhode Island citizens." Additionally, Lynch's office
maintained all criminal records. It was an enormous amount of power
in one person's hands, a construct that could create potential conflicts
in cases where the government itself was criminally culpable—the attorney general was tasked with prosecuting the crime, yet defending the
state's interests, and he would control the records that allowed for public
scrutiny of the process.

Although the investigation was still underway, Lynch and his team
looked at Jeffrey immediately. "We don't know if it's a crime. But if it

was, plain to see he's involved in the managing, development of the place," Lynch later said, recalling his conclusions about Jeffrey on the night of the fire.

The Derderian brothers' press conference had provided fresh ammunition for the attorney general. While the brothers thought the statement would show that they had nothing to hide, Lynch saw it differently. He gathered the press corps for his own news conference a couple days after the Derderians made their statement.

"You may recall that Jeffrey Derderian had given some tearful commentary regarding the incident," Lynch said. "I am hopeful that the Derderians are as cooperative with law enforcement as they have been with the press, because neither of the brothers had responded to questions for which we remain hopeful today of answers for all of us on, but specifically to see whether or not criminal charges can or should be filed."

Lynch said that Jeffrey had only answered "a couple of questions" the night of the fire, and his office wanted to ask more.

The comments from the attorney general to the media misrepresented what had actually happened behind the scenes. Jeffrey had spoken at length to police and a prosecutor from Lynch's own office at the fire.

At 2:20 a.m. at the Cowesett Inn, while the club smoldered across the street, West Warwick police detective George Winman interviewed Jeffrey. In that conversation Jeffrey gave details about the events that led up to the fire, including his check at about ten o'clock of the number of people who'd been let inside the club, which Andrea Mancini told him was around two hundred and sixty. Jeffrey told the detective about the moment he looked over from the bar and saw the wall on fire. The detective then asked Jeffrey to make a written statement.

"Around 11:00 p.m. the band started to perform—shortly after while at the main bar I turned and saw fire coming from the stage. I then went to the front area and grabbed a fire extinguisher and handed it to someone, I then went to the entrance to help people get out of the building," Jeffrey wrote by hand in nearly all caps.

In his report on the interview, Detective Winman did not note that Jeffrey was traumatized and likely in shock, but instead came to conclusions that raised suspicions. "Jeffrey Derderian was vague and unsure in answering many questions. He wasn't able to provide the last names of a number of his employees. He didn't know where the egg crate sound absorbing material had been obtained from or when," Winman wrote, referring to soundproofing foam on the club's walls. The detective also wanted the full names of the booking agent for the band and Great White's tour manager, which Jeffrey couldn't remember or didn't know, since his brother had handled some of those details for the show. The detective asked Jeffrey to call his brother Michael for that information, and then Winman interviewed Michael over the phone.

At 3:30 a.m. Winman was part of a second interview with Jeffrey, this one conducted by Randall White, a prosecutor with Attorney General Lynch's office. In that interview, where Jeffrey was joined by his father Archie, the prosecutor repeatedly asked about fireworks.

"Randy White asked Jeffrey Derderian a series of questions regarding the use of pyro-techniques [sic] being used in his club during past concerts by various bands. Jeffrey Derderian stated that no pyro-techniques [sic] have ever been used in his club. Randy White described a number of examples of pyro-techniques [sic], such as sparklers, flash pots that sit on the floor, devices that deploy open flames of any kind. Jeffrey Derderian adamantly denied this use of any described devices," Detective Winman wrote in his report.

Jeffrey would later say that the men tried to convince him to omit certain details from his recounting of events, including the fact that the club had hired a West Warwick police officer for crowd control and safety, and that the officer was stationed inside the front entrance when the fire started. When Jeffrey insisted that the police officer's presence be included in the statement, he remembered someone saying, "Uh, sure, if you think it's necessary."

At the time Jeffrey did the two interviews with investigators he was glad he'd spoken. He had nothing to hide, and he had not hesitated to talk with the men since he knew some of them from years covering the local news, and he was already on a first-name basis with prosecutor White. Later Jeffrey would describe the interview as collegial, with police and prosecutor acting as if they were looking out for Jeffrey's best interests. Jeffrey told them they needed to find the clicker that counted the number of people entering the club in order to determine how many were inside, and gave them his phone numbers, both cell and home numbers, plus his family members' phone numbers, and told investigators where they could find him if they needed to ask additional questions.

At his press conference the attorney general also told reporters that Michael Derderian had not spoken to investigators or responded to any questions, even though Detective Winman interviewed Michael by phone the night of the fire.

Michael and Jeffrey had only stopped talking in the wake of the statement from West Warwick police chief Peter Brousseau to the Associated Press that the Derderians "most definitely" would face criminal charges, and the brothers' attorneys had advised them to cease speaking with investigators. It was foolish to cooperate with authorities that had already publicly concluded guilt before investigating.

Jeffrey's additional brief comment, after the press conference, to Channel 7 was seen as more evidence for the attorney general's case against the brothers.

"It appears, yet again, the medium they use is the press, rather than speaking to law enforcement. So through all of you, I suppose, I implore them to, if they would, contact the local agencies and not the Boston Press Association," Lynch said to the reporters. He said that Jeffrey's comment to Channel 7 seemed to indicate that the Derderians planned to launch their own investigation, something Jeffrey never said.

Lynch's comments were tame compared to how others in Rhode Island reacted to the Derderians' press conference and statement. Outspoken survivors and victims' families did not want to hear anything from the men they increasingly felt were responsible for the disaster—nothing the brothers had to say would offer them comfort, and they should just shut up. Many didn't believe a word from Jeffrey, and since he was a guy who had been on television for many years, some saw his weeping at the press conference as a performance, something any hackneyed actor could do. It was rehearsed drama for the cameras, and those were crocodile tears.

Instead of helping to clear the air, the press conference became a weapon that would be used against the Derderians for years. Jeffrey Derderian had finally achieved the level of notoriety he'd always desired. He was now a household name.

CHAPTER 26

GREAT WHITE'S LEAD singer Jack Russell shared his account of what happened the night of the fire with the news media, beginning the night of the tragedy, but the story would change. Russell maintained that the band had permission for pyrotechnics, but other details evolved.

After escaping through the stage exit, Jack Russell stood outside in the bitter cold watching the nightclub burn, stunned by the instant inferno.

"It went up like a Christmas tree," Russell told Karen Lee Ziner, a reporter for the *Providence Journal*, one of the first journalists on the scene. The quote would be turned into a headline.

As other media descended, Russell saw an opportunity and used the backdrop of the burning club to promote the band's upcoming summer tour.

Russell had no way of knowing—no one did at that point—that so many were dead and dying inside the club. Danger and destruction were evident, however, and Russell could not find Ty Longley, one of his band members. "We're missing a guitar player," Russell told Ziner.

The decision to talk up his tour while a band member was missing and mayhem surrounded would forever vilify Russell in many minds, evidence of callousness and moral bankruptcy.

Morality was never one of the calling cards of Great White. The origins of the heavy metal band dated back to the late 1970s when Russell met guitarist Mark Kendall in Los Angeles and they began performing together. That initial partnership ended abruptly when Russell, eighteen years old and allegedly high on PCP, better known as the hallucinogenic drug angel dust, attempted with a friend to rob a drug dealer's home in Whittier, California, to steal cocaine. "I borrowed a gun from this friend of mine and we went over there and we came in the house with ski masks and were like give us your fucking coke or we'll blow your head off," Russell later said. After a scuffle he shot through a door and the bullet struck the drug dealer's live-in maid. The woman survived, but Russell was sentenced to prison.

After serving about a year behind bars Russell was released and reunited with the band. Great White released a self-titled album in 1984 "in the metal vein of Judas Priest," wrote *LA Weekly*, and "it wasn't successful." Then albums in 1987 and 1989 went platinum and double platinum, selling one million to two million copies each, and included a cover of the 1975 Ian Hunter song "Once Bitten, Twice Shy," which received a Grammy nomination for Best Hard Rock Performance in 1989. The video for the song became an MTV favorite, with Russell seen arriving on a motorcycle and featuring the actress and model Bobbie Jean Brown.

Typecast as a "hair band" due to their large coifs, the group toured with some of the most successful rockers of the time, including Bon Jovi and KISS, and filled arenas. As the 1990s rolled on, Great White's follow-up albums sold fewer copies, and infighting consumed the band, often agitated by Russell's addiction problems. Lawyers and lawsuits further disintegrated relationships, even affecting the band's name. By the time of the show at The Station, the version of the band that played the nightclub was actually called "Jack Russell's Great White."

The band was also a long way from the days when it could draw thousands to arenas, and in recent years eked along with gigs at clubs that only held hundreds. Even for these small venues, Russell would have to hustle up an audience. In the hours leading up to the show in West Warwick, Russell was seen around town handing out free tickets to anyone who recognized him or knew the band's name.

Jim Gahan and Michael Ricardi, two students from Nichols College in Dudley, Massachusetts, and hosts of the *Jim and Mickey's Power Hour* rock music show on their college radio station, excitedly drove down to West Warwick to interview Russell and at 6:15 p.m. recorded their show on the tour bus. They were thrilled when they got Russell to tape a promo for the radio station. "Hi, this is Jack Russell of Great White. You are tuned into my friends Jim and Mickey on 95.1 WNRC, rock 'n' roll!" Russell invited the guys to stick around for the show.

Michael was nineteen years old and Jim twenty-one. The two young men had unexpectedly bonded one morning in 2001 in their college cafeteria when Michael wore a shirt from the heavy metal band Poison's "Power to the People" tour, and they realized they had a shared interest in the same type of music. That first conversation, however, was cut short when all eyes in the room suddenly turned to a tragedy unfolding on television monitors. It was the morning of September 11. Theirs would be a friendship bookended by days of horrific tragedies.

While Jack Russell's Great White could no longer fill stadiums, it tried to maintain some of the spectacle. At the start of shows band manager Dan Biechele ignited pyrotechnics called gerbs, giant sparklers that shot fifteen feet into the air for fifteen seconds. Russell would sometimes stick his head directly into the sparks, feeling that they were a harmless show business special effect. At The Station he was "standing in the sparklers like I always do," Russell told WHDH-TV from the scene of the nightclub fire. "It's not a hot flame. The next thing I felt this heat, so I turned around and I see that some of the foam's on fire." That's when Russell tossed bottled water toward the flames and exited, seemingly unaware of the scope of the carnage.

But in a videotaped interview years later with host Sally Steele, publisher of *Vegas Rocks!* magazine, Russell said he was actually fully conscious of the depth of the disaster as it happened, and tried to act heroically and save his fans from the flames, but he was physically restrained and prevented from helping.

"What do I remember? I remember every single thing, you know what I mean? I don't really want to get into the people screaming. Do you want to hear about all that? People burning up to death? You want to hear about that?" Russell told Steele.

"I had my water bottle. You see it in the video, I was just trying to throw it up there. There's no chance it was gonna put it out so I went and hopped off and jumped out the back door. I got out and I called my old lady at the time on my phone. I said, 'Hey, honey. There's a fire. I think I might lose the equipment. I'll call you back in a couple minutes.' Didn't ever think it was gonna turn into what it did."

Steele asked, "Did you guys, any of the band, try to go back and get some people out?"

"Yeah, I tried to go to the back door and somebody kept pulling me down, throwing me on the grass," Russell replied.

"Who was that?"

"I don't know. I was so focused on that door, and all of a sudden it was all dark. I thought they had shut the lights out, but it was just the smoke was so black. I remember the last time I tried to go in there, somebody grabbed me, threw me on the ground and said, 'Don't go in there. You're gonna die.' I never knew who did that. I think it might have been my tour manager at the time.

"I remember coming out the back and I remember seeing my sound man laying in the snow. I grabbed him by his forearms to pull him up, and his arms just, the skin just came off like bracelets on his arms. I remember putting him on the bus and then looking for an ambulance to get him into. Then I started trying to help other people get in the ambulances and find their friends and whatnot."

Russell's description of having full awareness and prescience of the enormity of the fire, coupled with his account of a life and death struggle to save others, is at odds with his known behavior of being outside and promoting his band's upcoming summer tour. Russell's account also conflicts with other evidence. Dan Biechele, the tour manager whom Russell thinks pinned him on the grass to prevent him from rescuing others, is seen on video during this timeframe helping arriving firefighters with their hoses at the front of the burning nightclub.

As for Great White's guitarist Ty Longley, "He went to the right for some reason, instead of going out the back door," Russell said.

"I remember distinctly Ty Longley looking back at the fire really concerned," said Michael Ricardi, the student deejay, who stood directly in front of the stage. "He obviously knew that the pyro should've been out already."

Ty Longley perished in the fire.

Michael Ricardi somehow found his way through the black smoke to a broken window and jumped out, thinking that his friend and fellow Nichols College student Jim Gahan was right behind him.

He wasn't. Jim never made it out of the darkness.

"A lot of people thought I was very unremorseful," Russell later said, "and nothing could be further from the truth."

QUESTIONS

CHAPTER 27

JOEL RAWSON STARED intently at the screen and its ghastly images. A stack of human beings piled atop one another like cordwood in a doorway surrounded by flames, their tortured faces a Dantean horror. Moments later many would perish.

Rawson had requested a visit to WPRI-TV 12 to view the raw videotape for himself. As the top editor of the *Providence Journal*, Rawson did not normally hunt down details for stories that would appear in his newspaper, but The Station nightclub was unlike any coverage he'd managed in the past. The disaster was so enormous it required all of his operation's resources, and studying the raw footage shot by Brian Butler would help Rawson decide the direction of the *Journal*'s reporting. That the tragedy was captured on professional video, something incredibly rare, meant there would be access to information seen with one's own eyes, so the editor took the unprecedented step of contacting the management at Channel 12 News, a competitor, and asked if he could come to the television station for a personal viewing.

Rawson often said, "Don't look for truth in journalism. No. Look for facts that can be verified. That's its value. Verifiable fact. That's the world we live in."

As he watched the raw footage for himself, Rawson began to piece together the facts he'd ask his reporters to pursue.

Rawson awoke to the news of the fire on Friday morning, and as he heard the initial numbers of casualties, his first reaction was as a parent. His sons Stephan, age thirty-three, and Gary, age twenty-five, were the types who liked to go out and have fun. Were they there? Rawson and his wife Janeen got on the phone and hunted down their boys. "Where are you? Are you alright?" They were not at the fire.

Rawson was in the newsroom by eight and jumped into discussions of the newspaper's coverage. Karen Lee Ziner, a veteran journalist with twenty-nine years of experience who had been banished to the overnight shift after a dispute with her bosses, was the only reporter in the Providence newsroom when police and fire scanners came alive with reports of a fire. "The Station," a dispatcher said. "People trapped." Ziner called the West Warwick police and learned that hundreds were in the club, and when the call went out for all of the state's units to respond, she got in her car and raced to the scene. When Ziner arrived the inferno raged and "people walked in a gruesome parade, flesh hanging from their extended arms." She called into the newsroom, "This is another Cocoanut Grove," referring to the 1942 Boston nightclub fire that killed 492 people, including a relative of Ziner's. With her dispatches from the scene, editors scrapped the previously planned front page and had detailed coverage in print on readers' doorsteps by sunrise.

Such coverage within the confines and deadlines of a printed newspaper was remarkable, but Rawson had assembled an exceptional team. Rawson had essentially "rebuilt" the newspaper's organization in 1996 to focus on comprehensive local news coverage, something he felt the paper had strayed from in recent years. The result at the time of the fire was a news organization with unparalleled resources in the region: an editorial staff of 280, larger than the combined newsrooms of all three local television stations, which were his closest competitors in Rhode Island. Rawson had been able to maintain that editorial heft despite the purchase in 1996 of the corporation that owned the *Journal* for $1.5 billion by Dallas-based media conglomerate A. H. Belo Corporation, owner of television stations and newspapers, including the *Dallas Morning News*. Belo was infamous for being flinty with its acquisitions, squeezing money from them while making sure its Dallas properties remained well funded, since the company's executives tended to live in that community. Rawson, who had worked his way up through the *Journal's* ranks from the copy desk starting in 1971, was certain he'd be fired after Belo took over, a standard industry practice in newspaper management, but the paper was left mostly untouched by its new corporate master. It certainly helped that the paper was enormously successful for its relatively small market size, with revenues of $155 million per year.

With the nightclub fire, television had one significant edge over the *Journal*: the video. It was a rare moment-by-moment documentation of the disaster that the printed word alone would struggle to match, and the video seemed to run continuously on local, network, and cable television news.

Now as he watched the raw tape at Channel 12, Rawson was able to study the footage carefully. The speed. *What the hell?* He said to himself. *Why did this thing burn like that?* And the faces of the people in the doorway. They were going to die. He was looking right at them, and they were going to die.

Rawson had witnessed people burned to death when he served as an Army pilot in Vietnam. Two things scared him most during his war service: getting captured, and fire. During those missions, sometimes spying for the National Security Agency, he essentially rode atop a container of fuel, and his trainers made sure Rawson and his fellow pilots understood the danger. "They told us, 'You have seven seconds in a gasoline fire.'" Just seven seconds to escape, or be consumed by flames.

That threat of imminent death instilled in Rawson an elevated awareness of safety. He was a pilot before he was a journalist, and in many ways he still considered himself a pilot first. "That is an intense safety culture, and what you do in that culture, we call tombstone regulation. There's a crash. They go back. They figure out what happened," he would later say. "They figure out: Is this a failing in there in the system? Is there a failing in the machine? And you fix it. The safety culture demands that you pay attention to what failed."

Watching the Channel 12 video, Rawson saw a clear safety failure. It wasn't just the fireworks. The club itself was not safe.

CHAPTER 28

INVESTIGATORS QUICKLY DETERMINED that the fireworks Great White used were four devices called gerbs. They were placed on the floor of the stage, in between a drummer's alcove at the back wall and Jack Russell and the other performers at the front of the stage. Two of the gerbs fired vertically, creating a shower of sparks up into the air behind the lead singer, and the two others were aimed at forty-five-degree angles to both the left and right of the alcove. The combined effect of the four gerbs firing off at once would produce a wall of white blaze, making the band appear as if emerging from a volcano.

A federal investigation would later determine that the exact fireworks were each a 15×15 silver gerb, meant to shoot sparks for fifteen seconds and out to a distance of fifteen feet. The distance between the walls and the gerbs set at forty-five-degree angles was four feet, and the direct contact of the sparks at that distance ignited the walls in about ten seconds.

Gerbs are considered larger versions of sparklers, similar to those used at countless backyard picnics on the Fourth of July, but gerbs work differently. Ground aluminum is pressure packed into a cardboard tube, and when a switch is flipped an electrical current of about six hundred degrees ignites the aluminum. One end of the tube is flame retardant, so the contents of the tube burst out the other end. Titanium particles are added to create white or silver sparks.

Such indoor fireworks had grown in popularity since the 1970s, possibly inspired by pyrotechnics at large rock shows, and were fairly ubiquitous by the time of The Station disaster. "During the past decade," Julie L. Heckman, the executive director of the American Pyrotechnics Association, told the *New York Times* the day after the fire, "you see that indoor pyrotechnics have been added to family bar mitzvahs, weddings, birthday celebrations, political conventions and openings of malls."

A receipt dated January 16, 2003, showed that Daniel Biechele, Great White's tour manager, ordered 105 15×15 gerbs, plus 120 electric igniters from High Tech Special Effects in Bartlett, Tennessee. Biechele received a 20 percent discount, so each blast cost fewer than ten dollars, making the price for the pyrotechnics at The Station less than forty dollars.

Great White's 2003 tour was the first time it had used pyrotechnics, according to Paul Woolnough, the band's manager, in an interview with the *Boston Globe*. Biechele told investigators that it was Woolnough who asked for pyrotechnics for Great White because "he wanted to spice up the show."

Two years earlier, when Biechele ordered gerbs from the company when he worked for a different band, he was told, in writing, that whenever he used the gerbs he needed to make sure he received clearance ahead of time from the venue and the local fire marshal, plus have extinguishers handy and abide by federal laws for transporting pyrotechnics. There was no evidence that Biechele followed any of these rules at The Station.

When the walls caught fire, witnesses said they heard Biechele say that he'd *fucked up*.

The gerbs themselves came with a written warning to obey national fire codes for igniting pyrotechnics in front of an audience: "Once a Gerb is ignited it cannot be extinguished until it burns out. Always test fire the setup before the performance to ensure that the setup is both safe and what is required." There was no test of the gerbs at The Station before the concert.

There had been fireworks used by acts at The Station before the Great White show. The nightclub manager, Kevin Beese, and the sound technician and stage manager, Paul Vanner, who were both at the fire and escaped, said they had witnessed pyrotechnics at the club in the past, some at shows before the Derderians owned it, but also at performances during the brothers' tenure. "Sometimes it slipped through" without prior permission, Beese told the *Providence Journal*. But Beese told the paper there had been no use of pyrotechnics when Great White performed previously at the club in April 2000. "That's why I was kind of taken by it this time because I didn't see it last time."

Other witnesses said they remembered a KISS impersonation group where one of the singers breathed fire from his mouth, and another band had burning tiki torches onstage, and there had been jack-o'-lanterns with lit candles.

Despite these incidents, all of which were apparent violations, Beese said he had never seen pyrotechnics on the scale that Great White had ignited and that caused the fire, and he said that any requests for permission for fireworks were denied. Beese maintained this position through several interrogations by police and prosecutors. In an attempt to get him to change his story, the state police conducted a wiretap sting using a friend to call Beese and trick him into implicating the Derderians, but even with his guard down Beese's explanations stayed consistent.

By one account, the misuse of pyrotechnics by some bands at the club had raised concerns, and action was taken to stop it. Vanner, the stage manager, told the *Journal* that four months before the fire he'd brought up the issue of pyrotechnics with Michael Derderian during drinks after a show. "I don't know these guys that are coming into your club setting up this stuff. They don't care. They want the big boom," Vanner said he told Michael. "I can't guarantee safety in this club if you continue to do this. If you want a guarantee, Mike: None." From that day forward, until the Great White show, there were no pyrotechnic displays at the club. "He seemed to take it to heart," Vanner told the paper, although he was not sure if there had been an actual pyro ban, or if it was just coincidence.

Julie Mellini, the bartender, told the grand jury investigation that she had not seen any pyrotechnics in the four months preceding the fire.

A "big boom" was what David "Scooter" Stone expected at the start of Great White's performance. He'd heard the special effect before at The Station, a type of pyrotechnic that makes a loud blast. It does not shoot out sparks like gerbs, but it is a form of fireworks nonetheless, and also illegal under Rhode Island law without permit.

Stone, a thirty-three-year-old maintenance supervisor at an apartment complex, was a longtime club regular, and over the years had developed a habit of jumping in during big shows to play with the lighting. He'd sit behind the lighting console and flick the buttons to the beat of the music. "It's somethin' that I've really just enjoyed doing, it was fun for me," Stone later told a grand jury investigation.

The club's owners or managers didn't schedule him, so Stone said he usually learned about upcoming shows by reading advertising, and he was not paid. He just showed up. When the Derderians took over, they began giving Stone fifty dollars in cash at the end of the night for his help, and around the holidays he received a gift certificate to the Stop & Shop grocery store as an additional thank-you. No one had asked or scheduled Stone to come and do lighting on the night of the Great White show. "No one had told me that I needed to be there. It's usually on shows of national nights that I would just go there," Stone testified.

At about seven thirty on the night of the show, Stone said that Biechele, Great White's tour manager, took him aside and asked him to have all the lights turned off when the band started its set. "He had said, 'I'm gonna set off some pyro,' and he just, he went like this, he said it was going to be real fast and then just go with the, go with the show."

"I thought he meant it was gonna be like a boom," Stone said under oath, and Biechele never mentioned that he intended to use gerbs.

That was the entire discussion about pyrotechnics, Stone said, and he did not share what Biechele told him with anyone else. Stone said he'd never had many conversations with either of the Derderian brothers during their years of ownership, and what little speaking they did was "small talk."

Just after the fire Stone also told police about the encounter with Dan Biechele, and in a sworn affidavit West Warwick detective sergeant Keith Azverde described the conversation this way: "Dan told David Stone that he would be using pyrotechnics which he described as 'gerbs.'"

But the word "gerbs" was not actually said, according to Stone's testimony. Confusion or misdirection about that, and about whether Stone was an employee of The Station, would eventually lead to a misunderstanding that infuriated survivors. Years later when the *Providence Journal* obtained a copy of Detective Azverde's affidavit, the newspaper reported it as proof that club management had given its permission for the explosives, writing that "the nightclub's operators knew Biechele's band, Great White, would use fireworks—called pyrotechnics in the entertainment industry—despite public denials by club owners."

"Scooter" Stone, in the newspaper's retelling, was elevated from being one of the bar's regular customers who liked to play with the lighting console to one of "the nightclub's operators," with a direct connection to Michael and Jeffrey Derderian. The moment when Stone listened to Biechele's instruction, and no gerbs were mentioned, was exaggerated to become official permission from club management.

The Page One revelation enraged survivors. "For the longest time, the Derderians said the band didn't have permission to use the pyro," Victoria Eagan told the *Journal*. Azverde's affidavit, Eagan said, showed the band "had verbal permission to use gerbs, and that's generally all that's needed."

The Station nightclub in West Warwick, Rhode Island. ANTHONY BALDINO III

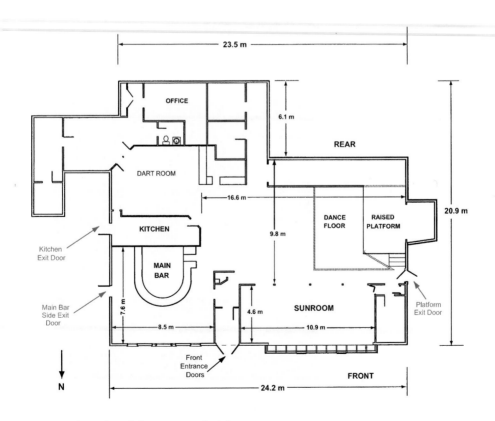

Floor plan of The Station nightclub. NATIONAL INSTITUTE OF STANDARDS AND TECHNOLOGY

Nightclub co-owner Jeffrey Derderian with twin sons
Jake and Max before the fire. LINDA DERDERIAN

Kristina Link and nightclub co-owner Michael
Derderian before the fire. They were married
after the tragedy. LINDA DERDERIAN

Great White in its 1986 "hair band" heyday in Los Angeles. Audie Desbrow, Mark Kendall, Jack Russell, Tony Montana, Michael Lardie. MICHAEL OCHS ARCHIVES/GETTY IMAGES

Bates College student Phil Barr, eight weeks before the fire. PHILIP BARR

Concertgoer Dan Davidson took digital photos as the concert started and captured the moment Great White ignited pyrotechnics. The second photo shows the trickle of flames eight seconds after the fireworks started. The third photo reveals surging flames nine seconds later. DAN DAVIDSON

Twenty-five seconds after the first trickles of flames, columns of fire reached the ceiling. The band stopped playing five seconds later. In the foreground, with a cigarette in his mouth, is club patron Scott Vieira, who helped with security at the show. Great White tour manager Daniel Biechele is seen standing on the stage behind Vieira. The cardboard box with the words "Danger" and "Explosive" contained the fireworks used in the show. DAN DAVIDSON

The next day. DAVID L. RYAN/*BOSTON GLOBE* VIA GETTY IMAGES

After the debris was cleared, friends and relatives of the victims created a memorial to them. SCOTT JAMES

Rhode Island attorney general Patrick Lynch.

Michael and Jeffrey Derderian, with attorney Kathleen Hagerty, listen to victims' families' testimony before receiving their fate in court.

Gina Russo at the dedication of the Station Fire Memorial Park on the site of the former nightclub on May 17, 2017. With WJAR-TV 10 news anchor Gene Valicenti and Rhode Island governor Gina Raimondo.
SCOTT JAMES

CHAPTER 29

GOVERNOR CARCIERI CRAWLED into bed next to his wife, Suzanne, to watch the eleven o'clock news. She'd been by his side throughout the aftermath of the fire, spending her days at the Crowne Plaza with victims' families. Sue had formed close, emotional bonds with those who waited for news of their loved ones, and families would later speak openly about the "love" they felt for Rhode Island's first lady because she was there in their hour of need.

The governor and his wife had not stopped since returning to Rhode Island to attend to all aspects of the crisis. One especially difficult moment came when families asked if they could visit the scorched remains of the nightclub. "If they lost a loved one, they want to see where they lost them," Carcieri said. "Their biggest fear was that they were burned alive" like the victims of the September 11 terrorist attacks. "When you love them, you just can't fathom them going through that." Once again, the governor tried to offer comfort by repeating what he'd been told by doctors, that nearly all died of asphyxiation. The state arranged for a bus so the families could visit the nightclub site and grieve in private, beyond the media glare.

The Station was the deadliest rock concert in American history, in an era of modern fire codes that were supposed to prevent such disasters, and the press was in a frenzy raising questions about how such a failure could happen in the United States. With news media interest further piqued by the Channel 12 video, there was an insatiable appetite for more information, and it seemed like some reporters did not care who or what they trampled for their next scoop.

As a crime scene that needed to be preserved, the site of the nightclub was sealed off with a chain-link fence and state police officers were stationed at the perimeter as guards. This kept intruders and the curious at bay, but also the media.

That led to a confrontation between the governor and Joel Rawson, the *Providence Journal*'s top editor. The paper had a storied history of taking down state officials with its coverage, so Carcieri figured he had to stop working on the disaster to meet with Rawson when the editor made contact and said they needed to talk. The governor had kept his promise to the victims' families that they would be the first to hear new developments, and that information would come directly from the governor's mouth in the privacy of the Crowne Plaza. Only after the families were briefed did the governor hold a press conference. This tight control was atypical of how the news business usually worked in close-knit Rhode Island, where reporters and government officials had developed relationships over many years and tended to be collegial, with information flowing more freely. By comparison, now that the biggest tragedy in memory had hit the state, information was in a lockdown.

When Carcieri met with the editor, Rawson took out a manila envelope and slapped it down on a table, complaining about the lack of access the *Journal* was receiving. He took from the envelope a series of photographs of state police officers at the nightclub site, looking intimidating in their militaristic uniforms. Carcieri listened as Rawson made note in the photos of the troopers' jackboots, an apparent reference to fascist regimes, and implied that the governor was acting like a dictator with how he treated the press. The editor demanded better access for the *Journal*, since it was the top local newspaper, and that meant being with the families of the victims.

"Joel, that's your opinion," Carcieri said. "Those people are dying inside. They deserve some privacy. If they want to talk, if they want to come out of the room and talk to your reporters, I can't do anything about it if you're sitting outside. But in that room, they're going to have that to themselves, and they're not going to be imposed upon by people that are trying to get a Pulitzer or whatever."

Carcieri would later say of Rawson, "He hated me after that. Never forgave me, actually."

The confrontation with the editor was a distraction from what the governor saw as his primary duties following the fire: making sure all the victims were accounted for, identified, and returned to grieving families, while also helping survivors. There was also the investigation to determine exactly what happened, not just for any possible criminal case, but also so action could be taken to prevent another tragedy. Carcieri wondered how many similarly dangerous clubs existed.

He'd ordered a blitz of inspections of more than 1,700 entertainment establishments spread across all thirty-nine cities and towns in the state, every place that might possibly pose a safety threat. A few places had already been closed as a result.

For a former business executive who thought of himself as a problem solver, the governor took stock as the number of challenges kept growing. Now, lying in bed, Carcieri was exhausted. He'd barely slept since receiving that phone call in Florida, and only when pushed to the brink of complete fatigue was he able to finally drift off. Real rest, however, was elusive. In his dreams he saw flames.

Carcieri and his wife watched the television as the newscast featured the names and photos of the latest victims identified by the medical examiner. Suddenly on the screen was the image of a beautiful young woman with a friendly smile and blond hair.

The governor and his wife knew the woman.

Katherine M. "Katie" O'Donnell, a twenty-six-year-old medical assistant from nearby Seekonk, Massachusetts, was the daughter of Carol and John O'Donnell, a former work colleague of Carcieri's. Twenty years earlier the two families were close and took their children to play together at a nearby lake. Carcieri vividly remembered little Katie.

It felt like "somebody hit me with a two by four" when the governor saw Katie's photo on the late news. Several times during the days following the fire the governor had found himself thinking of his own children, now in their twenties and thirties. They were the types who loved to go out and enjoy themselves, and could have easily been at a place like The Station. "It could've been one of my kids," Carcieri later said. Now it turned out that one of his children's friends was among those killed.

As governor, Carcieri mourned those lost in the fire, and forged unexpected personal bonds with survivors and victims' families. Until Katie, it never dawned on him that someone who had been so intimately entwined in his own life was also one of the fire's victims.

CHAPTER 30

RENE VALCOURT HAD never seen so many people. The line never ended at the funeral home for Freddy's wake. Rene knew his nephew was well liked, with many friends, but hundreds came to pay their respects. He thought he knew everyone who Freddy knew, but there were so many faces he didn't recognize.

Rene struggled to interact with the other mourners. He couldn't stop crying uncontrollably and kept uttering the same sentences to anyone and everyone who would listen. "He wasn't supposed to go," he said in a mix of grief and anger. "I'm supposed to go first." Rene had known Freddy since the guy was born, had helped to raise him from the days when he was a skinny towheaded toddler, and then watched as he evolved into a dark-haired giant of a man.

He was nicknamed "Change-back Freddy" as a little kid. They'd go to the corner store and Freddy was so amazed when he made his first purchase that he received change back from the cashier, so in subsequent visits he would always insist on change back, even if he wasn't owed any. The clerks loved it and always indulged the precocious lanky boy with at least a penny or two, and the nickname stuck.

Rene remembered how when Freddy was just three years old he had a collection of tiny toy football helmets, each with the insignia of one of a dozen different teams, and little Freddy, amazingly, memorized them all. "Dallas Cowboys!" he'd said in that excited innocent voice. Rene felt those toy helmets helped inspire Freddy's love of sports. More than just a fan, Freddy played football and baseball at Central High, and eventually became an announcer at the school's games. It seemed like just the other day Freddy was still playing games. He and Gina, her sons Nicholas and Alex, and Fred's kids Brandon and Nicole often came over to

Rene and Eileen's big house in Oaklawn for battles on the foosball table, or that *Super Mario Brothers* video game, or shooting pool.

Poor Gina. They said she might not make it. Rene remembered when Freddy had told him about Gina for the first time. He was in love. And then only a short time later Freddy told Rene that he had asked Gina to marry him, she'd said yes, and Freddy wanted Rene to be his best man. Rene was so honored. It reminded him yet again how they were so much more than just uncle and nephew. Now there was no Freddy, no marriage, and maybe no Gina. It was too much. With each memory came a new burst of tears.

Mourners around the room swapped their own stories about Freddy, a man they saw as larger than life, the one who always had a hug, a laugh, or a joke—and often all three. The younger Rene, Freddy's cousin, had lived as Freddy's roommate for a time and would always remember how he talked about Gina. "She's gonna be the one," Freddy had said. "I'm going to propose to her." Rene recalled how nervous Freddy was when he talked about popping the question. "He had feelings he never had before," Rene said.

Cousin Brian liked to tell the story of the day he wasn't feeling great but Freddy insisted they go to a rock concert at Great Woods, a live music venue in nearby Massachusetts. Freddy showed up at Brian's place and dragged him off his sick bed. "An amazing time," Brian would tell everyone. Whatever bug had brought him down was long gone by the time the show was over. Freddy's verve for life was more infectious.

Remembering moments like these at the wake became all the more painful and shocking when anyone approached the coffin. Freddy was in an open casket, looking the same as he did when he was alive. He was not burned like everyone expected for someone who died in a raging fire. When found among the victims his wristwatch was cracked, the time stopped at 11:13 p.m., but his body was almost perfectly intact. Freddy was one of four victims of the nightclub tragedy who would have open casket services.

The next day came Freddy's funeral, and the line of mourners wrapped around the block waiting to get in for the service. Five condolence books were filled with remembrances and signatures.

The older Rene sat through the full Roman Catholic mass and remained overcome with grief and rage. He seethed that Freddy had been stolen from him. It wasn't supposed to be this way. He was supposed to die before his nephew. That was the natural order of things. Not this. When it came time for the family to drive to St. Ann Cemetery in Cranston for the service to bury Freddy at the family's gravesite, Rene refused to attend. Something about going there and seeing that tombstone with Freddy's name etched onto it represented a line that Rene simply could not cross. Seeing it would mean that Freddy was really gone forever. In Rene's heart he needed to reject the idea that Freddy was no longer here. No, he would keep Freddy's spirit alive.

That day he made a promise to himself to never see Freddy's grave.

Rene also vowed to never go anywhere near the site of the nightclub.

CHAPTER 31

Somebody has to pay!" John DePetro shouted on his talk show on WHJJ-AM. Nestled in the talk radio station's rundown studios in East Providence, DePetro's rant had become a mantra since the fire, a demand for justice for the dead. "Who is gonna scream if somebody goes to jail?" DePetro added.

The nightclub's co-owner Jeffrey Derderian was DePetro's longtime friend, dating back to the days when they attended Rhode Island College and worked at the school radio station. But when Lynne Duke* of the *Washington Post* asked if his pal might be the villain imprisoned for the tragedy, DePetro said, "Could be."

Talk radio WHJJ-AM shared its building with sister station WHJY-FM, the rock music broadcaster that sponsored the Great White show. It was their deejay, Mike "Dr. Metal" Gonsalves, who warmed up the audience and died in the fire.

DePetro's coverage of the tragedy was considered even-handed compared to most—speculative outrage and talk of revenge filled the airwaves in the days after the fire, fueled by comments from local and state officials that the tragedy was a crime, even though no investigation had been completed. "We will get to the bottom of why it happened and who made that decision, and we will prosecute to the fullest extent," said Governor Carcieri the day after he arrived from Florida.

That the fire was a criminal case, and not an accident, seemed obvious. The Channel 12 videotape showed Great White set off the fireworks that ignited the club, and Rhode Island had some of the toughest laws in the

---

* Author's note: Lynne Duke was my classmate at the Columbia Graduate School of Journalism.

nation regarding pyrotechnics—such explosives were banned, unless a special permit was obtained. There did not appear to be a permit, and just transporting fireworks into the state without permission was also a crime. Based on those facts alone, Great White had broken the law.

The depth of public agony and anger was also understandable. Rhode Island was so small and parochial that it felt like everyone knew someone who was killed or hurt at the fire. "People say in the world it's six degrees of separation," said Attorney General Patrick Lynch. "In Rhode Island, it's probably a degree and a half."

Like ripples from a stone tossed into a pond, the swells from the tragedy had reached every nook and cranny of the tiny state. In the media, and in the minds of many locals, there were comparisons to the 2001 terrorist attack on the World Trade Center, simply due to the scope and impact on such a modest population. "This was our September 11th" became a common expression.

However, unlike September 11, the investigation and discussion quickly shifted its focus from those responsible for setting off the explosives, Great White, and turned toward those whose establishment was destroyed, the Derderian brothers. Investigators fixated on how Michael and Jeffrey operated the nightclub, and their casual, typically Rhode Island way of running the business was now being contorted into something nefarious. The Derderians paid some employees in cash, under the table, a common practice in the local club scene. Stories also emerged that the brothers didn't pay bands in full if the groups failed to perform as promised, a tactic that created bad feelings. No one claimed that arguments over gig fees and paying workers in cash caused the fire, but the controversies were seized upon as signs that the club owners did not always play nice or follow the law, and the logic followed that perhaps The Station was mismanaged in other ways that actually contributed to the deaths.

Prosecutors and police were not alone in pursuing the brothers. Just days after the fire, one of the nation's premiere journalism institutions issued a decree to the news industry to target the Derderians.

"Journalists who are covering the West Warwick fire must ask very hard questions about the role played by The Station owners and managers on the night of the fire," wrote Bob Steele. His article, "Rhode Island Fire: Scrutiny of Club Owners Too Tame," was published thirty-six hours after the fire started by the Poynter Institute, a then-influential journalism think tank in Florida.

Steele, the institute's Nelson Poynter Scholar for Journalism Values, questioned whether the Derderians had received preferential news media treatment because Jeffrey worked in television news, implying that his journalism peers were failing to report on the brothers due to favoritism to a colleague. Steele based his call for action against the Derderians on an analysis his colleagues at Poynter had conducted of Google search results, which said that in the first eleven hours of coverage of the fire, Jeffrey Derderian was not mentioned once by name in 629 articles. Steele compared this to the case of a Chicago nightclub disaster where the club owner was mentioned by name in 426 stories in about the same time frame. "Even if this search failed to recognize some stories that named Derderian by that time, the comparative coverage raises important questions. Are journalists covering the West Warwick fire less aggressive in reporting on the club owners? Even now, 36 hours after the fire started, the coverage of the owners has been unusually tame, certainly in comparison to the Chicago story," Steele wrote.

It was a provocative attack on the news media, even if specious in its reasoning and research.

Steele and his Poynter colleagues did not seem to take into account that the Rhode Island and Chicago tragedies were different in distinct ways. Compared to the Chicago reporting, the nightclub fire remained a developing story for days, as the facts were largely unsettled, with new dramas constantly emerging. Within those first eleven hours that Poynter surveyed, by 10 a.m. Friday morning, news coverage concentrated on the number of victims, which remained unconfirmed and grew by the hour. Understandably, this was the focus of news organizations, many overwhelmed by the task of reporting on dozens dead and hundreds injured.

The Rhode Island catastrophe also differed from Chicago because the nightclub fire was primarily a television news story, due to the unprecedented video shot by Brian Butler of Channel 12. Such rare images made the fire a quintessential television story, and for Poynter to analyze TV news coverage with a Google search would have been impossible. In 2003 Google search results would not have included live broadcast news, and in those days, before the rise of YouTube, video content was not widely or accurately indexed by Google.

Additionally, Steele raised ethical issues about Jeffrey and WPRI-TV 12 for having a photographer in the club to videotape for an upcoming story. "Jeff Derderian clearly had a profound conflict of interest in covering this story about fire safety in night clubs. He was a major stakeholder through his ownership of a business that was at the heart of the story. He had a vested interest in the story that was in tremendous contrast to his journalistic role," Steele wrote. "What was Derderian thinking? What were his bosses at WPRI-TV thinking? Didn't they recognize the serious conflicts of interest in having these dual, competing roles as journalist and business owner?"

The Poynter Institute's public conclusions that Jeffrey Derderian was unethical, that there had been a possible media conspiracy to protect the brothers, and that the news media should now go after the club owners aggressively was picked up by the Associated Press and published nationally.

The *Providence Journal*, however, had not waited for the marching order from Poynter to aggressively pursue the Derderians.

As grief and rage consumed the state, pushing emotions to their heights, the *Journal* published the home addresses of Jeffrey and Michael Derderian and their families, including the street numbers. In the days and years of news coverage that followed the fire, the *Journal* would not publish the exact home addresses of anyone else considered complicit in the disaster, including the band members or their manager, who ignited the deadly explosives.

News organizations, as a general rule, are hesitant to publish exact home addresses, and have fierce debates about the value of releasing that information to the general public, especially when a particularly volatile issue is involved. It is understood that publishing an exact home address could pose a danger and facilitate retaliation or violence against someone, so newsrooms consider whether a greater public good is served by sharing such private information. In some states there are laws that restrict publishing the exact home address of public officials, because it is considered a dangerous form of harassment and intimidation.

Such rules no longer seemed to apply to covering the Derderians. In the media the brothers were no longer just fair game, they had become prey.

CHAPTER 32

BRIAN BUTLER'S CHANNEL 12 videotape documented how quickly the flames spread, and investigators immediately recognized this was not normal. There was something highly flammable on the walls, and even while the fire still burned, the culprit was determined: foam.

It was charcoal egg-crate-style convoluted polyurethane foam, bought in large blocks and cut into smaller pieces and pasted with glue to cover the walls and ceiling. This type of foam was typically used for packaging, and when exposed directly to flames, it was like a solid version of fuel. As the foam burned it became molten ooze that dripped from the ceiling, the "black rain" that scorched the scalps and skin of the fire's victims. The amount of foam on the walls of The Station was the equivalent of thirteen gallons of gasoline.

That level of combustion ignited the building, a wood-framed structure, which quickly led to a flashover, the spontaneous combustion of everything in a room.

Flashover happens when a fire is in a confined space and hot gases rise to the ceiling, spread out to the walls, and then descend down in a dark black smoke. Different objects ignite at different temperatures, but in a flashover, when the heat at the ceiling reaches 1,100 degrees, anything combustible at floor level begins to ignite, including human beings. Fire experts describe a flashover as the phase "when a fire in a room becomes a room on fire."

Flashover is considered the most dangerous phase of a fire, unpredictable in its timing, and even a firefighter in full protective gear is unlikely to survive if caught inside a building when it happens. In the nightclub, because the foam was such a powerful accelerant that fueled the flames, flashover happened very soon after the fire started. In a fire not stoked by flammable foam, reaching flashover can take several minutes.

Flammable foam is everywhere in America, in upholstered furniture and mattresses, and in the three decades before the nightclub fire had been linked to more than thirty thousand deaths in the United States. Foam played a role in the World Trade Center towers collapse during the terrorist attacks of September 11. The jet fuel from the planes that struck the towers burned off, but those initial flames ignited the buildings' contents, including furnishings filled with foam. Heat fueled by those contents combined with other factors and weakened the building's structure. Even Osama bin Laden did not expect the towers to be completely destroyed by his attack. One of his accomplices was foam.

At The Station temperatures reached more than 1,000 degrees within ninety seconds of the walls igniting from Great White's fireworks. Skin began burning at 124 degrees, and asphyxiation started when the air reached 300 degrees.

Up to two-thirds of the people inside the club headed back toward the way they'd entered, through the narrow passage where tickets were collected, out to the main entrance. It was human nature to try to escape using the same route taken to enter, but so many people trying to leave by just one exit led to panic, a stampede, and bottleneck.

"They tried to go out the same way they came in. That was the problem," said West Warwick fire chief Charles Hall. "They didn't use the other three fire exits."

Anyone still inside near the stage, where the fire started, was likely dead or severely incapacitated within one minute due to the heat and smoke.

The area near the main bar was the last to become superheated, and patrons there had a few more moments to escape. About one-third of the people who got out of the building went through windows instead of exits.

A federal investigation later determined that a second type of foam was also attached to the walls of the club: closed-cell polyethylene foam. This older, stiffer foam was apparently placed on the back walls and drummer's alcove by the club's previous owner, Howard Julian, in 1996 for sound abatement. Polyethylene foam was also flammable, and the two foams emitted deadly gases when burned, including carbon monoxide, carbon dioxide, and hydrogen cyanide.

But it was the black smoke, which contained superheated particles, that ended most lives. When inhaled these particles scorched airways, prevented breathing, and led to unconsciousness before the flames could reach most victims.

Hand-held fire extinguishers were no match for a fire fueled by the foam, federal investigators concluded, but sprinklers could have saved every life.

This wasn't just speculation. Three days before The Station tragedy, on February 17, 2003, the rock band Jet City Fix played at the Fine Line Music Cafe in downtown Minneapolis. The band set off pyrotechnics as part of its act, which ignited highly flammable foam on the nightclub's ceiling. The building's sprinkler system kicked in and smothered the flames. Everyone escaped and no one was harmed.

The Station did not have a sprinkler system. It was not required.

The flammable polyurethane foam, however, was in violation of local fire codes. The Derderians placed it on the walls in the summer of 2000 after West Warwick police chief Peter Brousseau threatened to revoke the club's entertainment license if noise complaints continued from neighbors. The foam was painted black and sprinkled with glitter for rock roadhouse décor.

Several fire inspections were performed after the foam was installed, and the deadly danger was never noticed.

The failure of the fire marshal, and the details of how such a deadly version of foam was installed, would cause outrage and lead to years of finger pointing. The foam would also be the linchpin in the government's case against the Derderians.

CHAPTER 33

FROM A DEEP darkness, Phil Barr abruptly opened his eyes. He was in a room, in a bed, not his own.

What's happening? Phil realized there was someone else present. It was his former high school history teacher from Moses Brown, Doug MacLeod, in his signature tan leather jacket, the one he always wore to school. Phil had fond memories of those days, when they'd talk about American and European history. Doug was also the school staffer assigned to the swim team, and would drive Phil to meets when he was often the only student from Moses Brown to qualify for the next level of competition.

Wait. That was ages ago, Phil thought. Long before Bates College. It was good to see Doug, reassuring even, but also confusing. *Why is he here? Why am I here with him?*

Phil tried to say hello, but no words came out. It was as if something were stuck down his throat to prevent him from talking. Why couldn't he speak?

Doug looked into Phil's eyes and smiled. Again, Phil tried to talk, but choked on his feeble attempt at words. Then, just as quickly as he had appeared, Doug vanished into blackness.

THE WHITE WAS too bright, almost blinding, when Phil opened his eyes. He squinted and made out the details of ceiling tiles basking in sunlight from a nearby window. He was on his back, staring straight up, surrounded by unfamiliar faces. A team from the hospital's intensive care unit slowly explained that he'd been in a medically induced coma and intubated. He was in the hospital. He'd been in a terrible fire. He had burns. But he was getting better. He was healing. They had taken out the intubation, but he would not be able to speak yet because his vocal cords were badly scorched. As the nurses and doctors talked him through his revival, Phil became aware of the sharp, raw pain in his throat. It was all too much to process.

Moments later his father Philip walked into his room. "Hey, how are you?" his dad said, almost nonchalant, as if trying to not make a big deal of the situation. His father's presence immediately calmed and reassured Phil.

Dad was the family's wise elder, someone Phil had spent his life trying to please and emulate, even as a boy, like wearing leather loafers when the other kids donned sneakers. Phil craved to achieve the same level of excellence his father had attained as an accomplished attorney in one of Rhode Island's top firms, and later as a business executive. Phil never doubted his father's love, but his dad didn't coddle when it came to work, especially studies or the task of applying to the best colleges. If Phil sought his father's advice, it would sometimes arrive unsparing. "This is not to the best of your abilities. Is this really something you want to turn in?" Phil remembered his dad saying when asked to read a term paper that obviously needed work. They'd stay up late and wordsmith together until the assignment was perfected. Phil would later wonder if he'd developed a hypersensitive sense of self-criticism because of the dynamic with his father.

Hey, how are you? It was too strangely casual for his dad. With those few words and their tone, Phil realized something had changed between them. There were few moments growing up when Phil felt his father was relaxed to the point of being happy, but standing before him now was a different man. In his father's face he saw an emotion he'd rarely witnessed before in his dad: relief.

Unable to speak, Phil mouthed words and used gestures to try to communicate. What day is it?

"Tuesday," his father said.

That's not so bad, Phil thought, he'd been in the coma for four days.

Then Phil's father gently revealed that Phil had been sedated and asleep for more than three weeks.

Phil had suffered first- and second-degree burns to his face, back, and one arm. The wounds on the inside, however, brought him to the cusp of death. His respiratory system, from his throat down into his lungs, was burned when he breathed in the intense heat and smoke inside the nightclub. Three days after he was hospitalized he suffered pulmonary failure and would have died, if not for the hospital's extraordinary measures, including dangling him in the air face down to help open his airways. Air was vibrated to shake open spaces in his lungs, and he'd undergone forty bronchoscopies to remove burned lung tissue, some pieces the size of oysters. A ventilator kept him breathing, and eventually his body healed and he started inhaling on his own.

During those weeks Phil was never alone. His family worked in shifts to make sure that someone was constantly by his bedside. His dad would be there during the day, and his mother, Barbara, would stay all night, herself the survivor of a near death experience due to complications after she gave birth to her daughter, a trauma that had given her an intimate understanding of how hospitals operated. She'd also worked in healthcare as an occupational therapist, and during a training internship in Utah she'd done a rotation in a hospital burn unit, witnessing firsthand how vital it was to give patients hope. She knew that patients with advocates by their side tended to receive the most attention, better care, and the best chances for survival. In an email update from the hospital that was posted online for the Bates College community, where Phil's friends and classmates had followed his progress since the fire, Barbara and Philip explained the family's strategy of providing Phil with a hospital vigil. "We believe that this approach promotes the highest standards of care, develops effective two-way communication with his care givers and ensures that we have a full understanding of his medical condition and prognosis for recovery."

Evan Clabots, the friend from the nightclub who escaped, was among those who sat bedside. He pretended to hospital workers that he was Phil's brother, since only immediate family members were allowed in the intensive care unit. Somehow his high school history teacher Doug was able to reach Phil too, which happened to be the moment Phil briefly came out of sedation, just a few days into the induced coma. It had not been a dream—his former teacher was really there.

In the days following Phil's full awakening came a series of small victories. He breathed more on his own, and even though he still could not speak, he began to communicate and make sense as the effects of the sedatives dissipated from his mind. Nurses gave Phil paper and pen so he could express his thoughts, but as he tried to write, his hands would not cooperate, as if they'd forgotten how to function—a sign of atrophy. He'd always had terrible penmanship, something his parents criticized, and now his scrawl was even more unreadable. When his father asked him if there was anything he needed, Phil scribbled, "I hope to make progress every day." Such a line was trademark Phil, the hustler from the Bates swim team, and news of the note spread hope from Lincoln to Lewiston.

It was a brave face. Part of Phil was determined and hopeful, but anxiety brewed inside. No matter how hard he tried, he couldn't catch his breath, not really. Instead of the long, deep inhales he knew so well from swimming—he practically analyzed them when he did laps—he could only take little sips of air, like panting. The doctors and nurses assured him the short breaths were normal at this stage of recovery, but Phil became convinced that if he did not consciously force himself to take every single breath that he would die.

He refused to sleep. Phil believed that if he nodded off, he would forget to inhale, and death was certain. No doctor or nurse could convince him otherwise, despite admonishments of "Phil, you've got to sleep."

He kept himself awake for days, and his mother Barbara became increasingly alarmed. She told her son that if he allowed himself to doze off, she would remain by his side watching to make sure that he did not stop breathing. "Phil, I am right here. I'm not leaving. You can close your eyes for an hour or two and it will be okay," Barbara said. "I'm not going to let you stop breathing."

Only with these assurances, and feeling that he was beginning to take deeper breaths, did Phil's mania finally subside and he allowed himself sleep.

But not rest. Soon after emerging from the coma Phil was on his feet, urged on by a pixie-sized drill sergeant of a physical therapist. She was barely five feet tall and probably weighed only ninety-five pounds, with shoulder-length blond hair and piercing blue eyes and a demeanor of perpetual happiness. Yet she was tough and demanding, forcing Phil out of bed to walk at least three times a day. When she first brought over a walker to get Phil to his feet he compared his bulk to her tiny frame and asked, "What are you going to do if I fall?"

He learned to not underestimate the therapist's determination, and he needed plenty of his own. The trauma from the fire and the time in the coma meant he had to retrain his body to function—his muscles had forgotten how to work. Phil had to move to recover, but it hurt, and not just because of the burns—the one on his back was the most severe. With so little lung capacity, even the smallest effort left him exhausted. He wasn't getting the oxygen needed to fuel his ambitions.

He also noticed what he wasn't getting from his father. In the weeks he struggled to heal, Phil finally realized what had changed between them, something he sensed that first moment he saw his dad after emerging from the coma, but did not fully understand immediately. This was no longer the father who pushed and cajoled Phil to excel. Phil's near death was new territory for his dad. The once all-wise patriarch now asked questions like, "What do *you* want, Phil?" This was a man who seemed simply grateful to have his son alive. Phil realized they were no longer expert and student, and Phil was free to recover on his own terms and at his own pace, something not dictated by anyone else, least of all his father.

Phil wondered when he could return to Bates. It wasn't realistic anytime soon, to think and work at that level while his body suffered. Those Wall Street internships felt like a distant daydream. His confidence grew when he was weaned off supplemental oxygen and passed a series of "swallow tests," clearing the way for solid food. He could talk again. Perhaps anything was possible, he told himself, even a full return to the life he had before the fire. He asked his doctors when he'd be able to swim on his college team again.

Swimming, they explained, was not physically possible. The fire had destroyed his breathing capacity and damaged the upper tissues in his lungs that filtered out particulates from getting into his system. This meant that oxygen could no longer saturate his body as it did before the fire, and oxygen needed to get to his extremities for any activity that would challenge his entire pulmonary system, like swimming.

To compete again could not happen.

CHAPTER 34

O F THE 187 taken to hospitals from the nightclub fire, only one died in the first week. Those severely burned had a chance of survival, thanks to relatively recent medical advancements. Had the disaster happened a few decades earlier, the possibility of living would have been far less likely.

Burns are among the most common injuries in the United States, with nearly half a million requiring medical treatment each year. Forty thousand of those cases require hospitalization.

Treatments for burns have been documented back thousands of years, some on papyrus dated to 1600 BC in Egypt, but survival rates did not substantially improve until the twentieth century, when doctors better understood how infections and shock killed so many victims. Knowledge was often born in tragedy or the battlefield, as doctors scrambled to save burned soldiers in World War II. The Cocoanut Grove nightclub fire in Boston in 1942 was a watershed moment because penicillin, which had only recently been mass-produced, was used to treat a large number of burn victims.

The link between death and the severity of burns had been established since the 1500s and eventually developed into a degree system:

First degree: Heat, pain, and small blisters.

Second degree: Severe pain and large blisters.

Third degree: Damage to the skin and underlying flesh, with crust formation.

Fourth degree: Damage to all soft tissues down to the bone.

A variation on the degree system for burns exists to this day, but breakthroughs that greatly impacted survival rates did not begin happening until the 1960s and 1970s, with discoveries about the dangers of shock, fluid retention, and respiratory damage. Also, techniques were developed to more effectively remove dead skin. The development of artificial skin to improve survival happened in the 1990s. Specialized burn centers treat about thirty thousand cases each year, with a survival rate today of nearly 97 percent.

The medical world was more prepared than it had ever been when The Station fire happened, and the greatest example of how far medicine had advanced involved Joe Kinan, a thirty-four-year-old divorced salesman who loved live concerts. Joe worked as many as three jobs to make ends meet, and as an amateur bodybuilding enthusiast, he began and ended most days in the gym. The Great White show was the first time Joe had been to The Station, and he became the most severely injured survivor.

Joe stood fifteen feet from the stage when Great White shot off its fireworks. Joe wasn't a drinker, so he was sober and almost instantly aware that the club had ignited and he was in danger. Like so many other patrons he turned and headed back toward the way he'd entered, down the narrow passageway where tickets were taken. In the retreat someone stepped on the back of his foot. Joe fell and was crushed as others fell on top of him.

"All I saw was black smoke," Joe later told *People* magazine. "I was in terrible pain until my skin burned off. Then I had no feeling."

"I never lost consciousness during the fire," Joe said in an interview published by Massachusetts General Hospital, where he was treated in the burn unit. "The sounds of yelling were loud at first, but then everything got quiet. Two firemen pulled me out from a pile of people."

Joe learned from investigators that he was inside the inferno for between thirteen and sixteen minutes, with temperatures reaching more than a thousand degrees. When he was found he had third- and fourth-degree burns on 40 percent of his body. His scalp was scorched and gone, and he'd lost his left eye, his ears, toes, and all of his fingers. Joe was in a coma for three months, followed by nearly a year of hospitalization and rehabilitation. By 2020 he had endured nearly 150 surgeries and had effectively "died seven times," by his own count. He expected what he called "tune-ups," surgeries for his skin and problems related to scar tissue, for the rest of his life.

If one medical miracle weren't enough, in 2012 Joe was given the chance to regain working fingers via a hand transplant taken from someone who had recently died, one of only about one hundred times the procedure had been done. In a seventeen-hour surgery that began on the evening of October 7, Joe received the left hand of eighteen-year-old Troy Pappas of Bates College, the same school Phil Barr attended. Pappas had died from a head injury in a dormitory staircase fall. Five hours into Joe's recovery from the operation, he moved the fingers on his new hand.

A year of intense rehabilitation followed, and by January 2013 he held the hand of his fiancée, Carrie Pratt, a fellow burn survivor whom he'd met at a survivor's conference. Later they would have a daughter, Hadley, and get married.

But the drugs needed to prevent Joe's body from rejecting the transplanted hand created a new life-and-death struggle. Joe's immune system was so severely suppressed by doctors to prevent rejection that he sometimes required isolation and hospitalization. Exposure to common illnesses like the cold or flu threatened his life. "There's still a lot of guessing," he said years later at his home in rural Lakeville, Massachusetts, about the hand transplant, since such surgeries remain on the frontier of medicine.

The fire also ravaged Joe's psyche. Remarkably, he made his way back to live concerts about as soon as he was physically able, somewhat sheepish about his appearance since the scars on his head and face are so visible, but still determined. His first show was Metallica, the heavy metal band. "They fired off so many canons," Joe remembered, followed by "so much smoke." He found himself choking and unable to catch his breath. He had to leave.

Joe thought he'd fare better at a concert by Michael Bublé, the easy-listening Canadian crooner in the tradition of Frank Sinatra, but that show featured a "wall of fire" and Joe again "freaked out." He became less traumatized by pyrotechnics as years passed, but remained astonished at how many bands have continued to use fireworks in their shows since The Station tragedy. In Joe's observation, pyro became more popular than ever after the nightclub disaster.

"Why?" he asked.

CHAPTER 35

S*HE'S AWAKE!*
At her bedside, Gina Russo's brother-in-law Matt shouted. In recent weeks there were so many times when her family thought Gina had regained consciousness—her eye would flicker open, perhaps, and appear to look around her hospital room. Her mother, sister, and others talked to her, and sometimes a tear would drip down Gina's cheek, making everyone believe they had a connection. These were false hopes, and Gina remained deep in a coma. The family kept a steady vigil, but when Gina finally awoke, Matt was alone in the room with her, having stopped by while in Boston on business.

"Alex and Nicholas?" Gina mouthed. Her first thoughts were her sons. In those initial moments of awareness there was no memory of the fire, or even that she was hurt. Gina was just a mother who wanted to know where her boys were.

They're fine, Matt explained. In fact, Alex had a baseball game that afternoon.

Baseball? Gina was confused. It's February, and you can't play baseball in February. Not in Rhode Island, at least.

Fred?

Matt didn't respond.

Gina had been in the coma for eleven weeks. She was at Massachusetts General Hospital, transferred there from across the street at Shriners into one of the region's few level-one burns units for adults. Plagued by infections and a high fever, she was placed in the intensive care unit on the thirteenth floor in a so-called incubation room and put inside a sterile oxygen tent. Before leaving Shriners, doctors gave Gina a temporary tracheostomy and inserted a tube directly into her windpipe to assist her impaired lungs. While still sedated, doctors continued to work on Gina's burns, grafting skin from other parts of her body to replace what had been destroyed. It was a race against time to prevent further infections, which could lead to amputations or death.

As her recovery progressed, doctors dialed back the medications that kept her unconscious. Gina drifted into a dreamlike state where she imagined herself sitting alone in her sister's SUV outside a pizzeria, perhaps a manifestation of how isolated she felt trapped inside the coma. Then she envisioned herself on a playground carousel, happy and smiling. Gina loved merry-go-rounds as a kid, and even as a grown-up would sometimes take a spin, not feeling self-conscious or silly, just enveloped in a moment of joy. Others were on the ride with her, although their faces were indistinct and she couldn't figure out who they were. Then the carousel caught fire, and as Gina and the others went round and round it got hotter and blacker. A voice said to her, "I'm going to get you out. I'm going to save you."

In another hallucination a completely naked man, someone she did not know, wandered in and out of her room. This eerie vision stayed with her even after she emerged from the drug haze, and the image of the naked man was so vivid that her family reported it to nurses, worried it was an actual incident.

Fear swept over Gina in those first hours and days of her awakening. She knew she was in a hospital, although she did not immediately understand why. With the tracheostomy tube still down her throat, she could not speak and could only mouth words to try to make herself understood. She was frightened all the time, as if prodded from a nightmare she could not remember. Something terrible lurked, but she was unable to pinpoint the source of an overwhelming sense of dread.

She was introduced to lawyers her family had asked to represent Gina. In the weeks she was sedated, the work on civil lawsuits had started on behalf of survivors and victims' families against those responsible for the nightclub tragedy, and in some cases to fight healthcare insurers. Because the injuries were caused by someone else's actions, some insurance companies balked at paying hospital bills, even for those who had paid their premiums. So while some survivors dealt with horrific wounds and trauma, they also battled to receive healthcare coverage. It was the beginning of a long legal mess that would last for years.

The attorneys asked Gina if she had any recollections of the fire.

"What fire?" she responded.

One of the lawyers explained that she had been at The Station night-club when it caught fire.

A rush of images came back, with incredible clarity. The flames. The searing heat. The oozing black rain that dripped down and scorched her flesh. Horrible screaming. People with their heads on fire. Gina cried. She remembered being trapped inside and the moment when she thought she would surely die. Bits and pieces came together and began to make sense. She survived that horrible moment and was in the hospital recovering. Then she saw Fred. He pushed her through the smoke toward the exit, then disappeared in the darkness.

"Where's Fred?" she mouthed.

No one seemed to understand what she'd asked, as if they could not decipher her meaning through the tracheostomy tube. Instead they changed the subject to talk about her sons and how well they were doing. She had to focus on healing so she could be there for her boys.

Gina couldn't shake the constant fear. Over the next days her family gave her a few more details, telling her about her treatment at Shriners. Worried about upsetting her, they were careful not to tell her that anyone had died in the fire. Gina assumed Fred must also be in the hospital, also recovering. For short periods doctors removed the temporary tracheostomy tube to get Gina to breathe on her own, then for longer and longer stretches. During these breaks, as her strength grew and she became more fully conscious, Gina asked what hospital Fred was in. Even with the tube out, she could only whisper, and at first was ignored, again as if no one understood her.

Then she articulated each word distinctly. "Where's Fred?"

Her family couldn't stall any longer. With tears falling down her face, Gina's sister Stephanie said, "He didn't make it out of the building."

"What? Where's Fred?" Gina asked again.

"He died in the fire, Gina. I'm so sorry."

"No. It's not true. Nobody died."

"Oh, no. Ninety-nine people died, Gina. It wasn't just Fred."

CHAPTER 36

J OEL RAWSON DID not want his reporters and editors to forget why he worked them so hard.

In the fire's aftermath the editorial staff barely went home, including Rawson. The scope of the tragedy was unlike anything the *Providence Journal* had covered, and as the investigation continued, the story had evolved from a catastrophe into a tangle of intrigue and finger pointing. It took all of the newspaper's considerable resources to cover, and there were some staffers who'd gone days without leaving the office, prompting Rawson to pointedly tell some to go home and rest. He'd neglected his own personal life too, including a pressing need to buy a new truck. When he finally got away to get that done, the dealer said he would need a day or two to obtain the vehicle. Rawson didn't have a day, or even a spare hour, so he went to a rival dealership and bought a truck on the spot for cash.

The newspaper was full of people pushed to their limits, so Rawson started a ritual he hoped would keep them motivated. He'd walk into the newsroom, gather everyone around, and tell the story of one of the people who died in the fire. The newspaper painstakingly profiled each victim in the weeks following the disaster so every soul got his or her due. It was a difficult assignment for reporters, since they would often have to knock on the doors of grieving families who might be hostile to a media intrusion. For Rawson it was important that these people came to life on the pages of the *Journal*, so readers understood the totality of loss. That meant finding details like favorite sports teams, or where victims met spouses, or how they volunteered for causes they loved. Rawson did not call the articles obituaries. These were lifetimes.

In his newsroom speeches, Rawson shared the story of a victim the paper had profiled. That person could no longer speak for him or herself. Posted on the wall of the conference room, where editors and reporters gathered for editorial meetings, a full page from the paper featured the faces of the fire's victims. Rawson would point to a face and say, "This is who we're doing this for."

Reporters tend to be cynical, and during one stretch when Rawson worked the newsroom exceptionally hard, one said, "You're just pushing us because you want to win a Pulitzer Prize."

"You're not going to win a Pulitzer," Rawson fired back. "Why do we do this? We've gotta do this because this is what we do. That's what we're here for."

The paper was hardly alone in its pursuit of the nightclub story, and for the first time in memory the *Providence Journal* was being beaten. As the state's most influential news organization, the *Journal* was accustomed to being first on stories in Rhode Island, but it suddenly faced impressive competition on its own turf. The Station was the deadliest single building fire in modern American history, and the deadliest rock concert, and that led to questions across the nation about the safety of public spaces. Americans who once took their safety for granted now checked for exits when they went out.

Cementing the story in the public's mind was the Channel 12 video, and investigative teams from top news organizations like CBS's *60 Minutes* and NBC's *Dateline* dug in on the story. Their reports documented flaws in the nation's fire prevention system and helped lead to nationwide reforms of building codes.

Newspapers, however, gave the *Journal* its greatest competition, and reporters and editors on staff took notice. On a major national story it was common for top newspapers to dispatch reporters to the scene for a few days, but often it was the first time in town for those journalists, so their ability to beat local reporters was limited. In the case of The Station fire, newspapers like the *New York Times* and the *Boston Globe* sent some of their best journalists, who also happened to have been former star reporters for the *Providence Journal*. Rawson and his team helped nurture these people's earlier careers, and they'd come back to directly compete on the biggest story the paper had ever covered—not as strangers, but with experience and contacts that sometimes rivaled the *Journal*'s current staff. Reporters in the Providence newsroom griped that they were being scooped by people whom the *Journal* helped create, a bitter irony. No one beat the *Journal* in its own backyard, and yet it was happening.

Even outsiders noticed. In a May 3, 2003, column for the weekly newspaper the *Providence Phoenix* entitled "Losing the Beat: The Ability of Out-Of-Town Papers to Offer Better Early Coverage of The Station Fire Shows How the *Providence Journal* Has Become a Less Surefooted Institution," writer Ian Donnis concluded that "the way in which the *Journal* repeatedly got beat on its own turf marks, in the view of many insiders, a far cry from the not-so-distant time when the strength and depth of the paper's statewide coverage was a particular point of pride."

Rawson personally helped drive the paper's coverage. After viewing the raw footage of Brian Butler's video at Channel 12, the editor continued to be concerned that the safety of the nightclub itself was a major factor in the disaster. Rawson asked for a copy of the footage from Channel 12, which the station, a competitor, agreed to give, as long as the *Journal* never published the footage on its website or grabbed a frame to turn into a photo for the newspaper. The *Journal* was allowed to study and reference the video for its coverage, and Rawson had his staff inspect every frame. It was clear the fire spread extraordinarily quickly, and that people could not get out fast enough to save themselves. The fireworks started the inferno, there was no doubt about that, but the club was a deathtrap.

In Rawson's world as a pilot the cause of a crash is rarely just a single problem. "In aviation it's what we call a failure chain. Very seldom, it's one thing," he would later say.

The video indicated there had been a failure chain at the nightclub. It wasn't just Great White and pyrotechnics. The owners of the nightclub, the Derderians, must have played a role. The Derderians had said very little publicly, and refused repeated interview requests from the *Journal*.

The *Journal*'s coverage shifted away from Great White and the fireworks and fixated on the Derderians.

Some of the *Journal*'s coverage raised questions of fairness. On Sunday, April 20, two months after the fire, the newspaper published a front-page, six-column-headline, above-the-fold top story entitled "The Station: Two brothers and a legacy of death." In a lengthy exposé, reporter W. Zachary Malinowski connected facts from the Derderians' lives that documented a pattern of demise, from their grandparents' escape from the Armenian genocide, where "more than 500,000 of their countrymen had been slaughtered by the Turks," to the brothers' mother dying when they were children, and the shooting at the family's grocery store that wounded their father, Arshag, and brother Robert. Then came the nightclub fire, which had claimed ninety-nine lives at that point.

The Sunday *Journal* had the paper's highest circulation of all its editions, and when Jeffrey saw the headline and the specious connecting of family tragedies as a "legacy of death," he concluded, "We're done. We will never be treated fairly."

In the month following the tragedy, the *Journal* published forty-two articles that mentioned or focused on the Derderians, and that number would swell to 122 by December, covering the months when a grand jury convened to determine criminal charges.

By comparison, the man who ignited the explosives that caused the fire, Great White tour manager Daniel Biechele, received eighteen mentions in the *Journal* in the same time period, and his name appeared just once in the newspaper during the crucial final three months of grand jury deliberations, and that was only as part of a list of people who were inside the nightclub when the fire started.

The safety of the nightclub became one of the dominant aspects of the *Journal*'s coverage, and in the rush of coverage there were mistakes. A large graphic on the newspaper's front page purported to show the layout of the club, and revealed that it did not have the requisite number of exits for a fast emergency evacuation. But the newspaper mistakenly missed one of the exits in its depiction and was forced to run a correction a couple days later in which the paper admitted it did not have any confirmed information when it created the graphic. The tiny correction was published on an inside page.

The number of patrons inside the club at the time of the fire was a major concern, raising questions about whether the Derderians had exceeded the legally allowed capacity of the building. Rhode Island officials would not speculate on whether the club was over capacity, and Attorney General Patrick Lynch told reporters that it was a question they were trying to answer, but it was a challenge. "There were three bands that played there, and it's a fluid atmosphere where some leave and some go."

The *Journal* erroneously reported in the weeks following the fire that the legal capacity for The Station was three hundred, and it seemed clear based on the number of fatalities and survivors that there were more than that inside when Great White set off the fireworks. Conclusion: the Derderians broke the law. The newspaper would not discover until much later that West Warwick had set the capacity for the club at 404.

Presented as facts by Rhode Island's top news source, and repeated by other news organizations, these errors became damning for the Derderians and helped cement the public's opinion of them. The *Journal* was not alone in making mistakes in its early coverage, something that often happens during a large breaking news story when journalists must rely on sources, and the information they are provided in haste can be wrong. In time, the argument goes, genuine facts surface and the record is corrected. CNN, for example, broadcast an erroneous report during September 11 that there had also been an explosion on Capitol Hill in Washington.

Rawson was frustrated with what he saw as a concerted effort to keep reporters away from facts. He had noticed that ever since the plane crash that killed John F. Kennedy Jr. in waters off the Rhode Island coast, local officials had developed a policy of keeping the media away in the time of a crisis.

"Part of the playbook, now, which I found out when Kennedy went down, is that there is a protocol to isolate the press," Rawson would later explain. "When the plane went down, there's a protocol, a government protocol that says one of the things you do is you cut off the press. You make sure that it cannot approach anything." Rawson understood the reasoning: an accident or crime scene needed to be preserved for investigation, and families of victims wanted privacy.

It was Rawson's observation that Governor Donald Carcieri had adopted this playbook of isolating the press in the wake of the fire. At the ruins of the nightclub, which was surrounded by chain-link fence and guarded by state police officers, the media was kept at a distance, across the street. In the meantime, any ordinary person was allowed to walk up to the fence and take photos or leave flowers. Rawson had one of his photographers put on a baseball cap and join these onlookers to take photos with a nonprofessional camera, but he was irritated by such subterfuge. It was wrong to deny the news media access that the general public was granted.

Additionally, important answers about the club's capacity and safety record could come from West Warwick fire inspector Denis Larocque, who had inspected the nightclub several times recently and declared the club safe, but the media was banned from speaking to him.

Tensions came to a head when the *Journal* was told the media was prevented from covering an upcoming memorial service organized by the state. Rawson understood that if families did not want to speak to the press, that was certainly their right, but the state did not have the authority to stop the *Journal* from asking those families. That's when Rawson met with Governor Carcieri and confronted him about the problem, and the newspaper was allowed access to the service.

But that faceoff between the governor and the newspaper editor led to accusations by the *Providence Phoenix*, the small weekly newspaper that was virtually alone in doing any critical reporting about the quality and ethics of the journalism at the *Journal*, that Rawson's newspaper had abused its power and used its pages for an underhanded agenda aimed at manipulating public perception during the fire tragedy.

"Joel Rawson's anger over access issues during the first week of the story, although perhaps justified, appears to have influenced the paper's coverage in unusual ways. In particular, the *ProJo* delayed publication of a favorable column by political columnist M. Charles Bakst about Sue Carcieri, the wife of Governor Don Carcieri, and seemingly downplayed Carcieri's presence in the paper during his decisive handling at the forefront of a major crisis," wrote Ian Donnis.

Rawson declined to be interviewed by the *Phoenix* about whether the *Journal* had used its pages to punish the governor. When Donnis submitted his questions in writing, Rawson issued a statement via email that did not address the accusations of bias. Instead, the editor praised his employees. "I am extraordinarily proud of the work that the *Journal* staff did on the Station fire," Rawson wrote.

The *Phoenix* responded, "It's more than a little ironic that Rawson, whose newspaper sued to get access to municipal documents in West Warwick, adopts a fortress posture when it comes to discussing the *Journal*."

Rawson had long ago developed a tough skin when it came to running his newspaper. With Rhode Island's endemic corruption, the *Journal* was often the last line of defense in fighting for the public's interest, challenging the state's most powerful institutions.

One legendary moment came when Rawson was editor of the paper's Metro section and he met with Colonel Walter Stone, the imposing head of the Rhode Island State Police. The meeting took place in the empty backroom of a Howard Johnson's restaurant, and as Stone lunched on chicken pot pie he told Rawson that the chief justice of the Rhode Island Supreme Court has been meeting with known mafia figures, "not rumor guys, but guys who've been convicted," Rawson recalled. Stone's chief of detectives had worked on the investigation and took the evidence to the attorney general's office. "He laughed me out of the room," Rawson remembered Stone saying, so, "I'm giving you this thing." Following the *Journal*'s reporting on the chief justice's mob ties, the judge resigned in 1986.

It would not be the last time the *Journal* exposed corruption in the state's highest court. A different investigation in 1994 also led to the resignation of another chief justice, and the *Journal* won the Pulitzer Prize.

Holding government institutions accountable was one of the core tenets of the *Journal*, and the newspaper would hunt down the facts on its own as it always did, regardless of whether officials or Governor Carcieri cooperated. The *Journal* was the watchdog in a state that had shown repeatedly that it desperately needed one, and the argument that other factors were more important than transparency rang hollow for Rawson.

"Wait a minute. I live here," Rawson later said about the nightclub fire. "We live here too. This is our community, you know. We're just as affected by this thing as everybody else."

CHAPTER 37

GINA REACTED TO the news of Fred's death with silence. She couldn't speak. As the numbness subsided she was consumed by grief and wept uncontrollably.

"The heartache that followed was more unendurable than any of the physical pain I would experience as the result of my burns," she said later.

She wanted to die. The flames had consumed so much of her body, and to hear that the fire had also taken her love was too much. A psychiatrist was summoned to her bedside as her anguish pushed her mind into a deep netherworld. "I just tuned out my life, like a radio dial stuck between two stations."

Gina hovered in this state for days. Her family rallied around her, reminding her that she still had so much to live for, especially her sons. And Freddy wouldn't want her to give up. She knew that, right?

Memories of Fred and his intense love of life helped sustain her, but Gina could not shake the crippling sadness. Images of the fire kept resurfacing, reminding her that the only reason she survived was because Fred pushed her toward the nightclub exit while an inferno raged around them. He saved her, and perished in the process. A sacrifice like that could not be for nothing. Embracing that thought, that Fred gave his life so she could live, helped strengthen her willpower.

She needed every ounce of stamina. Even on high doses of painkillers, her treatments were torture.

For the first time while conscious, she went through agonizing debridement. Nurses gingerly removed dressings that covered Gina from head to toe. As each bandage came off, dead and dying skin ripped away from her flesh, causing her to scream. Nurses washed the skin to remove any remaining black flecks and rewrapped the whole body in fresh gauze. The process took three hours and was repeated two to three times a day.

Gina did not know the extent of her injuries, and part of her did not want to learn the truth. Being in a burn unit, she saw other patients and assumed she was just as disfigured.

What did it matter? Fred was gone. Who cared what she looked like? Still, she avoided seeing her reflection, and asked the nurses to remove all mirrors so she wouldn't accidentally catch a glimpse of herself.

A week after coming out of the coma, a nurse worked on Gina's scalp, coating it in silver sulfadiazine, an antibacterial cream that immediately hardened into a black eggshell when applied, then was picked off a piece at a time, removing the burned and dead layers of skin that adhered to the medication. Don't worry, the nurse said casually as she worked, they'll be able to rebuild your ear.

"My ear? What do you mean?" Gina asked.

She had no idea there was a problem with her ear. She could hear fine in both of them.

The nurse left the room crying and apologizing. She didn't know that Gina had not been told. A doctor and psychiatrist came to the room. With her voice shaking Gina demanded to know what other parts of her had been destroyed. The doctor explained that the left ear was gone, but nothing else had been lost. Gina's scalp, however, was another matter. She had suffered fourth-degree burns on her head, some of the most severe burns a human being can survive. Her scalp was an open wound, and she would likely never grow hair there again.

Surgeons had saved her hands, at least cosmetically. In time they would begin to look normal, but she would probably never use them as she did before the fire. Gina thought of her work as a secretary. Her hands were her livelihood, and if she couldn't use them she might never work again.

Her lower body, the doctor said, was mostly fine, except for a third-degree burn to one knee. However, they had harvested skin for grafts from both the front and back of her legs, leaving behind a patchwork of irritation and scars. On her back she had suffered severe burns, but there was an unusual pattern. Some areas were untouched by the flames, suggesting that the bodies of other victims might have landed on her, and their limbs protected her from the fire. An image of Fred flashed into Gina's mind. Did he shield her from harm?

Now informed about the extent of her injuries, Gina could not rest. She stared at the ceiling of her hospital room all night long, worried that if she slept she might die.

Pain was her constant companion. Everything hurt. New skin grew in unevenly, making it unpleasant to move. Calcium built up in her joints, creating jabs of torment and limited motion. Touching or getting touched was excruciating.

Doctors told Gina to manage her expectations for recovery, which in her mind meant that she could be like this for the rest of her life. It was in this state that a feeling of rage festered, and she lashed out at anyone who dared come near. "The pope himself could have come in to visit me and I would not have wanted to see him either," she said. Remarkably, despite the constant anger and venom, friends and family continued to be at her bedside, a source of relentless understanding.

Anna Gruttadauria, the mother of Pamela Gruttadauria, came to visit Gina. Pamela was another survivor of the nightclub fire, and she was also at the burn unit of Mass General. One of the worst injured, Pamela had her eyes sewn shut and both hands removed, and had been heavily sedated since the disaster. Pamela's mother had gotten to know Gina's family, so she wanted to give her best wishes after hearing that Gina would soon be transferred from the hospital to a rehabilitation facility for the next step in her recovery. Gina thought Pamela's mother was lovely and uplifting, and the visit brightened Gina's spirits.

Days later, on May 4, 2003, the *New York Times* published a report on the fire's aftermath and the struggles of those impacted. Anna and Pamela were featured, and the mother remained optimistic, even though her daughter had been placed on dialysis due to kidney failure.

"I still have my daughter," Anna told the newspaper. "This is between Pam and God. She could have died in the fire but she didn't. She could have died of infection but she didn't. I have to believe God is saving her for something. Pam is in God's hands."

Pamela, thirty-three years old, died just hours after the hopeful *New York Times* article was published, succumbing to an infection that caused multiple organs to fail. She became the one hundredth victim of The Station nightclub fire.

The news of Pamela's death devastated and frightened Gina, worried that soon she would become victim number 101.

CHAPTER 38

W HEN THE DEATH toll reached one hundred, The Station secured its place in infamy.

Yet the nightclub disaster was not the deadliest fire in Rhode Island history. During the Cold War, on May 26, 1954, a weapon malfunction on the aircraft carrier USS *Bennington* caused an explosion that set the ship ablaze as it entered Narragansett Bay for its homeport of Quonset Point. One hundred and three were killed and more than two hundred injured.

A deadly military accident, however, was not considered the same as a building fire. Service members face a certain level of risk, but civilians in a public setting have an expectation of safety. The lessons learned by Americans over the years about the dangers of fire have come at a terrible price, and seem predictable and preventable in hindsight.

The deadliest fire in United States history was a massive forest fire in Peshtigo, Wisconsin, that claimed as many as 2,500 lives, although it has been mostly forgotten since it happened on the same day, October 8, 1871, as the Great Chicago Fire, which killed about three hundred.

Chicago was also home to the nation's deadliest single building fire with the Iroquois Theatre disaster on December 30, 1903. Sparks from a light ignited a curtain during a Sunday matinee performance of the popular Drury Lane musical *Mr. Blue Beard*. The theater was filled to capacity, with more jammed in for standing room, for an estimated crowd of nearly 2,200, many of them children. The fire spread from the curtain to highly flammable painted canvas scenery, and with only one effective exit, a massive grand staircase, at least 602 people perished when they could not escape. The number of fatalities might actually be higher, since bodies were possibly removed before the count was completed.

Despite the tragedy of the Iroquois, the lesson of having enough exits and avoiding flammable interiors was not learned.

In 1942 Cocoanut Grove of Boston became the nation's deadliest nightclub fire as 492 people were killed and 166 injured when combustible decorations caught fire. Within five minutes much of the club was consumed in flames and black smoke. An estimated 1,000 people had crammed into a space rated for 460, and could not escape. Many headed for the main entrance, but it was a single revolving door that quickly became jammed and broken. Other exits had been bolted shut to prevent patrons from leaving without paying. Doors that were unlocked were designed to open inward, making them useless against the crush of a stampede desperate to get out. In the aftermath firefighters found several dead guests still sitting in their seats with drinks in their hands, apparently so instantly overcome by toxic smoke they didn't have time to move.

After Cocoanut Grove, new fire safety codes became law. For example, it became a requirement that revolving doors be flanked by hinged doors. Capacity rules were better defined and fire prevention was generally improved.

Then on May 28, 1977, came the fire at the Beverly Hills Supper Club in Southgate, Kentucky, just outside Cincinnati. One hundred and sixty-five people died and more than two hundred were hurt when they flocked to see singer John Davidson in a cabaret room that could safely accommodate six hundred, but was packed with as many as 1,300. A smoldering fire caused by faulty wiring in the drop ceiling of an adjacent room burst into a flashover and quickly spread. Patrons could not evacuate in time to save their lives. The building, which had been added to with piecemeal construction over many years, did not have a sprinkler system. One victim lingered and died nine months after the fire.

Litigation followed the Beverly Hills Supper Club disaster and became a class action lawsuit, one of the first major cases pursued this way. Victims and their families won $43 million in settlements.

Nearly 7,400 Americans died in fires that same year, but the numbers of fire fatalities began to drop incrementally in the aftermath of the Beverly Hills Supper Club, and had averaged about 3,200 fire deaths per year at the time of The Station disaster.

Mass disasters weren't completely finished, however, and sporadic horrific fires grabbed headlines. On November 21, 1980, an electrical fire that spread due to a lack of sprinklers created toxic smoke and fumes and led to the deaths of eighty-five people at the MGM Grand Hotel on the Las Vegas Strip. The Happy Land social club fire in the Bronx on March 25, 1990, killed eighty-seven people when a disgruntled ex-boyfriend sought revenge on his former girlfriend who worked at the club and set it ablaze by pouring gasoline at the entrance to trap people inside. The club was unlicensed and had no fire alarm or sprinklers. The case is considered the deadliest mass murder by a single person in United States history.

These extreme cases aside, it remains a stubborn fact that more than three thousand Americans die each year in fires, a number that has remained consistent, even as medical breakthroughs save more burn victims from death, and billions have been spent on fire prevention and response.

There are several theories for why so many lives continue to be lost.

One involves the United States legal system. Most deadly fires have been unintentional—they were not purposely set to harm others. But in the safety culture that developed after tragedies like the Beverly Hills Supper Club, another trend emerged: the criminalization of accidents. Even though a criminal conviction often depends on the "intent" of the accused, thinking has evolved to hold those criminally responsible for violating safety rules, even if there was no intention to hurt others.

As a result, when a tragedy happens, the parties involved often turn to attorneys for protection, rather than being immediately fully transparent with investigators and authorities, fearful that any information they would honestly provide could be manipulated to create a criminal charge, rather than be used to determine the cause of an accident to prevent something similar from happening again.

It's a situation that some experts fear played out with deadly consequences in 2018 and 2019 with the crashes of two Boeing 737 Max jets. An equipment malfunction contributed to the first crash of a Lion Air flight in October 2018 in Indonesia, killing 189 people. The equipment issue, which some in Boeing and the Federal Aviation Administration apparently suspected, did not become public until after a second crash with Ethiopian Airlines in March 2019 claimed 157 lives. Had all parties been immediately transparent after the first crash, some believe the second tragedy would not have happened.

Criminalizing accidents, which in theory might hold people accountable and force others to follow safety rules, could actually have the unintended consequence of thwarting timely investigations.

"Criminalizing error erodes independent safety investigations, it promotes fear rather than mindfulness in people practicing safety-critical work, it makes organizations more careful in creating a paper trail, not more careful in doing their work, it discourages people from shouldering safety-critical, caring jobs such as nursing, and it cultivates professional secrecy, evasion, and self-protection," concluded safety expert Sidney Dekker, professor at Griffith University in Brisbane, Australia, and founder of the Safety Science Innovation Lab.

In the case of The Station fire, the remark within hours of the fire by the West Warwick police chief that the club owners would "most definitely" face criminal charges led the Derderian brothers to almost immediately limit their cooperation with the government, even though the brothers had key information about events that caused the fire.

For some in the government, seeing the disaster as a crime was more important than anything else. Little remained of the foam from the nightclub's walls after the fire, and Attorney General Patrick Lynch fought to keep that evidence for his criminal case, spurning federal investigators tasked with testing the foam to determine the fire's cause to prevent similar disasters. "All due respect, but to me there's nothing more important than the criminal investigation. And so we hold precedent, and we are the law," Lynch said. "So then, when you have these national organizations come in, and they want to test it for their report. I'm like, 'Really? You don't really matter to us. So stand by, we'll get back to you when we can. Or you can work off the work that we're doing.'"

In addition to this infighting over what best protects public safety—timely investigations versus effective prosecutions—there are other theories about why fire remains so deadly in the United States. For one, people are not sufficiently fearful of fire. Americans are more than a hundred years beyond the time when using fire was routine. People heated their homes with fireplaces, and cooked over open flames, and that proximity taught them the danger. In the modern world, people see fires when they're decorative in hotel or restaurant fireplaces.

At The Station, patrons watched the walls ignite from the fireworks and momentarily thought the flames were part of the act. Considering the number of rock shows that use fire as a special effect, this was understandable. However, that delay of up to thirty seconds to comprehend the danger cost precious time. Too few had noted the locations of the club's different exits when they arrived, so when the crowd realized the fire was out of control, two-thirds of those inside raced toward the one door they were familiar with, the entrance, and only about 40 percent would make it out that way. Those who survived rerouted and discovered other exits or escaped through smashed windows.

The speed of the nightclub fire was alarmingly fast because it was fueled by highly flammable foam on the walls, but fire spreads more quickly than people appreciate. Fifteen years after The Station disaster, the deadly wildfires of California were pushed by fifty-mile-per-hour winds, allowing the flames to move faster than human beings can run. Many residents had no idea fire could spread so quickly, and dozens perished.

"They don't understand its power," said Joe Kinan, the worst-burned survivor of The Station.

CRISIS

CHAPTER 39

IN THE MONTHS following the fire, after most of the injured were home from hospitals, a new crisis emerged. Many of the victims' families and survivors were destitute. Half of those hospitalized didn't have health insurance, and few had the means to cover their daily needs, since many had lived paycheck to paycheck before the disaster. With families' breadwinners gone or unable to work, there was no money to pay bills. Assistance was limited or difficult to immediately access, and even though civil lawsuits were filed within days of the fire, litigation would take time, with no guarantee of a payout.

The Federal Emergency Management Agency's denial of substantial disaster aid was an especially bitter pill for the victims' families and survivors. When six firefighters died in a warehouse blaze in Worcester, Massachusetts, a few years earlier, President Bill Clinton approved FEMA assistance within three days. A similarly swift response was expected with the nightclub fire, but requests for immediate help were rejected, and many victims and officials saw it as petty revenge by President George W. Bush against a state that historically voted for Democrats. It also didn't help with relationships in Washington that Rhode Island's liberal-leaning Lincoln Chafee was the sole Republican senator to vote against authorizing President Bush's Iraq War.

Phil Barr came from a different world than most at the fire. He attended a prestigious college, had health insurance, and his family had resources, so there were no worries about keeping a roof over their heads or their next meals. By Easter, less than two months after the disaster, the conversations in the Barr household shifted. After hearing about the needs of other victims' families and survivors via the media, the Barrs decided to help fill the needs that the government and aid agencies couldn't.

For Phil, it became part of his healing. He only had a vague understanding of the difficulties other survivors and victims' families faced, but he was hit with a feeling that he should get involved. His mother Barbara was equally determined, and the two soon bonded on the issue. When they learned that the Station Family Fund was being formed they attended an early meeting. Phil raised his hand that night in May, still battling at that point to regain his strength. "I want to help out in whatever way I really can," he told the crowd of about two dozen.

Phil struggled to breathe as he spoke, and noted that few people who were hurt in the fire were at the meeting, although many of the fund's volunteers had been in the nightclub when tragedy struck. Some suffered from debilitating survivor's guilt. One man couldn't go twenty minutes without breaking down into agonizing sobs. A woman with long black hair in a biker jacket, who had escaped as soon as the fire started, chain-smoked throughout the entire meeting and seethed with rage against anyone and everyone she thought culpable. With the Barrs' upper-middle-class affluence and education, Phil and his mother stood out from nearly everyone else in the room, and in time the group would nickname Phil "the college boy."

Jonathan Bell, a lawyer who lived in Providence but worked for a large firm in Boston, led the initiative. With his slightly oversized, pleated-front khaki pants, business casual polo shirts, and horn-rimmed glasses, Bell struck Phil as a typically nerdy lawyer, the kind of man Phil often encountered as the son of an attorney. From the start Phil recognized that Bell was the type of person who might have a chance to manage the cause and its eclectic group of volunteers. Bell was a listener. His thoughtful and reserved approach, allowing everyone to have their say while he barely spoke, made each person feel welcomed and considered. And because Bell did such little talking himself, when he did have something to say, everyone listened—it had to be important.

Bell's reason for getting involved was a mystery to Phil. Bell wasn't present the night of the fire, and wasn't a club patron. He had no direct personal connection to any of the fire victims or survivors, and he wasn't even in the state at the time of the tragedy. As a busy corporate attorney, Bell had been traveling overseas for work that night and first read an account of the fire in a foreign newspaper, and then like millions of others watched the Channel 12 video on TV news. In some ways, he was as far away from the tragedy as anyone could be.

But Bell was a lifelong Rhode Islander, born and raised in Providence, where his parents both graduated from Brown University. He grew up on the city's upscale East Side. Yet in a community so small, the fire victims were also his peers, intrinsically part of his everyday life. These people were the salt of the earth, as locals would say, the regular working-class guys and gals who formed the fabric of a uniquely tiny and insular state. Bell felt the government and "do-gooders" would quickly abandon the survivors and victims' families, because as blue-collar rockers they didn't fit a traditional demographic that appealed to charities. The survivors and victims' families also had very little clout and could be easily run over, forgotten, or dismissed. Bell's suspicions were quickly confirmed when a state resource center that opened with great fanfare in the aftermath of the fire was shuttered after just ten days when the state claimed it was no longer being used. Bell knew he had the expertise to help and first thought of setting up a fund of his own, but then he heard that survivors of the fire were meeting regularly at the Cowesett Inn. With another corporate-type friend Bell sat in on one of those early sessions, and when it became clear they were so unlike the other attendees, they found themselves confronted. "What are you doing here?" someone asked. Bell explained that he and his friend were there to help with issues like setting up a nonprofit with 501(c)(3) status with the Internal Revenue Service, so donations could be accepted and processed out to those in need. The group not only accepted Bell's help, but also named him the fund's chairman.

The Station Family Fund would be different than other relief efforts in the wake of the fire because assistance would be decided and distributed by a committee of survivors. Criteria for receiving help were set up based on need, and those who qualified could get money. If someone was turned down, the decision came from others directly impacted, not some faceless government or charity bureaucrat.

The group began meeting regularly in private homes and at the Cowesett Inn, the same restaurant across the street from the fire that had served as the blood-soaked triage center. By then little remained of the nightclub itself—the building had been bulldozed and the lot surrounded by a fence as a crime scene. Each time Phil attended a meeting of the fund he'd look across the street and remember that awful night. *Spooky,* he thought, what an odd choice for a place to meet. But many involved in the fund were former regulars of the club, and somehow the location helped them process their overwhelming feelings of grief, guilt, and rage.

It quickly became clear to Phil that the situation with the victims' families and survivors had devolved into a full-blown emergency. Many of those impacted by the fire were on the verge of homelessness, unable to pay their rent or mortgages. Their vehicles, a lifeline in a time of crisis, were being repossessed. Initial donations brought in about $70,000, a pittance compared to the enormous need as requests for assistance came in by the hundreds. Seventy-six children, some born after the fire, lost one or both parents in the disaster, and twenty-three people lost spouses. Some couldn't even afford to buy pencils for their children for school. One man required money for groceries, but also a ride to the market, since the fire had taken such a toll on his respiratory system that he struggled to walk. Once again the Cowesett Inn became a place of triage, where the most desperate were assessed and helped.

Desperate. That word kept going through Phil's head as he worked on the fund. So many had lived close to the edge before the fire that it took little to push them into the abyss.

One eighteen-year-old girl who lost her mother in the fire, and whose father was no longer in the picture, came home to find her belongings out on the front lawn. The landlord had evicted the girl because no one had paid the rent. The teenager ended up living in her car, but coincidentally saw someone from the Station Family Fund selling T-shirts. The girl had never heard of the fund until then, and shared her story with the volunteer. The fund rallied and found the girl a new apartment and a job.

The fund did not have enough money to meet urgent needs like these. Even when there was money, there were situations Phil had never encountered, like how to actually give people money—some in need couldn't cash checks because they didn't qualify to have bank accounts.

Replenishing the fund relied on herculean efforts by volunteers like Todd King, a Great White fan from Framingham, Massachusetts, and a first-timer at The Station who had escaped the inferno with his wife,

Theresa O'Toole King. Todd's boundless energy sent him to nearly any rock performance in New England with a big plastic jug and sign asking for donations. He established connections with bands and stars of the metal rock scene, including Dee Snider of Twisted Sister. There were also scattered fundraisers, but they were small and when successful raised less than $2,000 per event, a drop when a lake was needed, Phil thought.

Years later Phil would come to understand that the nightclub fire also predated the rise of social media and the Internet's ability to instantly raise money in times of crisis. By comparison, in 2013 when the Boston Marathon bombing killed three people and injured 264 others, $26 million was raised in ten days. No such infrastructure existed in 2003.

Instead, efforts were modest and local. Arlene Violet, a former Roman Catholic nun who became Rhode Island's attorney general and then a popular radio talk show host, raised thousands of dollars on her broadcast. But Bell noticed that most of the pledge calls came from working-class people similar to those hurt by the fire, in amounts of ten, fifteen, or thirty dollars—a genuine sacrifice by those with little to spare. There were few pledge calls from the state's wealthy enclaves of Barrington, East Greenwich, or the East Side of Providence. As Bell predicted, the typical do-gooders did not see the victims of The Station fire as a legitimate charitable cause.

As the need grew, and money only dribbled in, Phil and the rest of the board were forced to consider an offer from an unlikely and reviled source: the band that started the fire.

Jack Russell, the lead singer of Great White, through his manager, proposed that proceeds from the band's upcoming tour be used to aid fire victims. Again, it wouldn't be much, perhaps $2,000 to $5,000 per appearance. But with the need so acute, even a deal with the devil had to be considered.

This eventually led to a meeting with Russell's representative, Great White's newly hired manager Obi Steinman, with fourteen members of the fund's board. Steinman gathered everyone around a long rectangular table at a restaurant with himself seated in the middle, like a king holding court. Steinman wore a black buttoned-down shirt with blue jeans, reminding Phil more of a bartender than a veteran confidant to rock stars. The only bit of rocker flash was a chunky bracelet.

The table divided into different perspectives. Those who sat closest to Steinman still revered Great White and saw lead singer Jack Russell as a rock god. They wanted to be regaled with anecdotes about Jack and other rockers, and Phil thought Steinman all too willing to share gossipy tales recalling tour hijinks, including a yarn about drinking with Sebastian Bach, the former lead singer of the metal group Skid Row. Sitting farther from Steinman were those deeply conflicted and skeptical of any offer coming from the band, since Great White had lit the spark that caused so much suffering. These board members questioned the band's intentions. If the funds were accepted, were strings attached? Did they really want to be associated with a donation from Jack Russell? Phil sat with this group.

Farthest away on the periphery of the table were those board members simmering with fury, outraged to have any contact, even if tangential, with those who had stolen lives with their irresponsible behavior. They listened to Steinman, with arms crossed, barely able to contain their enmity.

Jack Russell, the board was told, wanted to do the right thing.

The right thing, Phil thought. What a strange choice of words. *The right thing* would have been to not light off giant fireworks inside a room with a low ceiling. Phil wondered about Russell's real motivations. A public relations stunt? Did Russell think this would help get him off the hook? A grand jury was convening to determine any criminal charges, and any possible trial jurors would come from the Rhode Island public, whose opinion could be shaped by any act of charity by Jack Russell and Great White.

Phil tried to be open-minded. On one level he thought Steinman's presentation was heartfelt—on Russell's behalf. The lead singer himself had publicly blamed others for the tragedy. However, Steinman's contrition was undercut when he made it clear that any donation by the band would be promoted. Russell wanted his generosity acknowledged.

Steinman proposed what would eventually become a forty-one-city national tour beginning at the Logan County Fairgrounds in Sterling, Colorado. The board members brainstormed with the agent about ways to help raise additional money at the concerts by selling Station Family Fund T-shirts for twenty dollars each.

As the money started coming in, other fundraising ended. By

September, seven months after the disaster, the Station Nightclub Fire Relief Fund, the official main recipient of public charity via the United Way and the Rhode Island Foundation, announced that it was winding down. Much of $510,000 in remaining funds would go to college scholarships for the 156 children whose parents were hurt or died in the tragedy. The effort had raised a reported $3.27 million, with much of the money spent on funerals and initial support for survivors and victims' families, although some complained that getting aid was confusing and difficult.

The decision to turn donated crisis aid into scholarships angered those in the smaller, grassroots Station Family Fund, who saw that daily needs remained urgent. "People were put in the streets, almost homeless, no food on the table," said Todd King, the group's president.

But the backlash against the Station Family Fund for accepting Great White's tour money was immediate and lasting. Insurance companies refused to provide coverage for some shows, fearful that people angry over the band's role in the fire would be disruptive, or perhaps even violent and destructive. Some performances had to be canceled, and there would be no show in Rhode Island. There was even a momentary scandal and accusations that Great White had not turned over all the money it promised to the charity, although that allegation was not substantiated and the band was ultimately credited with raising more than $100,000 for the fund.

Far less controversial and ultimately more fulfilling was Phil's work on the fund that involved the children of the fire's victims, especially at Christmas time.

Phil and his mother Barbara were matched with the two sons of one of the most gravely injured survivors, Gina Russo. Later in the year, after Thanksgiving, Phil and Barbara traveled to Gina's modest cape home in Cranston and met with the boys, Alex and Nicholas, to ask what they hoped to receive for Christmas. At that first meeting Phil sized up Gina as a woman who had been pushed to the brink. She wore a hat to cover the bandages on her head, and had dressings on her arms to protect her wounds. The boys ran wild all over the house, or at least it seemed like that to Phil, who was raised in a household where such rambunctiousness was not tolerated. Gina seemed exhausted as the Barrs asked what they could do to help, but her weariness turned to surprise, Phil thought, that these strangers had come to her home with an offer to bear gifts. Phil and his mother learned that the boys most wanted hockey skates that year. A neighbor down the road had flooded part of a field enough for it to freeze over and form a makeshift hockey rink for the local kids, and the boys were eager to play. The Barrs made sure skates were under the tree that Christmas, along with a mountain of other gifts.

As he got to know Alex and Nicholas, and all of the children of the fire victims he'd met, Phil marveled at how wise and resilient they were. Somehow kids knew how serious the situation was, and how fortunate they were, even if a parent sustained painful injuries. The level of empathy in the children was remarkable, and regardless of age they found ways to help their families—an incredible sense of responsibility when they should be carefree.

In time the Barrs would become close with Gina Russo and her children, forming a type of extended family born from the ashes of their shared trauma, one that would last years.

CHAPTER 40

B ARRY WARNER, THE nightclub's neighbor who had complained for years about the noise, pulled up to the Kinko's on Main Street in West Warwick. It was May. Three months had passed since the fire, and it was time for the world to learn the secrets he knew.

Warner had poured his tortured soul into the pages he was about to fax anonymously to the media and the authorities. It was all there. That the Derderians weren't properly informed that the foam they bought and glued to the walls of their nightclub was highly flammable, that the company that sold the foam was incompetent, and most of all, that Warner was not to blame.

Warner knew it all. In fact, he knew too much. That's why people wanted to shut him up, and so far they'd been successful. That was about to change.

After that night when he witnessed the horrors of the fire—he could never forget the sight of that singed woman who looked like a ghoul—Warner drove to work the next day, Friday, listening to the radio for the latest news about the disaster. At that point they said seventy-four people were dead, an astonishing number. As newscasters talked about how quickly the fire spread, Warner got a pit in his stomach. He began to put the pieces together in his mind, and the pain in his gut soon churned into bile.

Warner no longer worked at American Foam. He'd been there for about twenty-seven years, starting when he was twenty-six and eventually becoming a salesman responsible for hundreds of accounts. He loved his job but disliked the owner and boss, Aram DerManouelian. That man had too much money for his own good, and acted like it: he didn't treat Warner with the respect he deserved, so he left for Flock Tex, a competitor in nearby Woonsocket.

By Sunday, three days after the fire, Warner wasn't the only one figuring out what went wrong with the foam. A West Warwick detective rang Warner's bell at eight in the morning and threw out an accusation. More police and confrontations followed, and within days Warner's name was published in the *Providence Journal*, publicly damned as the person who sold the Derderians the foam that killed all those people.

Warner ranted: It wasn't true! He didn't actually sell them the foam. Did anyone see him sell them the foam? No! That's because it never happened. He didn't personally make the sale and process the order. Yes, the deadly foam came from American Foam. And, yes, he had discussed the idea with the brothers of using sound foam to control the noise coming from the nightclub. But it wasn't the only idea he suggested. He told them about curtains and false walls too. There had been some follow-up questions from the brothers about the foam, and at one point they asked for a sample, so Warner grabbed one at work and dropped it off. Neither of the Derderians was in the club that day, so Warner left the foam with the bartender. Later the brothers asked Warner about glue that worked with foam, and he made a recommendation.

But he did *not* make the actual sale! As best as he could figure, the Derderians called in the order. The girl working the desk—a fill-in, Warner thought—took the order. There was an email too, dated June 9, 2000, that specifically asked for "sound foam." Sound foam is required to be flame retardant. When asked about this mandate years later, Warner said, "It's supposed to be. It's its nature," then added emphatically, "Is a football player big? Yes. It's A-B-C."

But the information that the Derderians' ordered "sound foam" apparently did not get properly processed by the fill-in, a person Warner would not name—why ruin the young girl's life?—and highly flammable packing foam was delivered to the nightclub instead. It would have taken a special order to get sound foam, since it wasn't something American Foam typically kept in stock.

A month later, in July 2000, Warner saw that he was credited with the sale to the Derderians on his monthly commissions statement, but it was only about twenty bucks and he would admit later that he didn't really pay much attention. Then after the Derderians installed the foam they kept calling and asking if the noise was better. Warner conceded that it was actually quieter, and the brothers repeatedly insisted that the neighbor swing by to see what they'd done.

After so much pestering, one afternoon Warner finally relented and went to the club to see for himself in person. It was before opening hours for the day, but workers were there and he was able to go in and look around. There seemed to be two types of foam on the club's walls, some new and pliable, and some that was old, hardened, and faded. Moments after his inspection began, a club worker yelled at Warner and told him he wasn't allowed on the stage and had to leave. He walked out. That was the last time he'd had an encounter with the club's foam, or even thought about it, until the aftermath of the fire.

Seeing the foam in person, and even touching it, would not have set off alarms. Flame retardant sound foam and highly flammable packing foam are visually indistinguishable, and they feel the same. They can even come in the same colors. One way to tell the difference is with the paperwork that comes with the foam, the material safety data sheet, or MSDS. It spells out the specifications of the foam and would warn the recipient of any fire hazard.

In Warner's experience, American Foam had a habit of not including MSDS info, an example, he thought, of Aram DerManouelian cutting corners. Instead, customers would sometimes have to ask for the spec sheets, and with reorders, they wouldn't even do that.

These weren't small details, Warner thought. People needed to know the truth. The ball was dropped at American Foam. And, more importantly, he was not the one who actually processed the order that sold the Derderians the foam. He was involved, but not in the way people were being led to believe by the news media, especially the *Providence Journal*.

Since Warner's name first appeared in the paper, he'd been denounced as one of the villains of the disaster. His new job was in jeopardy, and people gave him ugly stares in public. The windshield on his car was smashed with a rock in his driveway. He caught a news reporter hiding behind his garage. After an angry exchange over the telephone, Warner concluded that the *Journal* wasn't interested in hearing the truth. Lawyers who represented Warner, funded by American Foam's insurers, had told him not to talk to anyone. His life was spinning out of control, and there was nothing he could do to fight back.

If he couldn't speak up for himself in public, there had to be another way. Then he had an idea: be an anonymous whistleblower.

He wrote it all down. What American Foam did and didn't do. That written warnings that should have come with the foam did not. That the Derderians were not specifically told that the foam they bought was actually flammable. All of it, every detail he could remember. Incompetence. Cutting corners. That's why so many people died. The words poured out of his fingers in a stream of consciousness, page after page. It was cathartic, as if this was pent up inside and waiting to get out.

"This is a company that did little to educate their employees about the limits of polyurethane foam. In fact, they did the opposite," he wrote. "This is a company that did not want to lose a sale by telling the truth. Don't educate the customer was often spoken."

When Warner finished writing it turned out to be an eight-page fax. He knew he could not sign it, but there was so much detail that it would be clear to anyone that it came from a knowledgeable insider at American Foam. To keep his anonymity he went to Kinko's, where they would fax it from their phone number, making it untraceable to him. He sent the fax out to the media, including the *Boston Globe*, and to Attorney General Patrick Lynch. Prosecutors must learn the truth too.

As the faxes transmitted to the world, Barry felt relief.

It wouldn't last.

The *Boston Globe*, if it ever received the fax, did not publish a story about the tip from a self-proclaimed American Foam whistleblower. The attorney general's office did not make the fax public or present it to the grand jury, and concealed its existence for more than two years, hidden even from the Derderians, until November 2005.

Barry Warner remained silenced.

"It would have been both professionally irresponsible and legally unsound for prosecutors to have introduced the unattributed hearsay and innuendo contained in the fax to the grand jury," prosecutors argued when accused of covering up evidence that was exculpatory and helpful to Michael and Jeffrey Derderian.

In fact, prosecutors knew within days of receipt that Warner was the author of the fax. Investigators "went to the copy shop from which the note had been faxed and secured video of the individual who sent it. It was

Warner. We did that very soon after we received the fax," prosecutor Ferland said years later.

Even with confirmation that Warner was the author, the fax was kept from grand jurors who sought as much information as possible to determine whether anyone should be criminally charged. Warner was not asked about the fax or its revelations when he testified before the grand jury the month after the fax was sent.

In Rhode Island it was legal to withhold information from a grand jury that might prove someone's innocence.

CHAPTER 41

PHIL BARR RETURNED to Bates College on Memorial Day to visit a ghost.

It was the final weekend of the year at the college, when students sift through the debris of another semester, pack their belongings, and move out of the dorms. Phil went to box up his possessions too, not knowing if he'd ever return. His old life here in Lewiston, Maine, was gone forever. The ghost he came to visit was his own.

Memories flooded back as he drove onto campus to his third-floor single at the Parker residence hall. It was his first time back since the fire, and a spooky feeling swept over him as he saw that his room remained intact from that day he left in February, when he was full of hope and anticipation and headed to Manhattan for those investment-banking internship interviews. His bed was still made, exactly as he'd done it. Nothing touched. Nothing moved. This wasn't really his room, he thought. It belonged to someone else, a version of Phil that no longer existed. The man who lived here was not the same man moving out today. *Maybe it should all be tossed into a dumpster, and then just walk away.*

With morbid fascination he studied his surroundings. There were the term papers he'd been working on, still on his desk. He glanced down at the macroeconomics report he was preparing on English monetary policy of the 1800s. Phil grinned as he reviewed his paper's premise of taking old notions of merchant banking and applying them to modern business. He'd been full of clever ideas like that at Bates, and so determined about the direction his life would take.

"I'll start over here," his father, Philip, said as he began to fill a box.

Phil wanted to come up to Bates alone, insisting that closing this chapter of his life was something he needed to handle by himself, but he was not allowed to drive. The fire had melted the corneas of his eyes and they required time to heal—he needed to pass a vision exam at the DMV to get his license back. The doctors said his eyes would recover, and Phil was grateful. Another fire survivor's cornea was so badly singed that he'd lost sight in one eye.

There was also the gaping wound on Phil's back. The burn was severe and doctors disagreed on whether to do a painful skin graft, so they left the decision up to Phil, who opted to let the wound mend on its own, even though that meant it would take longer to heal. Months later it was still an open wound and the dressing was changed every evening, something he couldn't do on his own. He needed his dad's help.

Phil thought back to the moment he'd first moved into the dorm. He and his friend Derek felt they had pretty sweet deals, both able to get single rooms across the hall from each other. Having his own room made dating easier, although one relationship had been too much drama. It'd be great for a while, and then they'd break up and hate each other before reuniting. If living through the fire had taught Phil one thing, it was that he would be more deliberate. The cliché was true: life was simply too precious and short. That emotional pendulum relationship was unhealthy, and he was done. From this point forward nothing is the same, he thought as he looked at his room, strangely frozen in time. The truth was that nothing in his life was untouched or unchanged from the fire.

Phil wondered if he was finished with Bates forever. His recovery was frustratingly slow, from his perspective. In the weeks after he'd come out of the coma he'd refused to stay in bed, forcing himself to walk to regain his strength, although not being able to fully inhale was maddening. The doctors, however, seemed downright gleeful about Phil's progress, and he remembered the big day, Friday, March 21, at six in the evening when he was allowed to go home. It had then been one month and one day since the fire, and Phil's journey from near death to release was considered miraculous. Indeed, his parents sent a dispatch to the Bates community that said, "We believe that the power of prayer by so many relatives and friends around the world, coupled with his youth and excellent physical condition before the incident, have combined to produce this joyous result." The family popped a cork and celebrated with champagne when Phil returned home.

Despite his progress, Phil feared he wasn't ready to go back to school, not now and maybe not even when classes restarted in September. Physically it wasn't clear that he could be completely on his own anytime soon, away from the healthcare and the support system that continued to nurse him, especially his family. There had been an emotional price too. He was rattled by the horrors of that night, his entire system shaken. There was even concern about whether the drugs that placed him in a coma for so long would have a lingering effect. Before returning to Bates he needed to put his intellect to the test, since there would be no sense going back if he couldn't do the work.

If he did return, it could never be the same without the swim team. His doctors were adamant: "You can't do that." When Phil was released from the hospital, his lung capacity was less than half, just 45 percent. Without enough oxygen intake, there was no way he could do any activity that required so much pulmonary strain. Swimming defined his time at Bates, and it was more than the joy he felt when he was in the water and the exhilaration of the race—the team had become the majority of his social circle at the school: he hung out with the same fifty people for at least twenty hours every week over the course of years. They practiced together, competed as a team, and took long bus rides to New Hampshire, Vermont, Connecticut, and New York. He'd never been so close with any other group of friends.

The nightclub destroyed that too.

As Phil shoved his clothes and books into moving boxes, he decided to refocus. He would cut out trivial amusements and distractions, or people who were no good for him, like that former girlfriend. Such resolve was the only way he was going to get past this.

He knew his first two goals. Whether or not it involved Bates, he was going to find a way to have his shot at Wall Street.

And, somehow, he was going to get back in the pool.

CHAPTER 42

GINA HESITANTLY REMOVED her clothes. Not all. Just enough.
She was about to be released from Spaulding Rehabilitation
Hospital in Boston, finally allowed to return to her home in Rhode
Island. She had wanted to leave for a while, and had summoned the
courage to confront her doctor on June 9, rehearsing her arguments
ahead of time. Before she could utter a sentence the doctor unexpectedly said, "So, are you ready to go home?"

That was nearly a week ago and now she faced a moment of truth. In
the days leading up to her release her therapist had gently told Gina that
she should see herself in a mirror. It had been 113 days since the fire,
and Gina had avoided viewing her reflection. She'd never confronted
her injuries visually, and the therapist suggested it would be better to do
so now, surrounded by support, than have it accidentally happen back
home.

"It's not as bad as you think," the therapist insisted.

Gina's rehabilitation at Spaulding had been more agonizing than her
time at Mass General, and on some days she wondered if she'd survive.
Leaving the hospital had been traumatic. She'd bonded with the nurses
and doctors there, and she didn't want anyone else changing her bandages or touching her. They'd taken care of her most intimate bodily
functions, which she still couldn't do on her own, and now that would
be left to strangers. Gina's connection with the hospital staff was further
demonstrated when just before leaving for the rehabilitation center a
nurse came and painted Gina's toenails. "You cannot leave Mass General
without feeling pretty," the nurse said.

Each day at Spaulding began with stretching in bed, a painful ordeal since Gina had been bedridden for so long that her muscles had atrophied and she was extremely weak. At the first session her body was shifted so her legs could drop over the side of the bed, but they jutted out straight, unable to bend. Gina's lack of movement for months had caused heterotopic ossification, a buildup of calcium in her joints that thwarted motion. To break up the calcium deposits, therapists manually bent Gina's knees, creating a loud crunching and sharp jabs of torment. The same problem afflicted her right elbow and threatened other joints. Just seeing the therapist arrive for the daily sessions caused Gina to burst into tears.

The therapy worked. Sooner than she imagined possible, Gina found herself using a walker to take steps. One morning the therapist came into the room and removed the walker. "You're not going to need this anymore," she said. Those first steps without the walker reminded Gina of a six-month-old baby learning to walk, but she had such a sense of accomplishment.

Those moments of joy were tempered when she heard about the investigation into the fire and those who caused it, and her anger grew with each new detail. No one had been criminally charged, and the probe by the attorney general moved slowly. The state had public hearings, which included testimony from survivors and victims' families, and it was clear that fire safety codes were woefully inadequate and out of date. Changes were in the works, which caused some solace, but that did nothing for those already suffering or dead.

Gina seethed when she thought of those who were directly responsible. The bouncer who prevented her and Fred from leaving through the stage door exit, trapping them to their fates. The Derderian brothers who ran the club. And in particular, Great White and its lead singer, Jack Russell. She was enraged when she heard that Russell wanted to have a concert tour to benefit the Station Family Fund, the charity created by survivors to help those impacted by the fire. To Gina, no matter how worthy the cause, no good could come from any concert involving that band, and she was appalled that Jack Russell and his bandmates would even consider showing their faces in public so soon after killing and hurting hundreds of people. Any funds raised would be blood money, an attempt by Great White to buy forgiveness. Thanks, but no thanks.

For positive thoughts, her mind turned to Fred. She felt his spirit, and she would sometimes find herself talking aloud to him. *The nurses must think I'm nuts*, she thought, but at the worst moments of the painful rehabilitation she would look up into the heavens and ask Fred to help her get through it. She spoke to him every day for months.

By June her recovery reached a plateau. She struggled with walking and sitting, and stairs were especially challenging, but going forward it would be a matter of continuing her physical therapy to keep improving, and she could do that as an outpatient. She suffered from contractures, the tightening of her skin when it healed, and her eyesight was limited, due to damage caused by the heat and smoke of the fire. Her healing and therapy could continue at home, and now that she had the doctor's blessing it was time to finally look in the mirror.

"It's not as bad as you think," the therapist said. In the months Gina had suffered and persevered, she'd concluded that she probably looked something like Freddy Krueger, the melted demon from the movie series *A Nightmare on Elm Street*. She prepared to face that image as the therapist brought a full-length mirror.

Gina felt her heart pound as she stepped in front of her reflection and slowly lifted her head to meet her own gaze. She breathed a deep sigh . . . of relief. It wasn't as terrible as she'd envisioned. It wasn't good, but considering it had been only four months since the fire, she was elated. One side of her face was pink and speckled with scar tissue. She knew she'd lost her left ear, so she was ready to see only an opening there. She turned and viewed the burns on her back for the first time.

Seeing her scalp was hard. All of her hair was gone, and it would probably never grow back.

Yet she felt strong. Spaulding had done more than heal her physically—it had taught her about courage, dedication, and inner strength. The staff threw a party for Gina in the lobby, a send-off that was bittersweet. Gina knew there were other survivors of the nightclub fire that still had months of recovery ahead, and she'd become friends with some of them at the rehabilitation center, so the elation she felt for her release was tempered by feelings of guilt for leaving them behind.

She noted the date on the calendar: Friday the thirteenth. How ironic. This was, after all, her lucky day. Everything was about to get better, not worse.

Her mother and stepfather drove her home to Cranston, and Gina delighted in the sights from the car window. Spring was changing into summer, with trees full of leaves, flowers in bloom, and birds chirping. Gina smelled pollen in the air. When they pulled into the driveway, Gina sobbed, harder than she'd cried since the fire. It was overwhelming to be home again, and through her tears her eyes soaked up the mundane little details: the weeds at the corner of the garden that had somehow escaped the lawnmower's blade, and the section of a repaired fence that needed painting.

The exact time of her arrival home had been hard to predict, so the boys were both in school. Once they were picked up they ran into the house, laughing and crying at the same time. That night, although still bandaged up, Gina attended her son's Little League baseball game. She was picking up the pieces of the life she left behind.

It was daunting. Unable to work, how would she support her boys? In the days after her return she felt useless. Unable to walk down stairs due to the stiffness in her legs, she scooched down on her behind, a step at a time. Her relationship with her boys had been put on hold for months and needed work. During her time at Shriners, normally a hospital for children, Nick and Alex received age-appropriate education about burns and had interacted with kids in recovery, which prepared them for Gina's return home, but she felt a distance, perhaps even fear. Gina hated the idea of being a burden, and no longer surrounded by doctors, nurses, and therapists, she dwelled on how much help she required. With young boys and older parents, she should take care of her family, not the other way around.

Mulling around the house, the loss of Fred hit Gina especially hard. She obsessed over the final minutes of his life, and how he must have suffered as he pushed her to survival. And now what did her survival mean? Freddy was supposed to be her future, and now she was left with pain, disfigurement, and guilt. As her bitterness and resentment grew, Gina lashed out at the nurses and therapists who provided her in-home care. They were constantly around, changing her bandages and dressings twice a day, and Gina craved to be alone in her misery. She didn't want to speak to any of these people, or allow them to touch her, and she was especially offended by the idea of strangers poring their eyes over her wounded body. When an insurance company insisted on yet another full examination to determine the extent of her injuries, Gina flew into a rage. "If all the burn surgeons I've seen already weren't enough for them, then I didn't want their money," she said. "It wasn't worth the humiliation." The insurer backed down and used existing records.

News about the fire further provoked Gina's anger. There had still been no criminal accountability for the Derderians, the band, the fire inspector who had somehow declared the building safe, the foam sales-man, or anyone, and Jack Russell had put himself back into the limelight with an interview about his efforts to help the victims. Gina believed Russell had ordered the pyrotechnics and held him especially responsi-ble, yet the man seemed to have no shame.

Gina channeled her fury into writing, and on August 9 wrote a letter, one she would never mail, railing against those she felt most culpable for so much suffering.

"I have so much anger for the Derderian brothers, the bouncer who would not let us out the door because it was a club policy not to open the door except for anyone but the band (well, what made their life more important than mine) I cry every day for all that I have lost and for what I will never have or be able to do again," she wrote.

She expressed her love of Fred, telling her list of villains, "you have no idea, and never will, of the loss I feel for him and all the independence you took from me. I can no longer work at a job I've had for 19 years. I have to watch every dime I spend because of having to live on social security for the rest of my life at the age of 35.

"Your stupidity and greed has cost 300 people so much heartache and grief you will never understand the depth of this pain until the day the you are sentenced to spending your days in hell where you will feel the pain of fire and the smell of burning," she wrote. "I can only hope that the justice system will take into consideration the life sentence you have given to 300 people when your times comes to pay for what you have done.

"This is not the end of my story," Gina concluded, "it's just the begin-ning of what will be a lifetime of pain and suffering."

CONSEQUENCES

CHAPTER 43

For months a statewide grand jury met to determine whether criminal indictments would be handed up in The Station fire. Jurors started convening, just five days after the fire, at Camp Fogarty in East Greenwich, a gated National Guard facility that kept the news media away.

On the first day members of Great White entered the camp, and drummer Eric Powers was the first to testify. Prosecutors asked Powers about places where the band performed and when pyrotechnics were used. Powers made an impression with an apparent photographic memory and could relate details about venues and audience sizes. He explained that tour manager Daniel Biechele ran the fireworks and would inform the band minutes before show time if fireworks would be used. Sometimes it depended on the size of the audience. Based on his years of experience, Powers estimated the crowd at The Station on the night of the fire to be between 350 and 375.

Week after week new witnesses appeared, with the focus on pyrotechnics and the safety of the club. There were accounts that special effects had been used by bands in the past, including flash pots, which create a flash for a fraction of a second, followed by a small mushroom cloud of smoke, like magicians use when taking rabbits out of hats.

In May the West Warwick police reported it had received a tip that the band Red Hot, impersonators of the heavy metal group Mötley Crüe, used flash pots at The Station. If true, it might prove that the Derderians, or at least their staff, allowed pyrotechnics, albeit minor compared to gerbs, and that made it plausible that Great White had approval for its fireworks. The Derderians steadfastly denied that the band had permission to use explosives.

Detective Sergeant Keith Azverde of the West Warwick police told the grand jury he'd spoken to Thomas Phelps, a band member of Red Hot, who "stated that the band played The Station nightclub approximately 15 times with 3 to 4 performances played under the Derderian ownership in front of crowds of approximately 300 patrons." Detective Azverde further testified that Phelps said, "the band performance is the same for each show to include the use of pyrotechnics." The band would play two forty-five minute sets, with two flash pots ignited at the first song of each set.

If that weren't enough, the detective said that Phelps "states he is in possession of a videotape of the band's performance at The Station nightclub that depicts the band's exact routine performance."

"Do you have the video?" the prosecutor asked.

"The video is not in our, yet in our possession," Azverde answered, but the detective pledged to get a copy.

If true, the video would be a breakthrough in the investigation. There were witnesses who said they'd seen special effects used at the club, but undeniable proof that the Derderian brothers approved fireworks was elusive. One person said Great White used pyrotechnics when it first performed under the Derderians' ownership in April 2000, but more people present that night said the band had not used fireworks during that show, and the band's manager Paul Woolnough said the group did not use pyrotechnics prior to its 2003 tour. Members of another band, Lovin' Kry, testified that they'd used gerbs during performances at The Station, but most of their shows happened before the Derderian brothers' ownership. A videotape provided by the band, shown to the grand jury, was an edited compilation of various performances with fireworks purportedly exploded inside the club, but the footage did not have time stamps to verify when it was recorded, and the band's guitarist and drummer who testified admitted that they would not have any direct knowledge of permissions and discussions involving pyrotechnics, and they had never spoken about such matters with the Derderians.

That pyrotechnics were sometimes used at the club was confirmed by the club's manager Kevin Beese, both in his grand jury testimony and in news interviews. But Beese downplayed the incidents, and said most involved minor special effects—nothing on the scale of Great White's fireworks.

So expectations were high when Phelps from Red Hot finally testified, two months after Detective Azverde told jurors the band member possessed a verified video of fireworks inside The Station during the Derderians' tenure. It promised to be damning, incontrovertible evidence.

Prosecutor William Ferland asked Phelps, "As it relates to your appearances there at The Station, did your band ever employ any sort of special effects at all?"

"Yes, we did," Phelps answered.

"Did you have any appearances there at The Station since March of 2000?" Ferland asked, referring to when the Derderians bought the nightclub.

"No," said Phelps.

Phelps explained that he and his group had not played at the club in years, and that he'd never met anyone named Derderian.

That the band had not performed for the Derderians did not seem to matter to Ferland, and the prosecutor asked Phelps about Red Hot's pyrotechnics history. Did the band ever get a permit? Never.

Eventually, Ferland circled back to the dates. Didn't Phelps originally tell investigators that his band had played at The Station just a year ago?

"That's what I thought at the time," Phelps said. "However, I—I do close to 200 shows a year and it's—it—the last time I played there was sketchy in my own mind just because time seems to go by so fast."

Even though Phelps testified that he never played for the Derderians, had never met them, and had never used pyrotechnics during the brothers' club ownership, Ferland said he still wanted a copy of any videotape that showed how Red Hot used flash pots.

"I don't have them in my possession," Phelps testified. "My ex-wife kept all the tapes."

Ferland asked if Phelps had spoken to his ex-wife about the videotape.

"I can't find her. She's disappeared into the sunset."

"Do you know what her name is? I can find her. Do you want us to find her?" Ferland asked.

"I can give you the name, yes, no problem." Phelps spelled his ex-wife's name for the record and gave her address.

"Any date of birth on her?" Ferland asked.

"Something in 1970. We were married six months. Very short marriage."

"Your inability to remember her date of birth might explain that."

"Actually, her ability to take money."

It was unclear how a wayward, possible video of flash pots that did not involve the Derderians' ownership of The Station was relevant to the investigation. It was not the damning evidence the grand jury had been led to believe existed.

Another tape did surface of the Creed tribute band Human Clay, allegedly at a recent New Year's Eve performance at The Station, using a gerb sparkler similar to the kind used by Great White. Frank "Grimace" Davidson, who said he oversaw pyro for Human Clay, testified that he went into the club a day ahead of time for a demonstration test of the gerb for the club's manager, Beese. The test worked, but Davidson said he changed both the angle and distance of the sparkler blast because of concerns the spray could hit the ceiling. The night of the show, with the stage flanked by two men with fire extinguishers, the special effects mostly failed to ignite, but one gerb went off and that was captured on video.

Trying to link the pyrotechnics to the Derderians, however, was problematic. Davidson admitted that he'd never met them.

"Would you know them if they walked into the room?" the prosecutor asked.

"Nope," said Davidson. The Derderians had never given him pyrotechnics permission for either the test or the show.

Prosecutors did not bring in Brian Loftus or Dave Fravala to testify before the grand jury—the two men who said they witnessed suspicious activity involving the fireworks ten minutes before the Great White show. Their testimony would have reinforced statements by Kevin Beese, the club's manager, that the band's tour manager Biechele asked to borrow a flashlight at this same time because he needed to do something for the show in darkness. Another witness, club patron and fill-in security helper Scott Vieira, said Biechele was secretive when asked directly about wiring he was seen installing just before the performance, referring to it vaguely as "something to start the show." Loftus and Fravala also said they witnessed band members trying to conceal possible evidence in the aftermath of the fire, and reported this to the police.

Neither man spoke to the grand jury, even though Fravala said he offered, through his attorney, to testify. Instead, a constant stream of other witnesses talked about fireworks, even when there was no proof, and planted the idea in grand jurors' minds that surely there must be evidence out there somewhere that the club's owners had approved pyrotechnics. And if that were true for other bands, perhaps there had been permission for Great White.

Finding that smoking gun seemed impossible. However, one thing was clear. Prosecutors had two specific targets in their sights: Michael and Jeffrey Derderian.

CHAPTER 44

PHIL STOOD ON the edge of the pool. He had to know if his swimming days were really finished.

He'd come by himself to the Smith Swim Center at Brown University in Providence to go through the routine he'd known so well from years of competing. He wore his black Speedo under a red training suit. At the poolside he put on his beloved Swedes goggles, placing the two straps in the perfect spots on the back of his head, one low and one high.

It was open swim time for laps at the sprawling aquatic center with its huge pool, fifty meters on one length for Olympic-style competing, and the shorter side of twenty-five yards for college and local races. Phil noted that the lanes were set in the Olympic configuration, making the distance more than twice the length he swam in the NCAA. He'd also have to swim over the fifteen-foot deep end and there'd be no ability to stand and rest if he found himself in trouble. If the pool had been set the standard way, he could have picked a lane in the shallow end where the water was just four feet deep. Fate was making this tougher.

Well, I need to see how this goes, he said to himself. At least there were lifeguards. He noted their locations if he had to shout for help. He adjusted his goggles again and stretched his shoulders, just like he would before a race in college. *This is it.*

He dove in headfirst. It was only from the side of the pool, and not from one of the elevated competition blocks. Anyone would have understood if he'd slowly lowered himself into the water, but Phil wasn't there to be careful.

That first contact with the water brought up a feeling Phil had not experienced in many months: joy. It was exhilarating to be embraced once again by the chlorinated fluid of better days. He'd missed this so much.

"You can't do that," doctors said when Phil asked about returning to swimming after his injuries. Others were slightly more diplomatic. "That's a very far out possibility. I'd be very surprised if you could ever do that again," he remembered his pulmonologist saying.

As Phil's face submerged into the cool waters he knew that he would soon learn if they were right. He'd confounded them before, leaving the hospital after only a month. But that initial optimism had been replaced with a practical reality. It was September, and he had not returned to Bates. He wasn't well enough to live on his own.

He'd enrolled in a summer course at Brown, an English literature class about novels that had been made into films, and it felt good to be learning again. The subject was less important than the challenge the course represented—after what he'd been through he had to determine if he was capable of being a student again. He worried that he'd been exposed to oxygen deprivation during the fire, and such traumas could cause brain damage. He had to prove to himself that the injuries and drug-induced coma had not taken a toll on his intellect. To his great relief, the course went well, and he took it as a good omen that a swimmer he knew from his competing days was in the same class.

During the summer he worked with a personal trainer who thought Phil could enhance his recovery with weight training, so he was in the gym lifting despite the sweltering temperatures of a humid Rhode Island August. The weights improved his sense of balance, which had been damaged during his recovery. Deep breathing during the workouts helped rebuild his lung capacity. His breathing steadily improved, but making use of newly healed sections of his lungs—getting them to expand to bring oxygen into his system—was painful and exhausting.

As challenging as weight lifting was, pulmonary exercise like running or swimming was of an entirely different magnitude. He'd improved his lung capacity from the paltry 45 percent on his hospital release day, but he still didn't bring in enough oxygen to fuel a strenuous effort. Doctors had advised against it, but Phil had to know if swimming, such a vital part of his life, was gone. In a conversation with his trainer they'd concluded, what do you have to lose?

Now that Phil was in the pool at Brown, the stakes became vividly clear. As he surfaced from his dive he took a few small strokes and kicks to get himself up to the water's level. Then he reached out with his right arm, arched, to swim freestyle. After a few strokes he paused to assess.

Okay, he said to himself, *I feel okay*. Head down, he kept going. Another stroke. Then another. Then a breath. His old methodical routine kicked in. Stroke, stroke, breath. Stroke, stroke, breath. It was working. He was back in the pool. He inhaled the smell of chlorine, so comforting now with its familiar fumes of bleach and chemicals.

Then he hit a wall. Something wasn't right. A debilitating weariness enveloped his body. He had to stop. He lifted his head and realized he was less than halfway down the long lane—he'd actually only traveled a short distance, and his body screamed that it could go no further. There was no easy escape: the safety of either end of the pool, forward or back, was too far. He wheezed.

I'm going to finish fifty. I have to finish fifty. Stroke, stroke, breath. Stroke, stroke, breath. *I have to finish fifty*.

Phil kept his head down and focused. Stroke, stroke, breath. Stroke, stroke, breath. He'd done this a million times, and it used to be so simple, so routine. In the old days he could swim five hundred yards before feeling a twinge of fatigue, but now an overwhelming exhaustion hit. Stroke. Stroke. Breath. After what felt like an eternity, his fingertips finally made contact with the other end of the pool. As he lifted his head from the water, he panted almost uncontrollably. He pulled himself out of the water and sat on the lip of the pool, in a daze and losing track of time.

Enough. That's enough for today. Just one length of the pool—that's all he had accomplished, and his body was crushed. Years of training and competing and making it to the NCAA level were reduced to just fifty meters and he could have drowned. As he struggled to catch his breath Phil wondered if he'd ever be able to return to the life he once had at Bates.

CHAPTER 45

EDITOR JOEL RAWSON'S concern that safety failures at the nightclub were a primary cause of so many deaths reached an impressive height on September 21, seven months after the fire. Rhode Islanders woke up to read the *Providence Journal's* bold front-page headline: "412 people inside club on night of Station fire: A *Journal* investigation puts the number of people inside at the time of the fire above the governor's estimate and above the limits set by the West Warwick Fire Department."

It was a startling number, more than Governor Carcieri's estimate of 350, far above any previous headcount. The newspaper said it "exceeds all of the various limits on the club's capacity," meaning that the Derderians had broken the law. No government investigation had announced a confirmed number high enough to make that conclusion.

There were previous attempts by investigators and other journalists to derive the number of people inside the club, but the obstacles were prohibitive. The Channel 12 video was considered key, and a headcount was pursued by analyzing the footage frame-by-frame, but the camera's viewpoint was limited to where the lens pointed, leaving many offscreen.

Counting advance ticket sales was also unreliable, since admission that night covered three different bands, including a local group, and it was common for patrons to get a ticket for the whole night, but leave after watching their friends perform. It was likely to have more tickets in circulation for an evening than people inside the club at any one moment.

Further adding to confusion over ticket sales were performance agreements, originally used by previous owners and continued by the Derderians, which sometimes overstated the capacity of the nightclub. The engagement agreement for the Great White show created by Tapestry

Artists, a California-based booking company, put the capacity of The Station at 550, and Jeffrey Derderian signed that contract. With the comings and goings of patrons during three different bands, that number might be aspirational for a night's total attendance, but it was an exaggeration of the allowed capacity for any single performance. That number, 550, would come back later to haunt the Derderians as evidence that they were liars, and the controversy further muddied the waters about how many people were actually inside when the fire started.

Procedures the club had in place could have helped answer whether the club was over its legal capacity, but a crucial clue was missing. Andrea Mancini, who checked in guests at the front entrance, had a handheld clicker-counter to track the number of people let inside, but Andrea perished in the fire, and the clicker and the number it held was never reported found by investigators or the attorney general's office. When Jeffrey Derderian checked the clicker at 10 p.m. it noted about 250 patrons.

Eyewitness testimony offered mixed messages about the crowd size. Anthony Bettencourt, the uniformed West Warwick police officer hired by the Derderians for the show, a club policy for larger events, initially estimated the number of people inside the club when the fireworks sparked at about three hundred. Officer Bettencourt would go into further detail when he testified under oath before the grand jury on June 9, putting the crowd size at between 250 to 300 when he arrived at nine o'clock. "The club didn't look like it was packed or anything," Bettencourt said. When Great White took the stage, the officer said the crowd had grown by about fifty more people. Two on-duty West Warwick police officers also stopped by the club just before the band took the stage, and they did not halt the show for being overcrowded.

Other accounts were also confounding. Minutes before Great White performed, Gina Russo later said, "We began heading closer to the stage to get a good spot to watch the show. There were definitely a lot of people inside The Station that night, but strangely there was plenty of room to move around easily or stand comfortably."

Kevin Beese, the nightclub's manager, told the *Journal* the crowd was a good size, but far from the largest he'd seen there. "He said he knows it was smaller than 400 people because, when the audience reaches 400, concertgoers spill over from the main stage area to the front bar where he was working. But that night, the bar area was free of overflow," the *Journal* reported. The club's sound manager, Paul Vanner, told the newspaper he guessed the crowd size at 325. "I've seen it busier," Vanner said. "It wasn't that bad."

It was also not enough to simply determine who went to The Station that evening for the show, since patrons routinely wandered in and out during performances, something Officer Bettencourt noted in his testimony, and some people were not actually inside the building at the time of the fire, even if they genuinely "attended" the event. Attorney General Patrick Lynch, at a press conference just days after the disaster, told the media that determining an exact headcount inside the club was difficult because "it's a fluid atmosphere where some leave and some go." Club regulars were less vague in their description of a typical show: the parking lot of The Station was a hotbed of illegal drugs, drinking, and sex in cars. It was a rock 'n' roll crowd, and although smoking cigarettes was allowed inside, lighting up a joint was not, so patrons went outside to get high. That wasn't a detail Rhode Island State Police and prosecutors highlighted in their press conferences—it would have been considered disrespectful to those killed or injured.

With these different factors at play, a precise headcount seemed impossible. The fact that the nightclub was a deathtrap, and that the large number of people inside could not evacuate in time from such a fast moving fire, was not debatable. For editor Rawson, whose core belief was that news was about providing verified facts, it seemed incredible that on a question so central to the tragedy—was the nightclub illegally overcrowded?—no answer was forthcoming. "You need data. You also need different levels of data," Rawson would explain.

The newspaper was told and erroneously reported in the immediate aftermath that the legal capacity of the club was three hundred, and with that wrong number concluded that the Derderians exceeded that limit. The *Journal* would eventually learn the club's capacity was much higher and more complicated. Depending on the club's configuration, and with certain restrictions, the legal limit was 404. Rawson and his team decided to do their own investigation to see if the nightclub had exceeded that higher limit. "We were the only people who really wanted to find out," Rawson said.

It became a months-long investigation of unprecedented scale for the

Journal, involving sixty-two staff writers, five members of the paper's news library staff, five editors, and a graphic artist.

The *Journal* began building its headcount list with the names of the one hundred who died, even though there had been reports that some of the victims were actually outside when the fire started and ran into the inferno to rescue others. The paper then added 192 survivors the newspaper had interviewed for its coverage.

"We had asked people, 'Were you there? Where were you? How did you get out?' We knew how to re-create this thing accurately. It wasn't a guess. It wasn't a random throw-so-many-digits-in-there and run it," Rawson explained. "We knew where people were in that building. We knew where the dead were located. We knew where the injured were injured. We knew where the people got out. So this is part of knowing what really happened. This is in detail. The act of will is to really know this is the fact, and this is how I know it. I don't know if we found everybody, but boy, we got pretty close."

The tragedy had been beset by fraud almost immediately, with one person caught trying to fake a death while the building still smoldered, and there had been the case of a man caught claiming to have lost a loved one so he could take advantage of the donated hotel rooms and meals served to victims' families at the Crowne Plaza. With such a track record of deceit established so early in the fire's aftermath, how did the *Journal* know who told the truth?

"You don't," said Rawson later. "You rely on Mark Arsenault to say, 'Does this make sense or not?' That's why we pay reporters."

Mark Arsenault, a lean, clean-cut, affable reporter in his midthirties, had his desk near Rawson's office, and with that proximity the top editor would casually chat up the reporter and they'd become friendly. Arsenault was assigned to be one of the *Journal's* lead reporters on The Station fire and worked on the capacity investigation. Later he would say that two people he interviewed who claimed they were at the fire were ultimately cut from the list because he didn't believe them.

But journalists of Arsenault's caliber did not vet everyone on the newspaper's list of 412. The newspaper disclosed that it had not directly confirmed each individual on the list, relying instead on other sources. While the paper reported that it had interviewed nearly 200 in its tally, 57 others on the list were noted as identified by survivors. The *Journal* reported that another 49 on its list were identified by lawyers who claimed to represent fire victims. Seven other people on the newspaper's list were forwarded by their relatives, and hospitals provided five other names, plus there were two taking photographs at the time of the tragedy, including Channel 12's Brian Butler. These caveats noted by the newspaper indicated that 111 on the *Journal's* list were not rigorously verified.

The paper's investigation also looked at why the nightclub's capacity was raised in recent years to 404. The death toll was proof that the building could not be evacuated in such a swift-moving blaze, so it seemed logical to Rawson to question how and why West Warwick fire officials had determined the legal capacity and deemed that number safe.

"They kept upping it, and what I wanted to know was what was the conversation between the fire marshal and the Derderians when they were negotiating this thing upwards," Rawson said. "I don't know. I don't know, 'cause they talked about it. They had to."

Unknown to Rawson and his newspaper's team of investigators at the time they published their story was that these answers were already known to police and prosecutors, and the details were different from what the *Journal* reported. When the newspaper published its front-page findings in September 2003, the grand jury was convening to decide any criminal charges. Proceedings were secret, although the paper had published unverified leaks. The grand jury testimony would eventually be made public at the request of the attorney general's office, years later.

What the *Journal* did not know was that three months before the newspaper published its investigation, on the morning of June 25, the grand jury heard the testimony of Denis P. "Rocky" Larocque, the fire marshal for West Warwick.

Larocque was a mustached twenty-six-year veteran of the force who was promoted to fire marshal in 1998. He had a reputation for being a tough inspector who wouldn't even cut townie friends a break if he spotted a violation. Larocque told the grand jury he first met Michael Derderian on March 3, 2000, before the brothers bought the club. The prospect of a transfer of the business's liquor license to a new owner triggered a mandatory fire safety inspection, one of Larocque's duties as fire marshal. Even though the Derderians did not own the club yet, Michael tagged along for the inspection.

In past years the club's capacity had been increased, set by state laws that determined how many patrons were allowed into a space based on the layout of a room. If an area had tables and chairs, the fire code required that a minimum of fifteen square feet per person was required. When tables and chairs were removed, only seven square feet per person was required. In 1999, according to Larocque, Howard Julian, owner of the nightclub then, asked for a new capacity based on removing tables and chairs from three lounge areas during performances. With that in mind, the capacity was increased from 253 to 317.

During the March inspection for the possible liquor license transfer, Michael Derderian asked Larocque if it would be possible to increase the capacity to four hundred if pool tables and other furniture were removed from other areas of the club during performances.

Larocque told the grand jury that he researched Michael's request and determined that the capacity could be increased, not just by removing furniture, but also because the club was subject to a "grandfather" clause and was not required to abide by the newest fire codes. The club's very first incarnation in 1946 was as Casey's, a live music venue that featured orchestras and dancing, and although it had gone through many variations since then, it had not officially changed its use from a "place of assembly" and was therefore subject to the state's 1968 fire codes. Under those laws, with furniture removed, Larocque testified, the club qualified to have its capacity determined based on a "standing room" crowd, which required only five square feet of space per person. After Larocque measured the spaces where the public would stand during performances, he set the capacity at 404.

The same grandfather clause also meant the building was not required to have sprinklers.

Larocque communicated his findings on the club's capacity to Police Chief Peter Brousseau in a memo, and then told Michael Derderian during a conversation later at the club. Michael, who was not eligible to receive the information in writing since he did not yet own the club, wanted the decision documented. He wrote a letter to the town clerk summarizing the capacity decision, and then said that as the new owner he would take the additional step of having police and fire department representatives present during large events. This was not automatically required* under state law for a club the size of The Station, according to Larocque's grand jury testimony. The presence of a uniformed fire-fighter at events could be mandated, but solely at the discretion of the local fire chief, who had made no such demand.

Larocque speculated to the grand jury that Michael made the offer to have police and fire representatives on site for larger events to help seal the deal for the increased capacity. "I believe in his mind if that would help him get to that four hundred number he wanted, that was the initiation of his offer."

Even though Michael's offer was not required, it became the de facto agreement covering the club's capacity with the city, and the *Journal* investigation would point to the deal as evidence that the Derderians had broken their word and violated capacity rules the night of the fire. The brothers did not hire a firefighter for the night of the Great White concert, only a police officer, and the *Journal* concluded that this meant the Derderians violated their arrangement for larger events.

The details were not so simple.

When asked during his grand jury testimony about how the club owners were supposed to determine whether an upcoming crowd would be large enough to prompt the need for a firefighter, Larocque indicated that guesswork was involved, possibly based on advance ticket sales. Larocque testified that in March 2000 he told Michael Derderian that if a larger crowd than expected showed up, Derderian "could notify the department and we'd have a detail there within the hour."

Larocque also testified that he was not completely sure if he'd given Michael the exact number of patrons that would have necessitated a firefighter on site. "My recollection is he was given that in writing. I'm not positive. My recollection is I would have put it in writing, although I don't have that copy. But I remember handing someone, and I'm not sure if it was this time or the first time we have come up with occupancy numbers, thinking to myself there's no doubt as to what these numbers are. Everyone knows what the number is."

---

* The math: Larocque told the grand jury that under Rhode Island's fire code venues with more than 1,000 patrons, called Class A, are required to have at least one uniformed fire-fighter present, but venues with 301 to 1,000 patrons, called Class B, must only hire a detail if ordered by the local fire chief. The Station was Class B.

The *Journal* concluded that an on-site firefighter was required when the number of patrons exceeded 317.

Michael would later say that a huge audience was not expected for Great White, based on advance ticket sales and the fact that a previous performance by the band shortly after the Derderians bought the club did not draw an overwhelming crowd. It was a night in April 2000 that Michael remembered well, since there had been trouble. One of the band members apparently had a sexual liaison on the tour bus with a local woman he picked from the audience. The woman's boyfriend became enraged when he discovered that his girlfriend was on the tour bus performing oral sex on the band member. In his anger the boyfriend took a brick and shattered a bus window, and the club's security staff chased the man through the streets of West Warwick.

With the middling attendance that memorable night, Michael did not anticipate a huge draw three years later. He also said his arrangement with the town had evolved. About a year after the brothers bought the business Michael said he was summoned to meet Police Chief Brousseau, and they came to a new understanding that an off-duty police officer would be hired by The Station when any significant-size crowd was expected, and not both an officer and a firefighter. That police officer was hired and in place the night of the fire.

Years later Brousseau said he did not remember amending the agreement with the Derderians that allowed them to only have a police officer present for significant events, but said, "I had good dealings with the Derderians. They were reasonable. Whatever we asked them to do they would do."

There were other problems with the *Journal*'s conclusion that the club exceeded its legal capacity. By some accounts, even if the newspaper's headcount was correct, the math did not add up.

Larocque's measurements and capacity decisions were based on the parts of the nightclub open to the public, the "standing room" areas. Places that were off limits to the public were not counted in Larocque's measurements, according to his grand jury testimony. "You would not include bar, behind bar areas. You would not include the stage, you would not include any office or kitchen area," Larocque testified. It is unknown exactly how many people were in these nonpublic areas of the nightclub at the time of the fire, but counting staff and performers, the number was as high as thirty. Yet all of those people were erroneously counted in the *Journal*'s 412 to make the case that the top legal capacity was violated by eight persons. If those thirty people were subtracted from the *Journal*'s total, the number was below a capacity violation.

The *Journal*'s headcount would face other doubts in the years that followed.

A computer analysis by Stanford University published in 2006, based on data from an exhaustive federal investigation, put the total number of people inside the nightclub at about 350, a number that included those behind the scenes that would not be counted as part of the venue's legal capacity.

The results of civil lawsuits also put the *Journal*'s investigation in doubt.

In the civil suits, those inside the club at the time of the fire who were killed or hurt were eligible to receive money. Payments were eventually made for 305 plaintiffs, representing both victims and survivors, versus the 412 the newspaper claimed were inside the building at the time of the fire, most of whom would have been eligible to receive thousands of dollars in compensation. If the *Journal*'s number is to be believed, a huge percentage of people who were hurt or had their lives threatened did not accept money to which they were entitled.

Investigations for the civil lawsuits lasted years and involved multiple law firms that aggressively sought every person who might have a claim. Lawyers were incentivized to find any angle that could be leveraged, since the potential to make money was based on the number of clients they brought to the case, even if a claim was marginal. At least two people who were not inside the club when the fire started, Dave Fravala and Brian Loftus, the man with "the roach that saved my life," were among those who received money, due to the trauma they experienced.

There were no costs to survivors or victims' families to join the civil litigation, and the case was highly publicized. The idea that a valid victim did not know about the suit was highly unlikely. "It's not possible," said Max Wistow, one of the lead attorneys in the civil case.

Some inside The Station when the fire started did not want money because they were not hurt and thought any settlement should go to those truly in need. Phil Barr's fellow college student friend Evan Clabots felt this way and did not participate in the civil suit. Other survivors might have shunned the civil case, simply because they find such litigation distasteful. "There are people who have a natural aversion to lawsuits," explained Wistow, speaking in general about civil litigation, and not directly addressing The Station case. In the nightclub case, however, if the *Journal*'s headcount was to be believed, then more than 40 percent* of the survivors inside the burning building who were injured, traumatized, or whose lives were threatened declined compensation, a questionably high percentage in a state where people were famous for working all the angles, and where the unofficial mottos were "one hand washes the other" and "I know a guy."

Nonetheless, the *Journal*'s front-page assertion of criminal levels of overcrowding by the Derderians caused a sensation when it was first published in September, and afterward even more people came forward to the newspaper and said they too were inside the burning building. Later the *Journal* updated its investigation and included some of those claims too, increasing the number to 430 by October, and on February 20, 2004, to 440, and eventually on December 3, 2007, to 462, after combining its list with a then-released accounting of possible attendees compiled by the attorney general's office. That high number became a fact often cited by other media, and even made it into the official federal investigation.

But for some, the *Journal*'s headcount was specious. Survivors recognized names on the list of people they knew were not inside the club during the fire.

Bob Stephens was included on the *Journal*'s first list, and in its final count in 2007. Stephens was originally reported as missing by the newspaper, which in many minds meant he was presumed dead. Then the *Journal*, without explanation or correction, reported that Stephens was "found." After that Stephens's name was included in the newspaper's list as someone inside the club, confirmed because he was "interviewed by

---

* The math: subtract from the *Journal*'s count of 462 the people inside the club who could not sue because they were defendants in the case: Jeffrey Derderian and some band members. Of the remaining people reportedly in the club, deduct the 100 fatalities to determine the number of survivors. That leaves about 360. The number of non-deceased plaintiffs was 205. Removing Brian Loftus and Dave Fravala, who were outside, leaves 203 litigants inside the fire. Comparing that to the 360 in the *Journal* number means 44 percent of the survivors the *Journal* said were inside the burning building declined thousands of dollars in compensation for which they were eligible.

the *Journal*." But Stephens was actually part of a local camera crew that heard about the fire and raced to the scene to capture it on video, and he's heard on the tape arriving at the scene after the building is fully engulfed.

The *Journal* story also misidentified Police Chief Peter Brousseau as the town's fire chief.

It's unknown how many headcount errors were included in the *Journal*'s investigation, but the paper was not alone reporting people inside the inferno who were not. WPRI-TV Channel 12 News, the same television station where Jeffrey Derderian and Brian Butler worked, would later report that Dave Fravala was inside the club when the fire started, when he was actually outside smoking pot with his buddy Brian Loftus.

But these types of mix-ups—typical in covering a huge, complex story—were only part of the problem. Fraud was another. Investigators were worried from the start about people lying to say they were inside the burning club when they were not. Greg Best, Stephens's friend who shot the video of the engulfed nightclub, said, "The FBI came to my house the next day" and an agent retrieved the footage. "I made him a copy of my video, he took off with it, and he said it was very important because there was people that were claiming that they were in the building, and they weren't even there. So I had a scan of who was around me and everything. They could tell who they were, each person."

Online forums about the fire, where survivors, victims' families, and people interested in the tragedy have developed a network in the years since the disaster to swap information, are also peppered with postings that contradict the *Journal*'s headcount reporting, naming names of those whom they believe falsely told the paper they were inside the club. Many years later, when a memorial to the fire's victims was built, a group of survivors would pronounce their accounting of the number of people inside the club when tragedy struck, and that number was also dramatically lower than the *Journal*'s claim, and below the legal limit.

The Derderians immediately disputed the *Journal*'s report of the club being criminally over capacity, but did not publicly challenge the newspaper. With the grand jury convening, attorneys advised the brothers not to speak, despite requests by the *Journal*. The Derderians' representatives also did not talk to the newspaper for its investigation.

West Warwick's fire marshal, Larocque, also did not speak to the paper for its story, and his testimony to the grand jury was not made public until 2007. Had the transcripts been available, Larocque's account would have given Joel Rawson and the *Providence Journal* a few new headlines: despite multiple inspections of the nightclub over the course of years, Larocque told the grand jury he never noticed the highly flammable foam that covered the walls and ceilings of the venue.

Larocque could not explain how he missed the foam during his first two inspections, but on his inspection in December 2002, two months before the fire, he said he was distracted by a problem with an exit door. He had cited the club previously because the stage door exit had one side that opened inward and another outward. Both are required to open outward. The door problem was corrected after the last inspection, but now it was back. In the fire's immediate aftermath Larocque told the state police he was "blinded by anger" when he saw the blatant violation of the door, and this is why he failed to notice the foam. In his grand jury testimony, under oath, Larocque did not repeat the same hyperbole, but said he was upset and diverted from doing his job.

The door was a legitimate concern. Club employees told the grand jury they put it back up after being removed to pass the previous inspection because it was more effective at containing sound than the other door. After Chief Brousseau's threat that he would close the club if there were more complaints about noise from neighbors, sound abatement was an existential threat. The federal Occupational Safety and Health Administration would eventually fine the Derderians $70,000 for the "willful" door violation, although a separate federal investigation would find that the door did not play a role in the deaths on the night of the fire. It is seen wide open in the Channel 12 video.

The reason the illegal door was so effective at containing sound was that it too was covered in foam. Larocque told the grand jury he did not notice the foam there either, even though he said the door had raised his ire. The inspection was primarily focused on a checklist of other items to review, he said, such as examining emergency lighting and fire extinguishers. Had Larocque noticed the foam, he would have been required to determine if the foam was the flammable kind, probably by cutting off a piece and touching a flame to it in the parking lot. If the polyurethane had ignited during such a test, as it surely would have, the club would have been shuttered until the foam was removed. Without the foam, Great White's fireworks would not have turned the nightclub into an inferno, and no one would have died.

While Larocque maintained to the grand jury that he never noticed the foam during years of inspections and follow-up visits, he did testify that during his inspection in March 2000, before the Derderians bought the club, he discovered a different safety violation: an exit sign that directed patrons to a fourth exit through the kitchen in case of emergency. Larocque said it was improper to direct people through a kitchen, a fire code violation, because, "Kitchens and storerooms and other rooms subject to locking, you're not allowed to exit through." Larocque ordered then-owner Howard Julian to remove the sign. As a result, on the night of the fire, patrons did not realize there was another emergency exit so close to where they stood, and only club regulars and employees knew to escape through the kitchen. Twenty-four people killed in the fire were closer to the unmarked kitchen exit than any other.

Larocque had carefully considered the exits when determining the capacity for the club. Each door was rated, based on its width, to allow 150 people to quickly exit. There were four exits, but effectively eliminating the kitchen exit meant there were only three ways to escape. A bouncer, at least momentarily, allegedly prevented patrons from using the band's door, and since the fire started in that area, the heat reached nearly one thousand degrees in seconds and made that exit impassable. That left only two exits for escape, and it was human nature for most people to double back to where they entered, down the narrow passageway where tickets were collected. The pileup in that doorway and behind it was where the bodies of forty people were found, and where the most severely injured survivors were discovered, including Gina Russo. Some were only feet away from the kitchen exit that Larocque had nixed due to the fire code.

All of this was on the record with prosecutors and the grand jury, and it was information that would have made the *Providence Journal*'s investigation more accurate. But when the paper went to press with its story, Larocque's testimony was secret.

Criticism of the newspaper's capacity story would emerge over the course of years. On the day the *Journal* published its investigation and list of names, Joel Rawson saw the report as the latest example of the extraordinary work by his staff, and he concluded that their efforts were worthy of an award. "They earned it. Those people had earned it. They worked and worked and worked," Rawson said.

Rawson asked Tom Heslin,* the head of the newspaper's investigative unit, to take the capacity story and bundle it with other highlights from the newspaper's coverage to submit for journalism's highest honor: the Pulitzer Prize.

---

* Author's note: while news director at WLNE-TV, I worked with Tom Heslin to help organize a conference for the group Investigative Reporters and Editors.

JUSTICE

CHAPTER 46

O N DECEMBER 9, 2003, Rhode Island attorney general Patrick Lynch announced that a grand jury had indicted the Derderian brothers and Daniel Biechele, the tour manager who ignited the fireworks. Each man faced two hundred counts of involuntary manslaughter, two counts for each of the one hundred victims, under two different theories of law: one hundred counts of criminal negligence, and one hundred counts of misdemeanor manslaughter. One set of charges argued that the men had been grossly negligent, causing the deaths. The other legal theory was that the men had committed misdemeanor offenses that ultimately killed people. With Biechele that misdemeanor was the illegal use of fireworks, and for the Derderians it was in the installation of the flammable foam. If convicted, each count carried a prison sentence of up to thirty years.

"The words simply do not exist to describe the intense pain and immense grief that the victims and their families have endured in the 10 months since this tragedy occurred," Lynch said in a statement. "As much as I wish that I could change the timing of the announcement— when the suffering of the victims and survivors will be intensified by having to go through the holidays without their loved ones—I cannot."

Before announcing the indictments, at the same moment the men were arraigned in court, Lynch gathered the relatives of those killed at the West Valley Inn in West Warwick, across town from the nightclub site. Lynch wanted the victims' families to hear the news directly from him before it went public, but there were also reports that prosecutors feared victims' families might violently confront the accused at the courthouse, so families were lured to a different location.

Five hundred people crowded into a large banquet room, hoping for some measure of justice. Nothing could bring back their loved ones, but with the grand jury meeting for so many months there were high expectations that perhaps, for once, in a state with a notoriously corrupt legal system, the right thing would happen—that everyone culpable would be arrested.

Gina Russo sat in the assemblage, invited because Fred was her fiancé. In other meetings involving the families of those who perished in the fire, survivors were specifically excluded. An exception had been made for Gina this day.

It was one of the unfortunate truths of the nightclub tragedy that those whose lives were most impacted were bitterly divided into different camps, with some openly warring against others. Victims' families resented survivors, even those critically hurt, and blamed them for others' deaths.

"There were certain comments made that, 'You pushed my loved one aside. My loved one died because you survived,'" said Jonathan Bell, chairman of the Station Family Fund charity. "They certainly don't know it, and they don't mean it. They just mean, 'I'm experiencing a really deep loss, and your situation is different.'"

But Bell's rational understanding of the emotions could not change the brazen hatred and unite everyone.

"They could never meet together," said Gina, "because the victims' families wanted to shoot the survivors, like you could not mix them. And the mediators of those meetings knew it immediately, that they needed to separate them. The victims' family members could not even tolerate looking at a survivor."

Even among the survivors, there was sharp division. Some with physical injuries felt disdain for those who escaped without burns or "only" suffered psychological trauma. To some physically wounded survivors, mental health issues from the fire weren't real injuries, and were dismissed as exaggerated or even fake.

Gina personally experienced the divisions. On the six-month anniversary of the fire, with the urging of her family, she attended a remembrance at the nightclub site, and she was the only survivor there who had been severely physically injured. The grounds had been transformed into a makeshift memorial, with relatives and friends of the dead creating cairns of tributes, from stuffed animals and flowers to images of those lost and personal items related to their shortened lives. In time, it would grow into a sprawling, devastating grassroots reminder of the disaster.

At the gathering Gina felt isolated and apart. Others gathered there had not experienced the same horrors. Then came word that another survivor had died that day. Gina immediately feared it was one of the burn victims she'd left behind at Spaulding Rehabilitation Hospital, and she frantically tried to get information from others at the event. It became disturbingly clear that the people at the gathering, who mourned lost loved ones or who were uninjured survivors, had no connection to the severely wounded patients Gina had been with in the hospitals. "You've got to get me out of here," she said, overwhelmed with panic.

Later Gina learned that the person who died that day was thirty-three-year-old Lisa Marie Scott. She was hurt in the fire, had struggled to recover, and fell down a flight of stairs in her home in Johnston and suffered a head trauma that killed her. Even though the fall was likely the result of her injuries, Lisa's death was not directly attributed to the nightclub fire, and she was not added to the body count. In many minds, however, Lisa was victim 101. Her death was an example of the complex categories of victims and survivors that had led to so many deep divisions: Lisa escaped, Lisa survived, Lisa was horribly injured, Lisa went home, *and* Lisa died. Of the many angry factions, to which did Lisa belong?

There were deaths of other survivors. Some believed the 101st death was actually Jennifer Stowers, age twenty-three, a Boston-area teacher who died on May 21, 2003, from an overdose of antidepressants, which she had been prescribed after she escaped but lost two friends in the blaze. The medical examiner could not determine if Stowers had committed suicide, mistakenly consumed the wrong amount, or whether her body failed to metabolize the medication. Her death happened six weeks before her scheduled wedding and she and her fiancé had just received the invitations from the printer.

As Gina sat in the West Valley Inn waiting for the attorney general, she knew she was the embodiment of the conflict between survivors and victims. She was a survivor, but she did not simply walk away that night—she was among the most severely injured, putting her in a tier unlike those with lesser burns or just psychiatric problems. She also mourned the loss of a loved one, her fiancé Fred, although to some he was not really Gina's relative because they were not married. Even if they had been wed, there were families who had lost a son or daughter who thought their grief trumped all others, and outspokenly resented any comparisons.

Rhode Island law validated and inflamed the divisions between the survivors and the families of the dead. State laws did not allow for criminal charges against anyone for the injuries survivors suffered in the fire. There was no statute for it. In the months the grand jury convened to consider what, if any, criminal charges would be handed up, jurors could only issue indictments related to those who died, not those who were injured. This further enraged Gina. It was as if the government said that her pain and suffering did not matter. Maybe today she would hear about some possible justice for Fred, but no one would ever spend a minute in prison for hurting her. How was that possible?

The room became silent as Attorney General Lynch entered. Lynch looked scared, Gina thought, as he said the state would be pursuing criminal charges against Daniel Biechele, the tour manager who set off the fireworks, and Michael and Jeffrey Derderian, the nightclub business owners. When the attorney general stopped speaking, the room remained quiet. Gina waited, expecting to hear Lynch read out the names of the others who would face prosecution.

None came. *Three?* Gina thought. *Just three?*

Instead of more names Gina heard gibberish from Lynch's mouth, a mishmash of legal mumbo jumbo about why these three were the ones charged and how the state was going to proceed. Gina looked around her and everyone seemed stunned, unable to speak. Then Lynch did what Gina later thought had to be one of the most foolish mistakes of his political career: he opened the floor to questions.

The backlash was immediate. Families were furious about the short list of defendants. What about the band that set off the fireworks? Lead singer Jack Russell? The guy who put the foam in the club? The fire inspector who had declared the nightclub safe, even though it was a firetrap?

"I've got a few things to say to you," said a middle-aged man. Gina had noticed that the man had sat next to large windows. "Number one on the list, you have a lot of nerve bringing us into this building. I see six windows behind me that are nailed shut. Nailed shut!" he scolded. Then the man pointed. "And there's only one exit out of here. You probably didn't notice that, but many of us did. Because it's all the way across the room, if a fast-moving fire were to break out right now, I wouldn't be able to get out. After what you've brought us here to tell us, that's a lot of nerve."

The man's comments were blistering and humiliating to the attorney general. Lynch had surrounded himself with Rhode Island officials, including state police officers and fire marshals. Yet it was just this anonymous and ordinary man, someone who lost a loved one in the fire, who exposed that they'd been assembled in a building that was a potential fire hazard.

In the aftermath of the fire Rhode Island's officials had made a public show of updating antiquated fire codes, some dated to 1968, and created new rules that required sprinklers and eliminated safety exemptions for older buildings under so-called grandfather clauses. The nightclub tragedy had also led to intense scrutiny of the National Fire Protection Association, which set the fire codes that states followed nationally. An exposé by the CBS News program *60 Minutes II* showed how arbitrary the NFPA codes seemed, with weaker rules for smaller public venues that catered to three hundred patrons or less, as if those lives were somehow less precious. Correspondent Scott Pelley pointed out that the association's membership included building owners and developers who had a vested interest in controlling the costs of constructing and operating properties—an apparent conflict of interest when it came to requirements like mandating sprinkler systems, a technology that dated to the 1850s and was remarkably effective at saving lives. In the wake of the embarrassing *60 Minutes* report the NFPA changed national codes for both sprinklers and managing crowds at nightclub-type venues.

It was all too little too late for the families of the fire victims, and the man's outburst at Attorney General Lynch reminded everyone how government safety systems had failed to protect those who perished in the nightclub, and raised questions about whether the new promises for change were just more sloppy lip service rather than genuine. The nailed windows, plus the fact that the indictments ensured that no government official would be held accountable, were indicative to many in the room, once again, of corruption, insider dealings, and incompetence.

"Now I'm going out to my truck," the man continued. "I'm going to get my screwdriver and I'm going to unlock all the windows in the room." As the man headed outside, he confronted a towering Rhode Island state trooper, famous for their intimidating military-style uniforms. "Are you going to stop me?"

Instead of an argument, the trooper went out and returned with his own screwdriver, and the crowd watched in astonishment as the two men went around the room and unsealed the windows until every single one could open.

The tension soared from there, with families of the dead unloading their grief and rage on the attorney general. Gina knew she was there on behalf of Fred, but she had never stopped fuming over the idea that in the legal system injured people like her just didn't count. She knew she had to speak for those who were not allowed in this room: the survivors.

"You stand here and tell me that survivors don't matter, and we don't count," Gina said to Lynch when it was her turn, staring the attorney general directly in the face. "I have burns on forty percent of my body. I can't play with my kids. I can't do all the things I used to do with them before the fire. Tell me something, do you play sports and games with your kids?"

She didn't wait for Lynch to respond. "You can. I can't. And you're going to tell me that I don't count. None of the survivors count."

Gina heard a smattering of applause when she stopped. The room continued to erupt. Lynch was berated for two hours. Gina studied the attorney general as he faced an onslaught of outrage. She couldn't know what was going through Lynch's mind, but he looked completely surprised by each outcry. How could he not know that people would not be satisfied by three measly indictments?

The arguments that had so fiercely divided those impacted by the fire—that separated the families of the dead from the survivors, and alienated the maimed from those who escaped—were momentarily set aside by Lynch's indictment announcement. For once, everyone seemed to agree on something: they hated that so few would be held criminally responsible. The government had failed them.

Later that day, at a press conference, Lynch refused to say why the grand jury did not indict anyone else, claiming that state law prevented him from discussing the grand jury investigation.

When Gina got to her car after the meeting, she broke down. She cried so hard on the drive home that she had to pull into the parking lot of the Christmas Tree Shops store. She turned off the car and wept.

"God, that's it. I'm done," she said aloud through her tears. "This is yours. You don't want to take this away from me, well, then I'm going to find another way to deal with it."

CHAPTER 47

MICHAEL AND JEFFREY Derderian walked into 30 Rockefeller Plaza in Manhattan, nicknamed 30 Rock, home to the NBC television network. The stunning sixty-six-story skyscraper was part of a twenty-two-acre Art Deco complex built during the Great Depression, and at its centerpiece was Paul Manship's enormous gilded statue of Prometheus, the immortal that ancient Greeks believed stole fire from the gods. For his crime, Prometheus was sentenced to an eternity of suffering.

At street level sat the studios of the nation's top morning news program, NBC's *Today* show, and the Derderians were there at the invitation of one of the broadcast's shiniest stars, anchor Matt Lauer. Lauer was also a product of Rhode Island, having worked there in the early 1980s as cohost of the breezy *PM Magazine* at WJAR-TV 10, the NBC affiliate in Providence. Lauer eventually suited up and made his way to stations in Boston and New York before jumping to the network, but Rhode Islanders later would deign him a "favorite son," even though he was actually a New York native. Lauer was arguably the most successful of several national television news stars with Rhode Island connections. Meredith Vieira grew up there and reported for WJAR-TV before moving on to *60 Minutes*, *The View*, and *Today*, and CNN's Christiane Amanpour and John King both attended the University of Rhode Island.

It was April 2004, more than a year since the fire, and the Derderians had still not granted an interview. The nightclub fire remained in the headlines, with new developments gaining front-page coverage in the *Providence Journal*, which were often picked up by the national media. Yet the brothers remained silent, on the advice of their attorneys, warned that the trial should take place in court, and not the court of public opinion. When Jack Russell and others with Great White repeatedly claimed that they had permission to use fireworks in the club, the Derderians did not respond. After the *Journal's* report that there were more patrons inside the nightclub than were legally allowed, the brothers wanted to present a different set of facts, but held their tongues.

The Derderians felt there had been a relentless campaign in the news media, especially the *Journal*, to paint them as two irresponsible, greedy, gold-chain-wearing, cigar-smoking louts who would do anything to make a buck. That storyline even made its way into popular culture as prime-time television network crime dramas that depended on plots "ripped from the headlines" did their own versions of The Station nightclub tragedy, including the nation's top-ten program *CSI: Miami*, which portrayed the nightclub owner character as a mercurial and hook-nosed caricature, similar to the way Nazis portrayed Jews in the lead-up to the Holocaust.

WPRI-TV 12, the CBS affiliate that employed Jeffrey Derderian and photojournalist Brian Butler, who videotaped the real-life blaze, refused to air the May 5, 2003, episode of *CSI: Miami* called "Tinder Box," because it was so strikingly similar to The Station fire. The drama could still be viewed in Rhode Island via the nearby Boston CBS affiliate.

Other scripted dramas had similar plotlines, and television producers had plenty of material to inspire them. Prosecutors and the news media fed the public a steady stream of damning allegations that the brothers were obsessed with making money and as a result had cut corners that killed a hundred people. The *Providence Journal* published an essay by esteemed Harvard University economics professor James Medoff that accused the Derderians of relentless, deadly greed. Without citing evidence, Medoff told readers the brothers regularly ignored fire codes for profit. "Night after night," Medoff wrote, "the club filled above its licensed limit." The professor reported that Jeffrey rescued the club's cash drawer while dozens died. The source for Medoff's essay was noted in a footnote: "The ideas for his column arose from a class Mr. Medoff taught at Harvard with *Journal* Sunday Editor Peter Phipps."

Medoff, news reports, and talk radio shows also pushed the idea that the foam on the walls of the club was the flammable type because the Derderians were too cheap to pay for foam that would have been flame retardant.

To confirm this theory was videotape evidence in the form of a story

Jeffrey reported two years before the fire for WHDH-TV 7 News in Boston about how polyurethane foam could be deadly when ignited. In dramatic fashion Jeffrey's report showed how the foam, which is commonly found in furnishings including mattresses, can instantly turn into an inferno. "Polyurethane foam. Fire safety experts call this stuff solid gasoline," Jeffrey said in the story. Clips from Jeffrey's report were depicted as proof that he knew, more than most people would, that the foam presented a mortal danger, and in his avarice he simply did not care.

It was also reported that the brothers did not have required Workers' Compensation insurance coverage for Steven and Andrea Mancini, Tracy King, and Dina DeMaio, their four part-time employees who died. This too was presented in the media as confirmation of the brother's insatiable mammonism. To save a few dollars, the Derderians risked leaving the families of victims impoverished.

Michael's divorce was used to demonize the brothers, with reporters combing through the case to discover that the couple had debts, including money owed to the IRS. News reports noted that Michael's estranged wife, Judi, said in court filings that she wanted her husband to sell the nightclub, contending that it had been a drain on their resources. Surely all of this, common sense demanded and the media argued, meant that one hundred people were dead because Michael needed to squeeze every penny possible out of The Station.

The brothers, however, had answers for each of these accusations, which they planned to use at trial:

Yes, the divorce was acrimonious and there were arguments over assets, but that was not unusual, and Michael's tax issue with the IRS was fairly typical for a person who ran his own business.

From the brothers' perspective, Jeffrey's reporting on the dangers of foam for Channel 7 was not proof of carelessness. The clip from Channel 7 that had received so much media attention was from a story that Jeffrey did not write or research, but one where he was just the on-air talent, providing the voice to someone else's script and an on-camera stand-up shot in a producer's home. The story focused on foam used in mattresses, which was not anything like what the Derderians thought they had purchased for their club.

It was true, however, that Jeffrey had more knowledge than the average person when it came to foam. As a professional in broadcasting,

Jeffrey was familiar with sound foam, since it appeared in the studios and recording booths of every television and radio station where he'd worked. He had constant contact with sound foam, and from that perspective never had any doubt of its safety or its effectiveness. Jeffrey believed that was the same type of foam in the nightclub, and he would cite his experience and knowledge as part of his defense at trial. The Derderians ordered sound foam, they would argue, and when they received foam for the club that was not sound foam, they had been deceived.

The brothers also disagreed with the story that Barry Warner, the neighbor and foam salesman who first suggested they use the product for soundproofing, was somehow only distantly involved in the transaction. Warner knew exactly what they intended to use the foam for, and in the brothers' minds had convinced them to make the purchase. They had explored other options for containing the sound, but said that Warner had made the case that foam had the best chance of actually working in a place like The Station. Warner even helped them determine how much of the foam to order to cover the walls and ceilings, Michael said, noting that the order called for twenty-five blocks of sound foam, a quantity he would not have known to order if not for the expert advice of Warner.

Michael had placed the order himself in a short letter that was faxed:

> June 9, 2000
> American Foam Corp
> 61 John Street
> Johnson, RI 02919
> Att: Barry Warner
>
> Dear Barry:
> Please accept our order for 25 blocks of sound
> foam. If you have any questions, please give
> me a call at . . .
>
> Sincerely,
> Michael Derderian
> The Station
> 211 Cowesett Ave
> West Warwick, RI 02893

The letter was addressed to Warner at the company, and the foam salesman went as far as to recommend the specific type of 3M glue to hold the foam in place, something Warner admitted in his grand jury testimony, so the brothers thought it absurd for Warner to deny his role in the foam installation. Reports that the Derderians had demanded the cheapest foam in stock were also wrong—nothing like that had occurred.

As far as a capacity violation was concerned, the brothers thought the numbers reported by the *Journal* were wrong. The newspaper seemed more interested in creating a big scoop than facts, and had inferred that something underhanded had occurred between Michael and the fire marshal when the club's capacity increased to 404. For Michael, it was just a matter of math, and if the fire marshal said the number was safe, then the brothers had to rely on that expertise. The inspector had also deemed the whole building safe. The Derderians brought their children to play in the club, celebrated Michael's fortieth birthday there, and hosted Linda's office party, and would never have done any of that if they thought there was danger. They would also say at the trial that Jeffrey trusted the inspections so much that he picked the club as a place to shoot b-roll for his report on public venues safety. He'd be "an idiot," he later said, to invite a camera inside if he thought there were safety problems, since any issues would be broadcast for all to see.

Yet to the brothers, even that logical line of reasoning had been twisted against them. Media critics jumped in after the fire to condemn Jeffrey and WPRI-TV 12 for using the Derderians' nightclub in his reporting, charging a conflict of interest for featuring a business on television in which Jeffrey had a financial benefit.

"The station defended its actions, saying it had no plan to publicize or promote the nightclub in the story. But that argument doesn't hold up. The feature would have undoubtedly put the club in a good light," said Deborah Potter, a former reporter for CBS News and CNN, and executive director of NewsLab at the University of Mississippi School of Journalism, in an article in the *American Journalism Review*. "That positive spin alone might have brought the club more business, and Derderian would have benefited financially."

In Jeffrey's mind that was something an out-of-touch academician would say. Videographer Brian Butler was at the club shooting b-roll because Jeffrey was in a position to get past the hurdles of permissions for recording at a live music venue, something typically difficult. The visuals were a small portion of a larger story that had never been completed or aired, so it was speculation by Potter and others that the club would have been promoted by name in the report.

Butler would later confirm that he was specifically instructed to shoot "generic" footage. "Don't identify the place," Butler said the assignment desk told him. "Nothing with the club's name on it."

For Jeffrey, there was also one important point all the righteous media ethicists had failed to mention: the Derderians had just signed papers to sell the nightclub. If any story ever aired, and if the nightclub gained publicity, the benefit would belong to the new owner. Jeffrey would not profit.

These were facts, Jeffrey thought, but the media did not seem intent on facts.

To the contrary of how they'd been portrayed, the Derderians had not cut corners to squeeze money out of the club for their pockets. They were building a business, and had reinvested proceeds for improvements, like $60,000 for a new sound system, one with higher-quality acoustics and volume control. They'd also renovated the aging building, remodeled bathrooms, painted, and added new landscaping and furniture.

Instead of the money-grubbing failures portrayed by the media, the brothers considered themselves responsible businessmen who'd branched out in the music business to some success and acclaim. In 2002, with the nightclub's former owner Howard Julian, they'd formed Derderian-Julian Entertainment, and brought Aretha Franklin to the Providence Performing Arts Center, plus Earth, Wind & Fire to the Dunkin' Donuts Center, shows the *Providence Journal* praised as two of the top ten best concerts of the year.

In the brothers' minds, The Station was not a failing business, but a turn-around story in progress. Many of the problems that plagued the club before the Derderians purchased it had been addressed, and the brothers had been lauded for that at a meeting of the West Warwick Town Council. They also informed the town council when they installed the foam for soundproofing, but after the fire, the audio recording of the meeting where the Derderians talked about the foam was missing.

It was true the nightclub failed to carry Workers' Compensation insurance coverage for four part-time employees who died in the fire, but the brothers said they had been misinformed by the previous owner that it wasn't required. The Derderians also owned a gas station where they carried Workers' Compensation coverage for employees, so the idea that they were blatant scofflaws was untrue. They were simply confused about who was supposed to receive coverage.

The Derderians were hardly alone in their misinterpretation of the complexities of the Workers' Compensation system. After the fire and discovery of the Derderians' lapse in coverage, the Workers' Compensation Fraud Prevention Unit launched a statewide investigation of bars, clubs, and restaurants. In a sweep of 1,700 establishments, no coverage was found at 504, or about one-third. The rate of compliance was even worse when the investigation then looked at twenty campaigns of state and congressional politicians and found only four with coverage, just one in five. Caught in the sting was Sheldon Whitehouse, a former Rhode Island attorney general and candidate for governor, who had made reform of the state's "messy" Workers' Compensation system a centerpiece of his campaign. "There are 50,000 things you have to think of as a candidate," Whitehouse told the *Providence Journal* when asked about the failure to cover his workers, "but I don't think that was one of them." Also named in the sweep was the campaign of Attorney General Patrick Lynch, although Lynch contended that his campaign staff, including his campaign manager and press secretary, were not real employees but independent contractors, and therefore exempt. Other politicians, however, recognized their campaign staff as employees. Governor Carcieri, the former businessman, did have coverage for his campaign workers.

With such differing interpretations and confusion throughout the state about the Workers' Compensation rules, and with Rhode Island's former top prosecutor not in compliance, the Derderians felt unfairly singled out when the state fined them a record $1.06 million for failing to have coverage. Other businesses not in compliance were fined nominal amounts in the low thousands, and the brothers would eventually successfully argue the amount was excessive and have it reduced to a small fraction of the headline-grabbing amount.* In the meantime, despite the evidence that the Workers' Compensation system was widely misunderstood by employers, the media reported the brothers' fine as

---

* The math: the fine was appealed by the Derderians and sat in limbo for years until 2013 when a series of reports by the *Providence Journal* put the case back in the headlines. Eventually, the Derderians settled the case for $150,000, about 14% of the original fine, paid to the state in $833.33 monthly installments until 2030.

further evidence of their wanton greed, reckless mismanagement of the club, and disregard for human life. It became part of the public case against them.

The Derderians knew they could counter most of what had been alleged by prosecutors or reported by the media about them, and they felt like punching bags for remaining silent for so long.

Matt Lauer and the *Today* show offered a forum to set the record straight. The brothers, however, had something more than just an interview in mind.

At NBC's 30 Rock, after checking in with security and receiving mandatory guest passes to stick on their jackets, the brothers were escorted onto an elevator to the top of the skyscraper and one of the luxurious executive office suites. From the beginning of the negotiations for the interview the network had poured on all its charms, going as far as to offer to fly the brothers from Rhode Island to New York in NBC's private jet. The Derderians declined. With so many people suffering from the fire and its aftermath, the brothers thought it would be incredibly wrong for them to accept a private jet ride or anything of value, since it would feel like they were cashing in on the tragedy. The brothers opted instead to make the four-hour drive in a small two-door car in pouring rain.

Lauer was on the same elevator with the brothers, looking dapper in a light tan-colored suit with tie. He'd just finished working out at the gym, carried a small tote bag, and munched on peanut M&Ms. The anchor did not speak to the brothers on the ride up, and the Derderians guessed that Lauer had no idea who they were.

When they reached their destination introductions were made. The suite on the fifty-second floor was laden with a spread of high-end catered foods, and had a spectacular bird's-eye view of Manhattan. Lauer would later explain that the suite was regularly used as "a little bit of razzle-dazzle" to woo guests to appear on the broadcast.

Even though the brothers thought Lauer did not recognize them in the elevator, they were impressed when the anchor recalled that Jeffrey had appeared on *Today* a few times while working at WHDH-TV Channel 7 News in Boston, the NBC affiliate. Visiting the headquarters for NBC News and being schmoozed by Lauer would have been a career highlight for Jeffrey, had his life not taken such a turn, but now that he was finally here in the wake of the fire, he was no longer enamored with the news business. "I couldn't be further away from it if I was on Mars," Jeffrey later said. He had officially resigned as a news reporter for Providence's Channel 12 four months after the fire, never returning to the airwaves after the tragedy.

Lauer played up his Rhode Island bona fides, talking about his stint at Channel 10 and encounters with the city's infamous mayor Buddy Cianci. Lauer said he felt terrible for the Derderians, and offered to be the first one to tell the brothers' side of the story. Lauer would later say that there were questions about whether the brothers had been treated fairly by the local media in Rhode Island, and he hoped that by not being part of that—as a member of the national press—he'd have a shot at landing the first exclusive interview.

Jeffrey recognized Lauer's techniques. The setting of the executive suite was meant to showcase the power and prestige of television, and then the appeal to their vanity, and the show of sympathy. It was a reporter's standard playbook, one that Jeffrey had used countless times himself, and Lauer was a master.

Then the brothers broached their real agenda with Lauer.

Yes, they could do an interview, but in exchange for that exclusive they wanted Lauer to help them put together a benefit concert for the victims of the nightclub fire.

The brothers were keenly aware of the suffering the survivors and victims' families had endured, and that many were destitute from the disaster. Like others in Rhode Island, the brothers thought there needed to be a fundraiser similar to what was done in the wake of the September 11 terrorist attacks, when celebrities and performers fronted huge events that raised millions of dollars for those in need. The Station fire was the deadliest rock concert in United States history, and yet the rock music industry had done nearly nothing to help. When the Derderians were asked to do an interview with Lauer, they sensed an opportunity— they would endure the pre-trial risk of a media appearance, if the famed anchor would use his contacts to gather stars for a significant benefit show. Lauer was not just a morning newsman, he was one of the country's most famous people, and he hobnobbed with other celebrities. If he wanted to, he could use his contacts to help produce a charity show. And, of course, Lauer had a genuine connection to Rhode Island.

Jeffrey noted the look on the anchor's face when the brothers explained their real agenda: a concert for an interview. Lauer smiled slightly and seemed to have a moment of clarity. Lauer would later remember that the brothers were polite in their pitch—it was conversation and not a "direct quid pro quo" demand. But asking Lauer to effectively buy an interview violated journalism ethics. "I couldn't," Lauer said. "It would have crossed a big red line."

Jeffrey knew these were the ground rules of journalism, but he cared little for the axioms that once defined his career. It might be ethically compromising for Lauer to make such a deal, but Jeffrey no longer worked as a journalist, and he felt no shame in asking. Michael, who had never worked in the media, saw no problem with asking for Lauer's help. The stakes were too high, and the need too great.

The meeting ended with vague promises to keep in touch. They would never meet again, there would be no *Today* interview, and no Matt Lauer benefit concert for the nightclub victims.

Years later the Station Family Fund held its own fundraising concert, "Phoenix Rising! Musicians United to Benefit the Victims of the Station Nightclub Fire" at Providence's Dunkin' Donuts arena around the fifth anniversary of the fire on February 25, 2008, emceed by Twisted Sister lead singer Dee Snider with appearances by groups like Tesla, Stryper, and Winger. The show was recorded and televised the following month by the cable television music channel VH1 as *Aftermath: The Station Fire Five Years Later*. Ticket sales for the performance at the arena were reportedly sluggish, but the benefit raised a million dollars.

Michael and Jeffrey did not give up on the idea of helping the fire's victims. In 2007 the Derderians cofounded the Station Education Fund with Jody King, brother of the club bouncer Tracy King who heroically died in the fire. The charity obtained scholarships and benefits at seven Rhode Island colleges for the children of fire victims. Additionally, the fund provided books, clothes, and other supplies for students. Of the seventy-six children who lost parents in the fire, twenty-three received help from the fund by 2019.

The idea of Matt Lauer parlaying his celebrity status for disaster victims did eventually happen, but not for Rhode Island.

Even though Lauer would not help victims of the nightclub fire, the anchor went on to do exactly that for those hurt by Hurricane Sandy, which hit New Jersey and New York in 2012. Lauer told Billboard.biz that he came up with the idea to do a telethon benefit for those impacted by the disaster, and that he personally picked up the phone and called Jon Bon Jovi to book him for the show. Bruce Springsteen, Christina Aguilera, Billy Joel, Sting, and Aerosmith followed.

"It's been the easiest thing to book because everybody wants to be involved," Lauer said.

Lauer's "Hurricane Sandy: Coming Together" benefit raised nearly $23 million for the American Red Cross in one hour. But in time the veteran anchor would experience his own reversal of fortune. He was fired from NBC News in 2017 for sexual misconduct after coworkers said he coerced them into having sex, sometimes in his *Today* show office.

CHAPTER 48

I T WAS THE worst possible time for Phil to get pneumonia. He was
diagnosed days before the New England Small College Athletic Conference championships, forcing him to sit out the biggest stage of the
season and his last chance to compete at the college level. The Bates team
journeyed to Wesleyan University in Middletown, Connecticut, without
Phil to face their rivals and reigning champions, Williams College.

Phil had to return to Rhode Island to seek treatment from his doctors, who prescribed an intense regimen of antibiotics. Fighting the illness left him exhausted.

The lure of the competition was stronger. Phil didn't have the speed
to lift his team to the top, but no one was a better booster for his fellow Bobcats. Defying his illness, on a cold February day two years after the nightclub fire, he persuaded his mother Barbara to drive him to
Wesleyan. He'd already missed some of the competition, and he was too
diminished to race, but he could still contribute in his own way—he'd
become the swim team's unofficial head cheerleader.

A year earlier Phil could not have imagined being on the team in any
capacity and was unsure about returning to Bates. The summer class
he took at Brown in Providence turned into the entire fall semester. He
was not in any condition to be far away from his doctors and physical
therapists. He set a goal of returning to Bates in January, and as the
holidays approached his mother gently nudged, "Have you registered
for classes at Bates?"

The return to Bates became the source of many long family discussions, but Phil had been so focused on regaining his physical strength
that he'd underestimated the need for an emotional recovery. The com-
forts of being at home, and the structure his family provided, mattered

more than he realized. To be able to come home every night turned out to be vital to his healing.

"I'm not ready for that," Phil finally told his parents about returning to Bates. "I don't know how I feel about going back to Maine right now and being one hundred percent on my own." He signed up for another semester at Brown, yet continued to feel the call of Bates and the pull of the pool.

After that first scary day of struggling to swim just one Olympic length of the pool, Phil kept going. Years of training and competing taught him how to push his body to the next level. Building back from his fire injuries with such limited lung capacity was different than past training when he'd shave a fraction of a second off his best race time, but the overall theory was the same: press yourself harder and further. During his second visit to the Brown pool he did two Olympic laps, with a break in between to catch his breath. The third time they'd changed the lanes back to the shorter NCAA configuration of twenty-five yards, and Phil felt more confident, forcing himself to swim farther. In time he swam forty minutes twice a week, building his strength to the point where he could go two hundred yards without stopping, with flip turns. He didn't break any speed limits, and his body fought back with debilitating, painful coughing fits, but he felt his lung capacity expanding.

The workouts stretched the healed tissue in his lungs, returning utility to areas that had been damaged. The more he swam, the deeper his breaths became, and he felt himself getting more air and energy. When he drove himself too far he was overcome by a sharp, stabbing pain in his lungs, and he'd heave and wheeze. With each swim he'd get close to where his body would revolt, and then the next time he'd push the limit a bit more—a battle to determine and manipulate the line between exhilaration and collapse.

Initially he was self-conscious about the burn mark on his back, and occasionally someone would ask about it. Phil would tell them the story, briefly, not wanting to get into the details of the most infamous local tragedy, one that continued to make headlines. He was there to swim, not dwell on the past.

He'd kept in touch with Dana Mulholland, the coach of the Bates swim team. While back to clean out his dorm room on Memorial Day, he visited the coach, nervous about the meeting. As an invalid, Phil had little to offer his old team, and his future at Bates was still in question. It wasn't clear if he'd swim again.

"Dana, I want to come back, but I have no idea how this is going to go," Phil said, feeling like a disappointment to his old mentor. "I don't know if I'm going to be able to do much of anything."

Coach Mulholland was a consummate Mainer who wasted few words of his gruff provincial accent. In his midfifties with salt-and-pepper hair and silvery facial stubble that became present by midday, despite shaving each morning, he could have been mistaken for a local lobsterman. At five foot eight he was towered over by his lanky student swimmers, but the coach had a commanding presence with his thick eyebrows and fierce brown eyes atop a perpetual warm smile.

Mulholland assured Phil that he was part of the team, and welcome back in any capacity.

Phil remembered that as he continued his studies at Brown and pushed himself in the pool. He made plans to return to Bates in the fall of 2004, and he got closer to his other major goal too—in the summer before classes started he moved to New York for an internship with J.P. Morgan. Working up to eighty hours a week made his confidence soar. The old Phil was coming back.

Back on the Maine campus in the fall, a year and a half after the fire, Phil returned to the coach's office, this time undaunted. "Look, I'm ready to go. I'm going to swim in whatever capacity I can," Phil said. "I don't even know if I can competitively swim events, but I'll be at practice on November first," the beginning of the NCAA season.

In the months leading up to the official start of the season Phil swam laps led by his teammates at so-called captain's practices, four days a week. In the pool at Brown Phil had been by himself, at his own pace, and he quickly discovered that his body was nowhere near ready to race, even at informal practices. His relentless pushing built his lung capacity from 45 percent to 87 percent, but that still left him dramatically weaker than he'd been before the fire.

The demands Phil made of his body provoked excruciating coughing, and he no longer had the ability to swim the long races that were once his forte. In the past his best events were the 200-yard butterfly, eight laps of arguably the most physically demanding stroke, and the 500-yard freestyle, a relative marathon in competitive swimming at twenty laps. Phil now only had small bursts of energy, so he switched to shorter races like the two-lap 50-yard freestyle, and hoped to work his way up to 100-yard competitions in freestyle and butterfly.

When the official swimming competition season got underway Phil continued to push himself, but remained too injured to keep up with the team. He referred to his times as "atrocious," having once been able to swim the 50 freestyle in about twenty-four seconds, and now it took nearly thirty seconds, leaving him to finish "miles last." He practiced in the lanes reserved for the freshman women swimmers, and even there he was lapped.

None of it mattered. Phil was thrilled to be back on the team, and he channeled that enthusiasm by loudly cheering from the sidelines when he wasn't in the pool.

As the first meet of the season approached Phil figured he wouldn't compete—the team didn't need someone guaranteed to be in last place. But Coach Mulholland put Phil into three events. Let's see what happens, the coach said, pointing out that even a "DQ" would not matter at this stage.

DQ meant to be disqualified for failing to hit technical requirements, like touching the end of the pool with both hands in butterfly, or doing a turn incorrectly. Phil was anxious and self-conscious before his races, and he finished last, but he didn't DQ and in the process reached a remarkable milestone. Despite tragedy and debilitating injuries, he'd once again competed at the NCAA level. Coach Mulholland never made grand speeches or waxed philosophically, and yet by making Phil compete that first day he delivered an inspiring sermon about overcoming incredible odds, not just for Phil, but for the entire team.

Phil competed in every meet after that, despite constant hacking and torment as his lungs fought back. He suffered regular respiratory infections, but his race times got down to within a second or two of what he attained before the fire. A full second was an eternity in competitive swimming, and he remained in last place, but it felt more respectable, and his teammates seemed astonished. The story of Phil's unlikely comeback was the talk of the pool.

That made it especially devastating when Phil missed the championships because his latest infection worsened into pneumonia. As his mother drove him to Wesleyan to watch the competition, Phil became increasingly excited about rejoining the other men. Even if he couldn't race, he had his voice. Everyone joked that no one was louder than Phil at the meets, and he needed to be there for the end of the regular season, his last days in the NCAA.

When Phil arrived at the pool the other men were amazed, as if witnessing a miracle. Coach Mulholland would later say that Phil's appearance that day "inspired some great performances from his fellow swimmers."

The team clinched a spot in the finals of the medley relay, but had a remaining preliminary heat. The speed of that race wouldn't have any impact on the team's overall standing in the competition, and Coach Mulholland saw an opening to reward Phil's determination. If Phil was well enough to get into the pool, he could be in a championship race and swim the butterfly leg of the relay.

Butterfly was the third leg of the relay, and as Phil stood on the block he took in the moment. His mother sat in the stands, anxious about the prospect of her sick son racing. Phil's teammates gathered at the other end of the pool, waiting and cheering. Although it didn't matter how fast Phil finished, the stakes were still high: if Phil DQ'd during his portion, it would derail the team's standing. His time could falter, but his techniques needed to be perfect.

Phil felt no trepidation. Pumped with adrenaline, he suppressed his lingering sickness. Championship races always brought out fabulist thoughts in swimmers, that somehow the races were shorter at this level, or "the water tastes different." For Phil there was also the realization that more than half of his life came down to this moment. He'd traveled to swimming competitions since he was twelve, and now at twenty-three this was the finale. *This really is the last time I'll be doing this*, he said to himself.

His teammate tagged in and Phil shot into the water. After three whip kicks both his arms simultaneously surfaced into an enormous pull of force, like an embrace—one last bear hug from a guy with a football player's build who'd somehow beaten so many odds to be in that pool.

As he finished and his head surfaced, Phil scanned the pool and savored the feeling. He struggled to catch his breath, pushed through the pain, and looked over to where his teammates cheered wildly. The time for his leg, predictably, was the slowest. No one cared. Phil had competed in a championship competition two years after being left for dead inside an inferno. There was no greater victory.

CHAPTER 49

JOEL RAWSON GATHERED editors Carol Young, Thomas Heslin, and Susan Areson for breakfast at the Westin Hotel in downtown Providence. When the meeting was first scheduled, the plan was to celebrate.

"I have very bad news," Rawson told the editors. "We're not gonna win this thing."

Rawson received a phone call the night before with the news that the *Providence Journal* would not win the Pulitzer Prize. The newspaper was a finalist in 2004 in the prestigious Public Service category for its coverage of The Station fire, but an insider tipped a *Journal* executive that the top prize would instead go to the *New York Times*.

The official announcement was later that morning, and until the phone call the night before all indications were that the *Journal* would get the nod. Heslin created an extensive presentation that highlighted nearly a year's worth of coverage, from the initial breaking news, through the investigations into the Derderian brothers, the deadly foam on the nightclub walls, and the story that claimed the brothers criminally exceeded the club's legal capacity.

The newspaper's coverage represented a massive investment of resources, but also emotion. Reporters and editors felt a higher calling in covering the nightclub fire: a duty to hold those responsible accountable, and a need to keep a constant vigil.

"I was always haunted by what I perceived to be a vague community indifference to the suffering. Something about the venue, the working-class nature of the crowd, the remoteness of West Warwick," editor Heslin said later. "It seemed like this was a story Rhode Island—and America—could easily move beyond. And that was not going to happen on our watch. So, we used every resource, every ounce of staff, energy, brainpower, outrage, and professionalism to tell what happened, why it happened, who was affected and what could be done to prevent similar tragedies. We tried to tell stories and to make sure no one affected by the fire was overlooked."

It was not enough for the Pulitzer. Rawson told the editors they needed to return to the newsroom and inform the staff.

"I was not a happy camper," Rawson later recalled. "That's one of the memories of this thing that's still a pretty bitter memory."

In his announcement to the staff Rawson used an expletive to describe the Pulitzer judges.

In time, though, Rawson blamed himself. As a second-tier newspaper, it was unusual to win a Pulitzer. The prizes typically went to the *New York Times*, the *Washington Post*, the *Wall Street Journal*, and other nationally known newspapers. To be considered for a newspaper the *Journal*'s size, Rawson believed, required campaigning to create industry buzz so Pulitzer organizers were aware of the newspaper's accomplishments. Rawson wished he'd done that.

The Pulitzer rules at the time would have allowed Rawson to enter the *Journal*'s coverage in both the Public Service and Breaking News categories, where it might have been a shoo-in. But he only chose the most prominent Public Service category.

The *Journal* received a "finalist" award, but the Pulitzer board gave the top prize to a *New York Times* investigation of workplace safety. It was the year the *Times* had been shaken by scandal when one of its reporters, Jayson Blair, was caught plagiarizing and fabricating stories, and the fallout cost top editors their jobs. The Pulitzer for the *Times* was much-needed good news during an otherwise dreadful time.

Rawson and others felt robbed, and many in the Providence newsroom believed they were victims of Pulitzer politics that intrinsically favored the *Times*. Others joined the criticism. In an article called "The Pulitzers That Got Away," the Poynter Institute, the same journalism think tank that spurred the news media to focus its coverage on the Derderian brothers, questioned the Pulitzer decision. "The *Journal* had been far ahead of fire officials in determining the exact level of overcrowding in the club," writer Roy J. Harris Jr. argued.

For some at the *Journal*, the bitterness over the award loss lingered. Years later, when asked for their most vivid recollections about covering The Station fire, several reporters and staff members responded identically: what they remembered most about the nightclub tragedy was not winning the Pulitzer Prize.

CHAPTER 50

Gina caught her breath as she walked into the opulent Wang Theatre in Boston. Opened in 1925 and meticulously restored in the early 1990s, its 3,500-seat theater was a gilded visual treat. Adding to the glamour was staging for the current show, *Neil Goldberg's Cirque*, the chimerical acrobatic circus.

I could never afford to come to a place like this, Gina thought. Yet here she was, and soon she would be on that dazzling stage with hundreds watching and listening. She'd journeyed from a dark place to the golden theater. It had been less than sixteen months since the fire.

Following the demoralizing failure of the indictments and the continued agony of her recovery, Gina spiraled into vengeful and violent fantasies involving those who'd caused so much suffering. One night around the dinner table with her family Gina talked about torturing the nightclub bouncer and the Derderian brothers with the methods seen in the *Saw* horror movies, where victims were dismembered alive. She'd never do anything so barbaric, of course, but the fact that she thought and discussed it was troubling. Who had she become?

Psychiatric care had failed her since the fire. In the hospital, where doctors battled to keep her alive, the focus was her physical recovery. Gina remembered being told that she would likely experience crippling survivor's guilt for years, although it would probably diminish in time. The first therapist she saw wore a bowler hat and inappropriately giggled whenever Gina mentioned the fire. Gina saw nothing funny about the grim, personal details she shared, and when she walked out she vowed to never return. She guessed the therapist had no experience dealing with anyone who'd gone through this level of trauma. Another therapist wept when Gina spoke. *If she has a breakdown just listening, how in the world is she going to actually help me?*

Counseling from a local priest was sincere and beneficial, and despite everything, Gina maintained her faith and still believed in God. But in the months following her return home she had developed her own form of therapy: writing.

The fire had not destroyed her ability to use her hands, as doctors once feared. Her fingers worked differently, due to the regrown skin, but she could type. On a computer keyboard, rather than the old typewriter she used at work to fill in bureaucratic forms, she became fairly proficient again at typing. That embittered letter she had written, but never mailed, to the men who had destroyed her life was the beginning. Since then she'd found comfort by journaling, especially writing letters to Fred.

> *September 5:*
> *Today is your birthday and I miss you terribly. I want to spend this day with you and give you whatever would make you happy. I spent some of the day with your mother and Crystal. We went to the cemetery to be with you. Your headstone is beautiful but it's so hard to look at it because I cannot imagine your beautiful body in the ground even though I know your soul is in heaven. I want you here with me, Freddy. I need you so much all I do is cry for you and everything we lost. I hope our love is strong enough and you will wait for me to come to you and then we will spend all of eternity together. I love you and please wait for me no matter how long it takes.*

After the disappointing news of the indictments, she made another journal entry. She wrote on December 11.

> *I have been so sick and depressed since that meeting I just lost it and I realized I have no strength or energy left to fight this and am leaving this up to God. It's his call and he is the only one who can make things right.*

In a way that doctors and therapists could not help, the letters to Fred allowed Gina to release her emotions and find solace. She was hardly alone in her pent-up feelings, and others impacted by the nightclub disaster struggled in their own ways. At the site of the fire one of the makeshift memorials was vandalized. Diane Mattera, mother of twenty-nine-year-old fire victim Tammy Mattera-Housa, removed items dedicated to the memory of Ty Longley, the Great White guitarist who perished. Mattera threw into nearby woods a wooden cross, teddy bear, guitar, and photos of Longley's son, who was born after the musician's death, and left a note behind that said that Longley had "killed" her daughter.

"Ty's cross does not belong with my daughter's. That's it, pure and simple," Mattera told the Associated Press. "He was a victim too. But it was his band. He knew they were going to set off the pyrotechnics that night." Supporters of Longley, whom some believed died trying to save others, later replaced the trashed wooden crosses with one of welded steel secured in cement.

"They must have known, as I did, that Diane is also a very determined person," Gina later said.

The holidays were especially depressing for Gina. At first she thought the Christmas outreach from Phil Barr and his family and the Station Family Fund was degrading, proof of her maternal failings. "It was humiliating, it was embarrassing, and I remember at first saying, no way, there's gotta be someone worse than us. Like, I knew I had my parents. My kids were never gonna want for anything," she said. "It was humiliating to think that, crap, I might need that kind of help."

To relieve the burden on her parents, she accepted help from the Station Family Fund and got to know the Barrs. They eventually became friends. "They were good, good people who just wanted to give back even though their son could've—" Gina paused. "Life could've been very different for their own son."

Despite the outpouring of support, the holidays drove home the loss of Fred. Once again her therapy was to share her thoughts with him. She wrote in her journal on December 29:

> Christmas has come and gone without you and it was awful.
> I made it through the day because of my family but my heart
> breaks every time I think of you . . . I doesn't seem possible that
> it is coming up on 1 year since this tragedy nothing seems real to

me. I sometimes find myself wanting to call you and need to tell you something, but then I remember that you're not there for me to call so I can only say a prayer to you and hope you hear me. I love you so much and cannot accept your death.

Bearing her soul, even if only through a keyboard, helped Gina grapple with her anguish. She also found comfort meeting fellow survivors, and in small groups they'd ventured back to live music shows, although now they checked for emergency exits. She shared details of the shows and updates on their friends with Freddy. Storytelling became her self-medication.

Gina held the Spaulding Rehabilitation Hospital in high regard. Despite enormous odds, the hospital got her walking, using her hands, and even driving. When the hospital planned a fundraiser for expansion plans, Gina was asked to share her story of recovery with an audience at the Wang Theatre.

"I'll try," Gina said.

Three of Spaulding's patients spoke, including Dan Winston, a young tuba player who suffered a brain injury in a car collision involving an intoxicated driver, but after rehab was able to return to his high school orchestra. Also featured was Joseph Exter, a hockey goaltender critically hurt in an on-ice collision who went on to play for the minor league affiliate of the Pittsburgh Penguins. Gina learned that the hospital provided rehabilitation for many professional sports teams, including the New England Patriots, and star linebacker Tedy Bruschi was one of the hosts of the Wang Theatre gala. As fate would have it, Bruschi himself would later turn to Spaulding for treatment seven months after this night when he experienced a mild stroke from a blood clot, just weeks after winning the Super Bowl. The hospital helped nurse him back to health to play in the NFL again.

Gina had never done public speaking like this before, but she did not script her remarks, deciding instead to carry a few notes—this was her story, she knew it by heart. She was allotted five minutes, and was nervous when she walked to the microphone on the golden stage. The words poured out. The fire. Fred. Pain. Survival. It felt like an out-of-body experience, but it worked. The audience rose in a standing ovation.

"It was freeing to tell the story," Gina said. "It was better than sitting in a room with a therapist, because the reality was, that therapist couldn't answer me, couldn't tell me anything. So, if you just tell your story, you don't need to hear advice back, because there really isn't any when you've been through that kind of trauma. Unless that person sitting across from you has experienced it, they have no clue. No clue at all. All the books they've read and all the college degrees, it doesn't matter."

As she walked off the Wang Theatre stage she felt she got a look from the Patriots' star Bruschi that said, *How am I going to follow that?*

"This is your therapy," Gina said to herself, thinking back to the lesson she learned that day speaking to the crowd. "This is what you need to do. Tell your story."

This emotional healing led to other breakthroughs. In spring 2006 a mutual friend introduced her to Steve Sherman, a divorced father of three. The friend thought they'd be a good match. "What did you tell him about me?" Gina asked.

Just that you're a survivor of The Station fire and you have scars, the friend said.

Gina feared meeting someone new. Who would accept her with all her baggage? Gina was blunt when she met Steve, telling him that she had scars on her arms and her back, her head was burned so badly that she would never grow hair again, and she had to wear a wig for the rest of her life.

"So what," Steve said. "I'm going bald too."

PAYMENT

CHAPTER 51

D ANIEL BIECHELE STOOD before the court, his head bowed. His long scraggly hair from his days as Great White's tour manager was cut short and slicked back, the old rocker wardrobe of jeans and T-shirts replaced by a dark suit, white pressed shirt, and conservative tie. At twenty-nine Biechele could have been mistaken for a bank teller, not the person who lit the spark that led to America's deadliest rock concert.

On May 10, 2006, it was more than three years since the tragedy and Biechele had never spoken publicly. Now he was about to accept criminal responsibility for the deaths of one hundred people. Of all those culpable for the catastrophe, Biechele alone agreed to plead guilty to committing a crime.

"For three years, I've wanted to be able to speak to the people that were affected by this tragedy, but I know that there's nothing that I can say or do that will ever undo what happened that night." Biechele paused and succumbed to tears. "Since the fire, I wanted to tell the victims and their families how truly sorry I am for what happened that night and the part that I had in it. I never wanted anyone to be hurt in any way. I never imagined that anyone ever would be."

Biechele's statement, carried live by local television stations and national cable news outlets, came after two days of often furious, emotional testimony from victims' families, also broadcast live. Anger festered since the announcement in February that Biechele would plead guilty to one hundred counts of misdemeanor manslaughter in exchange for a reduced sentence of up to ten years in prison. The arrangement was an admission by the tour manager that he unintentionally caused the deaths when he illegally installed and ignited the pyrotechnics, the 15×15 gerbs that threw sparks fifteen feet for fifteen seconds, creating enough heat to set the nightclub's foam-clad interior ablaze. Like the Derderians, Biechele was originally charged with two hundred counts, two for each victim under two different legal theories. With the plea bargain Biechele would have one hundred counts dropped, forgo a trial, and face a possible maximum sentence of serving ten years in prison, rather than up to thirty years.

Many victims' families were livid that Biechele faced anything short of a life sentence—he'd killed so many loved ones, they reasoned, and he should pay, as should the Derderians, by forfeiting the rest of their lives behind bars. Anything less made no sense.

Criminal cases, however, tend to be decided based on the intent of the defendant, and there was no intent by Biechele to hurt or kill anyone, and the government never made that claim. The underlying crime the attorney general's office used to elevate the case to a manslaughter charge involved the failure to obtain a fireworks permit, a misdemeanor that incurred a fine, if that, and never prison time.

Such legalities meant little to those hurt by the fire, and in impact statements in the courtroom leading up to Biechele's sentencing many family members unloaded years of grief, bitterness, and frustration, vilifying those connected with the case and the criminal justice system. Biechele sat and listened to the outrage, and when it became his time to speak he openly wept.

"I know how this tragedy has devastated me, but I can only begin to understand what the people who lost loved ones have endured. I don't know that I'll ever forgive myself for what happened that night, so I can't expect anybody else to. I can only pray that they understand that I would do anything to undo what happened that night and give them back their loved ones." Biechele swallowed hard, but the tears consumed him for several seconds, making it impossible to talk. "I am so sorry for what I have done, and I don't want to cause anyone any more pain. I will never forget that night, and I will never forget the people that were hurt by it. I am so sorry."

Biechele sat down, bent over, and dropped his face in his hands and cried. His attorney, Thomas G. Briody, placed his arm over his client's shoulder to console.

Briody had been by his client's side from the beginning, hired within days of the fire, and had relentlessly attempted to shift blame to the

Derderians. A curmudgeonly contrarian with a gourmand's physique who also dabbled at acting, performing magic tricks, and writing mystery novels, Briody was personally familiar with the media spotlight and Jeffrey Derderian, since they'd both been reporters at WLNE-TV 6 News in Providence.* Derderian, a product of public schools, had succeeded in an industry where Briody, who bragged openly about graduating from the prestigious Choate Rosemary Hall private school, had struggled. With his law degree Briody was an oddity in television news, but he had distinguished himself as a reporter by uncovering Rhode Island's massive impending bank system failure. However, Briody could not convince the station's ownership to broadcast his revelation, due to fears the report would cause panic and a bank run. Briody was openly exasperated by the station's lack of support and eventually departed Channel 6, went to short-term assignments in Boston media, then left journalism to go into law. Briody was gone from WLNE-TV before Jeffrey Derderian arrived in the newsroom, but the two men knew each other from running in the same circles.

There was an old joke in the Rhode Island legal system that there are two strategies for defending a guilty client: IDDI and SODDI. IDDI stood for "I didn't do it," and SODDI meant "some other dude done it." Despite the fact that his client had lit the illegal explosives that set off the fire in the club, Briody opted for a version of SODDI and tried to assign the bulk of the blame for the tragedy, both in media appearances and in legal arguments, on Michael and Jeffrey Derderian. Briody argued that Dan Biechele should walk away without any jail time.

The maximum sentence Biechele faced was ten years in prison, but Judge Francis J. Darigan Jr. would determine the exact punishment. Prosecutors wanted Biechele to serve every one of those ten years.

"The devastation wrought by the conduct of the defendant is unparalleled in our state's history," argued prosecutor Randall White. "The suffering is endless, and the extent and depth of the pain is bottomless."

Briody, however, asked for leniency, stating that community service would be appropriate, not jail: "There is no question that the fire was an accident. Accidental death does not equal prison." Briody also noted

---

* Author's note: I was executive producer of the news at WLNE-TV during Tom Briody's tenure as a reporter.

that Biechele was the only person to take responsibility for the fire and was truly remorseful, and that "the punishment must be proportional to the conduct," which in this case was that Biechele "failed to get a permit. It was not murder."

Briody's oratory that Biechele was an honorable man because he was the "only" person to admit guilt in the tragedy was a trope the attorney would repeat for years in his campaign against the Derderians.

Had there been a trial, however, with evidence made public in court, the idea that Biechele was somehow noble would have been more difficult to support. There was a considerable paper trail that indicated Biechele had a long history of failing to get permission for pyrotechnics, and he'd been repeatedly warned, even in writing, about the deadly dangers.

Biechele purchased the gerbs from a company called High Tech Special Effects of Bartlett, Tennessee, initially while working for the band W.A.S.P. When Biechele indicated he intended to do his own pyrotechnics on the road, the company responded with two letters, dated May 2001 and July 2001, which explained what was required. "Here is a list of things that would need to be looked after if yu [sic] were to carry your own pyro."

The list of requirements included a steel-lined wooden box for carrying explosives and specific notice to the club and local fire authorities of the plan to use fireworks: "Advancement of the show to the venue, Fire Marshall [sic] and promoter." Also on the list were "Permits, local shooters, fire detail—if required," "Transportation of materials must meet all DOT regulations," and "Fire extinguishers."

Biechele failed to accomplish these requirements at The Station, and told investigators after the fire that he had received no instructions from High Tech Special Effects about the pyrotechnics.

"Did they provide to you any instruction material on their use?" prosecutor William Ferland asked Biechele in an interview eleven days after the fire.

"Not that I recall, no. I don't receiving any—" Biechele replied.

"No, no warning devices—" said Ferland.

"—manual or anything of that sort," said Biechele.

Despite the letters from High Tech Special Effects that detailed Biechele's responsibilities in writing, the tour manager inexplicably also told investigators that the company was the one that sometimes dealt with fire department permissions, "like pulling permits and everything else when the venues needed to pull the permits."

Transportation of the explosives was also done in a risky way, contrary to the written warnings. A photograph taken as the gerbs ignited showed that Biechele hauled the fireworks in a cardboard box with stickers that warned "DANGER" and "EXPLOSIVE," which he said was the original shipping package from the company. The pyrotechnics were illegally taken across state lines into Rhode Island on a tour bus, and Biechele did not have his own fire extinguishers at the ready if something went wrong—he told investigators he looked for one after the fire started, but could not find one. He did not pursue or receive permits, and did not give advance notice of his fireworks plan to West Warwick's fire marshal, Denis Larocque.

There was reason to be wary about approaching Larocque. In 1999, when The Station was owned by Howard Julian, correspondence between Julian and the band W.A.S.P., where Biechele was tour manager, about an upcoming performance described the fire marshal as "ass hole maximus."

Briody claimed that Biechele notified Michael Derderian about plans to use pyrotechnics and received permission, something the brothers consistently denied.

There was no mention of fireworks in the contract for the concert or the nine-page "Technical Specs and Explanations" instructions faxed from Great White to The Station one week before the show. The document contained details about every aspect of the show, including instructions and diagrams of how the stage would be set up, but had no mention of any potential pyrotechnics.

Biechele's defense, however, said there was other proof.

In Biechele's laptop were electronic records called "Advance Sheets" that noted the details for performances, such as arrival times, stage size, expected revenue, and catering. In a section of the spreadsheet was a box designated "PYRO" and for Great White's performance at The Station Biechele had entered the word "yes."

The spreadsheet information was entered and controlled solely by Biechele, so it was unclear how this was proof of anyone else's actions or thoughts, beyond Biechele's.

Additionally, there were doubts about the accuracy of the information in Biechele's laptop records, and questions could have been raised at trial about the chain of custody of the computer, and whether there was an opening for Biechele to tamper with evidence and alter records to try to cover his trail.

The laptop was not immediately seized by investigators, which gave Biechele possible access to both the computer and a device on his person he called a "pocket PC," which could be used to alter documents remotely. Biechele told investigators he had not changed the records after the fire. But, without being asked, he indicated that he had knowledge of timestamps, an electronic note on a file that indicates when it was last modified. Biechele said the timestamp on The Station advance sheet file would prove he had not changed the records. However, timestamps themselves can be altered.

The Rhode Island attorney general's office had a high-profile troubled past when it came to the chain of custody of important evidence. In the 1985 case of Claus von Bülow, a Newport socialite convicted of the attempted murder of his wife Sunny, guilty verdicts were reversed and von Bülow was found not guilty after questions were raised about the handling and sanctity of key evidence.

There were other questions about the validity of Biechele's laptop contents. An investigation by the Derderians' defense team showed that Biechele's spreadsheets were often at odds with reality. Several club owners and managers indicated that Biechele's laptop notes and statements about receiving permission for fireworks were false.

Biechele entered "PYRO yes" in the spreadsheet for Great White's show at the famed Stone Pony in Asbury Park, New Jersey, on February 14, a week before the fire. But owner Dominic Santana said there was no advance discussion and no permission given, and he confronted Biechele when the sparks from the gerbs hit the nightclub's ceiling.

At Russell's in Bangor, Maine, two days before the fire, the club's owner said he berated Biechele when sparks hit the ceiling and showered patrons. The owner said there had been no advance discussion or permission given, but the box in Biechele's laptop spreadsheet was left blank next to the word PYRO. Biechele seemed to forget the confrontation with Russell's owner and told the West Warwick police that the fireworks were used "without any problem."

At Crocodile Rock in Allentown, Pennsylvania, exactly one week before the fire, the owner said pyrotechnics were used without advance discussion or permission. In Biechele's laptop spreadsheet the box next to the word PYRO was left blank.

At Pinellas Expo Center in Florida, two weeks before the fire, the general manager said there was no advance discussion or permission given for pyrotechnics, and when the explosives went off at the beginning of the show, Biechele was ordered to stop. But the fireworks were used again during the finale. In Biechele's laptop, the box next to PYRO said "yes."

Even the advance sheet in Biechele's laptop for The Station had incorrect information. A box next to the word BARRIER said "yes," indicating that Biechele noted the need for a separator to keep fans back from the stage. But Biechele told investigators that there was never a plan to use a barrier at The Station.

In many of the shows in the weeks preceding the nightclub fire, Biechele's laptop notes were inconsistent with what actually occurred, according to witnesses, seeming to confirm a pattern of deceit or at least inaccuracy.

Biechele could not argue that he was ignorant of the rules. Correspondence from when he worked for the band W.A.S.P., before Great White, showed that Biechele previously asked venues for permission in advance and pursued permits. That seemed to change in the weeks leading up to The Station fire.

The victims' families, the survivors, and the public, however, would not learn about the instructions from the fireworks company, or how the deeper contents of Biechele's laptop raised questions about the tour manager's credibility. The plea bargain meant there would be no trial and no vetting of this evidence. Instead, the court heard Briody contend that Biechele had simply failed to get a permit. There was also no way for Biechele to foresee that the nightclub would ignite like a match due to the foam—he could not be held responsible for that.

Prosecutor White, however, pushed back against Briody's argument and countered that the tour manager "ignored common sense. Daniel Biechele's failure to get a permit in Rhode Island was not simply an unwitting, innocuous oversight, but a deliberate, intentional decision not to abide by Rhode Island law."

When it came time to pass sentence, sixty-three-year-old Judge Darigan read calmly from prepared notes, peering down onto his papers through metal-rimmed reading glasses perched on the tip of his nose.

"Over the past two days, I have heard the virtual voice of Rhode Island lamenting the loss of one hundred of its very talented, hard-working and yes, fun-loving young men and women. I have heard and I have seen mothers, fathers, sisters, brothers, and sons and daughters of these dead ask, why did this happen? How did it happen? How can we ever cope with the depth and breadth of the enormity of the loss each victim represents? All our voices of anguish, despair, and above all love, for those wrenched from the families of their grieving loved ones."

The judge disagreed with both the prosecutors and defense on what would be the appropriate sentence for Biechele. "This court finds that neither the state's recommendation nor the defense recommendation are appropriate in this case. This court must sentence the defendant for the offense for which he has pled guilty. That offense is misdemeanor manslaughter, occasioned by the defendant's conduct in not obeying the law regarding pyrotechnic uses," Judge Darigan said, periodically looking up from his notes to address the courtroom.

"What truly makes this case so serious and devastating to the families of the victims and to the Rhode Island community as a whole is the sheer almost incomprehensible amount of life lost as a result of the defendant's crime and a profound and everlasting effect it has had and will continue to have on the loved ones of the deceased. This court is most acutely aware that there is no sentence which could be imposed today, or in fact sustainable by law, which could possibly reflect the value of the lives lost or in any way bring back the wonderful, unique people into the lives of those who love them, or to extinguish the pain that all experience on a daily basis."

The judge said he had to take into account the nature of the offense, and not just the outcome, plus the fact that Biechele had no prior criminal record and had demonstrated "genuine and heartfelt remorse." Most importantly, Darigan added, was that "this crime was totally devoid of any criminal intent on the part of the defendant."

The judge instructed Biechele to stand before the bench.

"Mr. Biechele, the greatest sentence that can be imposed upon you has been imposed upon you by yourself: that is having to live a life, an entire life, knowing that your actions were a proximate cause of the deaths of one hundred people. The court can only fashion a sentence according to law and not according to the results of your actions. Any attempt by me here today or by others to correlate any sentence imposed today with the value of these lives, or to attach any other yardstick that may be applied, I believe would be a dishonor to the memory of the victims of this tragedy. You and the victims' families will be forever mindful of that fatal night, and it is not within the power of this or any court to fashion a sentence reflective of the enormity of this tragedy."

Darigan sentenced Biechele to fifteen years at Rhode Island's prison, the Adult Correctional Institutions, but suspended eleven of those years, plus three years probation. That made Biechele's sentence four years behind bars, and he would likely serve eighteen months.

The courtroom erupted into gasps and family members burst into tears. Diane Mattera, who vandalized the memorial to Great White's Ty Longley in her rage over her daughter Tammy Mattera-Housa's death, let out a shriek and fell into the arms of her husband, Raymond.

Patricia Belanger, who lost her daughter Dina DeMaio, the waitress at The Station who was supposed to be off but traded her shift so she could celebrate her thirtieth birthday watching Great White, shouted at Biechele's mother. "You get your son back after four years! Our children are never coming back!"

Outside the courthouse, Belanger berated the Rhode Island legal system as "a joke." Gerard Fontaine, whose son Mark was killed and daughter Melanie was injured, said, "One year for every twenty-five people that died—it's crazy. You can do what you want in Rhode Island and get away with it."

Attorney General Patrick Lynch also criticized the judge. "I do not think that the sentence was quite as severe as it should have been," Lynch told CourtTV.

Some victims' families thought Biechele's sentence was appropriate. "He didn't set out to kill anybody. It was a horrendous accident," said Sarah Mancini, whose son Keith died in the fire.

Such sentiments, however, were rarely reported. Media coverage focused on the outrage for weeks, with news stories and pundits concluding there was only one chance remaining for justice in The Station tragedy: the trials of Michael and Jeffrey Derderian.

CHAPTER 52

BY CELEBRATING THE best in sports, we set the tone for all of us," bellowed KSDK-TV anchorman Mike Bush in the packed posh ballroom of the Chase Plaza Hotel in St. Louis.

Phil Barr walked onto the stage with its dramatic black backdrop, perfect lighting, and dais for those being feted. Backstage he'd mingled with his fellow honorees, sports greats like the St. Louis Cardinals legendary left fielder Lou Brock, basketball star Grant Hill of the Orlando Magic, the NFL's Hollis Thomas, and speed skater Joey Cheek, who'd just won the gold medal at the 2006 Turin Winter Olympics. Phil felt privileged to be in the same room—that he was counted among them was astonishing.

Phil received a rectangular glass trophy, and was surrounded by a small group and instructed to turn and face the audience as cameras flashed. In his dark suit and tie, with white boutonniere pinned to his lapel and hair smoothed with styling paste, Phil broadly smiled for the photos and studied the crowd. The room was filled, not just with friends and family—his own parents were there—but with hundreds of faces he did not know, many of them children from junior sports leagues from throughout the St. Louis area, including Little League, Pee Wee football, and ice skating. They were there to see their heroes.

The National Sportsmanship Awards by the Citizenship Through Sports Alliance selected a representative each year from the nation's most prominent sports organizations, among them Major League Baseball, the National Basketball Association, the National Football League, the United States Olympic Committee, and the National Collegiate Athletic Association. Past recipients included baseball greats Sammy Sosa and Curt Schilling, and Olympic figure skater Michelle Kwan, for "exemplifying outstanding sportsmanship and community service." It wasn't solely how they played the game, but also how they gave back.

For the June 10, 2006, awards ceremony the NCAA picked Phil, and it was for more than just his miraculous comeback performance at the swimming championship at Wesleyan.

That day was a turning point, but there had been others. One by one, Phil accomplished the goals he set in the aftermath of the fire. He'd found Kara, a girlfriend finally his match. They'd met at a Bates College dorm party after exchanging smiles across a crowded room. Kara didn't just play hard to get, she was impossible. Later they would joke they'd had fifty first dates, with Phil asking her to coffee or group outings with friends. Each time Kara agreed to meet she'd grin and say, "But it's not a date." One night when they were scheduled to go with a group to a local steakhouse, Phil discreetly convinced each person to drop out, so when Kara arrived it was finally just the two of them. She knew nothing of the fire or Phil's injuries and his painful recovery, which included an inability to eat large meals due to a side effect of the feeding tube. When Phil only consumed a portion of a bacon-wrapped filet, Kara jokingly said, "A real man would eat the rest of that." Phil forced it down, smitten with someone so fun and challenging. They'd been together ever since.

Phil graduated from Bates, and then got the job he always wanted on Wall Street, a grueling eighty hours a week of mostly grunt work as one of the least senior staffers at J.P. Morgan in Manhattan. As he'd once daydreamed before the fire, he lived among the skyscrapers in Midtown, and Kara was nearby. Life was incredibly hectic, and he'd worked through the night on a bond offering before making his flight to St. Louis for the awards ceremony.

Memories of the fire rushed back as a video clip that summarized Phil's journey beamed onto screens around the ballroom. "Philip Barr, National Collegiate Athletic Association. A swimmer at Bates College in Maine, Philip Barr made the ultimate comeback," the voiceover began.

The other video tributes of the night featured joyous achievements. Phil's story began with tragedy, and he wondered how the kids in the audience would react. Phil and his father had provided the footage, some shot by his dad. They deliberately omitted the Channel 12 video, so ghoulish to watch since many in the images never made it out alive.

Instead, the video flashed the *Providence Journal* newspaper's front-page headlines of those terrible first days. "Families hunt for missing," "Days of Grief," "death toll climbs," and "Search for Answers." The scene switched to video of Phil in the intensive care unit on a gurney stuffed with tubes, then bracing himself with a walker down a hospital corridor.

"Philip suffered serious burns and lung damage and was placed in a drug-induced coma for three weeks," the voiceover continued. "Doctors said he would never swim competitively again. But after more than a year of intense rehab, he proved them wrong. Philip returned to the Bates swim team for his senior season, training as hard as anyone on the squad. Two days after recovering from pneumonia, he posted his best time of the season in the New England Small College championships."

Finally an uplifting scene in the video. There was Phil in his red Speedo diving into the pool, his arms lunging from the water in dramatic arched butterfly strokes, then reaching the end and turning to check his time. As he sat on the glamorous hotel stage Phil felt like he was back in that water.

"Philip's courage, selflessness, and determination inspired his teammates, and his compassion has its own legacy. Philip and other fire survivors organized the Station Family Fund, which has raised nearly a quarter of a million dollars to help victims' families."

Coach Mulholland nominated Phil for the award, but it was his work on the Station Family Fund that made it more than an overcoming-incredible-odds sports story. As Phil listened to the other recipients' stories, he saw the common thread. Whether at the NFL or the Olympics or in the NCAA like Phil, each had reached a peak of personal achievement, and yet found time to also work on behalf of others.

Swimming was one of Phil's goals for his recovery, but his real accomplishment at the Bates pool was bringing everyone together as a team, since his ability to win races was so greatly diminished. The idea of a swim "team" was something of a contradiction. In swimming, unlike most other sports, you only competed as a team in events like a relay—otherwise, you strove to beat others in your individual race, often guys from your own school. Coach Mulholland noted that Phil's inspiring recovery and return to competition, coupled with his relentless enthusiasm, helped elevate everyone's game, bonding the swimmers as something akin to a family.

Phil felt it too. But it wasn't just the swimmers. The Station Family Fund had brought him another family. Gina, Alex, and Nicholas were now an intimate part of his life, and he was grateful for it.

CHAPTER 53

T HE TRIAL OF Michael Derderian headed to the jury selection stage and both sides readied for a fight, one that many victims' families and survivors craved. They believed that with witnesses under oath, evidence would be public and dissected for the first time, so the whole truth about the nightclub fire could finally be laid bare.

The possibility of a plea bargain for the Derderians was impossible. With just three people indicted for the fire, and after Great White's manager Dan Biechele received a deal many considered too lenient, many believed the only remaining chance for justice rested with the trials of Michael and Jeffrey.

It took an extraordinary legal effort for the state to get this far. The attorney general's office used alleged fire code violations—some of the lowest forms of criminal charges a defendant can face, and not typically punishable by imprisonment—and applied legal wrangling to elevate the charges to two hundred counts of involuntary manslaughter against each brother, two per death based on two different legal theories. In other states, like nearby Massachusetts, the Derderians could not have been charged this way. To place even greater legal stress on the brothers, prosecutors maneuvered for separate trials for Michael and Jeffrey, increasing the legal costs beyond their means. The state also signaled to the defense that if there were hung juries in the cases, they would retry both brothers again individually, effectively meaning that the Derderians could face a total of four costly trials over the course of years, even if ultimately not found guilty.

That put pressure on the brothers to come to some sort of plea, even from some on their own defense team. It had been more than three years since the fire, with different defense attorneys at various times, and several ideas for resolving the case were explored, including an ill-conceived attempt by some of their own lawyers to get Jeffrey and Michael to turn against each other. The brothers remained steadfast in their support for one another, and they did not believe that either had done anything criminally wrong—there was no smoking gun secret to validate any type of betrayal, and the Derderian family bond proved unbreakable. There had been talk over the years that the government could be persuaded to settle if each man agreed to serve ten years in prison, an arguably light sentence for killing one hundred people. The Derderians felt responsible for the tragedy in the broadest sense, since they owned the nightclub business, but did not feel they'd acted criminally, and vowed never to plead guilty to something they did not do.

Behind the scenes, however, Michael's attorney Kathleen Hagerty had repeatedly presented to prosecutors a resolution to the case she called "buy one, set one free." As a former seasoned prosecutor herself, Hagerty believed that lawyers for the attorney general's office were personally torn about litigating the case, and some wished the grand jury had never returned the indictments against the brothers. The grand jurors themselves seemed conflicted about criminal charges against the Derderians. After the indictments were announced, Hagerty interviewed some of the grand jurors and discovered that some would not have indicted the brothers if the standard had been guilty "beyond a reasonable doubt" instead of just "probable cause" to justify a trial.

Prosecutors, in fact, knew their case against the Derderians faced serious problems. During trial preparation the attorney general's office secretly conducted a mock trial to test the likely arguments of both the prosecution and the defense. Jurors in that exercise would not convict the brothers.

Prosecutor Ferland later recalled about the mock trial "how disturbing it was to hear the jurors one by one gut the state's case. Despite the tremendous emphasis I put on my presentation that the charged crimes did not carry an element of intent to kill, the jurors could not get past the fact that none of the defendants meant to kill anyone. The band manager was easily convicted largely because he 'did something' that actually caused the fire and led to deaths. The club owners were a different story. If the randomly selected jurors were an accurate indication, the best we were looking at was a hung jury."

But the case was precarious for both sides because it came down to perception. Jurors would be asked to determine whether the brothers acted with criminal negligence, and the word "criminal" was subjective. That the brothers installed the foam was not disputed, but the fact that it was highly flammable foam would become a central question. Should they have known the danger? Barry Warner told the grand jury the brothers were not warned. The foam company owner testified that there was no warning paperwork included with the foam delivery. Michael's order asked for sound foam, which by law was supposed to be flame retardant, and the fire inspector deemed the building safe. But prosecutors could argue that the brothers should have known the danger anyway, should have become experts on the state's fire codes as business owners, and were ultimately responsible for the foam installation, regardless of whether vendors and the government failed to do their jobs. A jury could decide that the Derderians' ignorance that they received flammable foam instead of sound foam—they should have known to test it themselves—was "criminal," and convict the brothers. In another scenario, prosecutors could argue that the Derderians did not train their staff with fire drills, a situation that had deadly consequences when one of the club's bouncers reportedly refused to let some patrons leave via the stage door exit. Even though it would be argued that the fire inspector did not mandate fire drills, a reasonable juror could conclude that a responsible business owner should have taken such precautions anyway, and the lack of training was "criminal."

The government's own investigation had muddied some of the arguments against the Derderians, and that information would surely become public in a trial. In fact, conflicting grand jury testimony raised doubts about one of the most infamous "truths" of the disaster: that a bouncer refused to let patrons use the stage exit during the fire. In sworn testimony the two security workers in that area of the nightclub, Scott Vieira and John Arpin, both testified they did not turn anyone away from evacuating through that exit. The Channel 12 video showed the exit was wide open, despite a door that violated safety standards for the way it opened, and a federal investigation said that exit was impassable within seconds since it was so close to where the fire started and the heat soared toward more than a thousand degrees shortly after the band used that door. Whether patrons, like Gina Russo and Fred Crisostomi, were turned away from the exit before bouncers realized there was a fire would be subject to a bitter dispute in court.

Demonizing the bouncers during any trial would be problematic for the government. Bouncer Tracy King perished bravely saving patrons, and Scott Vieira's plight, like so many in the fire, was horrific, and the *Providence Journal* had already stumbled trying to use the man's woe for its own purposes. Vieira was not actually a staff bouncer, but a club patron, one of the regulars who pitched in a couple times a year during big events. He was tasked at the Great White show to sit by the stage door with his wife Kelly to make sure no one went in or out, a concern during performances because noise from the open door caused neighborhood complaints. Although he wore a black T-shirt with the nightclub logo, Vieira was not paid and not an employee, and he was instructed to find a staff bouncer if there was any trouble. When the fire started, Vieira testified, he ran into the nearby band's dressing room to get bottles of water to throw on the flames, but by the time he returned the blaze was overwhelming. In these moments Vieira's wife, Kelly, ran toward the main entrance to try to escape and became trapped and suffered severe brain damage—she never regained consciousness and died nine days later at Shriners Hospital in Boston in a room near comatose Gina Russo.

Kelly was forty years old, the mother of two grown daughters, and she and Scott were sweethearts since high school. The Vieira family's agony was thrust into the headlines when Kelly's distraught father, John Richmond, told the *Providence Journal* that Scott Vieira had told him that he knew the band planned to use pyrotechnics and that's the only reason his wife went to the show. "She went there just to see the fireworks, hear one song and go home," Richmond told the newspaper. It was a stunning revelation, since everyone associated with the nightclub had denied any prior knowledge of Great White's plan to use fireworks, and the *Journal* presented the story as damning evidence against the Derderians that "contradicts statements by club owners and personnel." The report ran on the *Journal*'s front page and was fed to the wire services and transmitted by United Press International to news organizations all over the world. But the story did not add up. Scott Vieira would swear under oath that he did not know about the band's plan to use explosives.

Additionally, as a club patron, not an employee, Vieira did not have access to the internal workings of the business, and his wife nearly always went with him to The Station—her attendance had nothing to do with fireworks. The day after the *Journal*'s page-one sensation, the *Boston Herald* newspaper reported that John Richmond's son, John "Jay" Richmond, said his father had lied to the *Journal*. "It's completely wrong. It's a stupid statement. She didn't know about the fireworks," the younger Richmond said. The *Journal* did not report on the doubts raised about its story, and never mentioned the disputed controversy again.

It was another example of how the facts of the fire, when given scrutiny, especially at a trial, would not be as black-and-white as had been presented by prosecutors or the media.

So the defense felt it could counter most of the state's arguments, but with emotions so high in the case, and the nonstop drumbeat from the news and state officials that someone must pay for the deaths, there was a risk the Derderians could be convicted. Still, Hagerty felt that if there was to be a plea bargain, it would have to be on more favorable terms than ten years in prison for both men. The "buy one, set one free" proposal was that one brother would serve time in prison equal to the sentence that the band's manager Biechele received, behind bars for about eighteen months with good behavior, and the other brother would serve no prison time. Hagerty felt one brother needed to remain free to support both their families.

The prosecution repeatedly rejected Hagerty's suggestion, and in many minds it was inconceivable that the government would make any deal and forfeit a televised, media-saturated public show trial, one possibly broadcast nationally by national cable news channels. With both sides dug into their positions, the case proceeded and Michael's trial was scheduled for September 2006.

In July, in Providence for a pretrial motion because the new Kent County courthouse had not yet opened, lawyers for both sides were conferring in the judge's chamber when one of the prosecutors, William Ferland, suddenly emerged and walked over to Michael, who sat alone in the empty courtroom. Michael stiffened, overcome by apprehension. Ferland was the man who had spent the last three and a half years trying to destroy what remained of the brothers' tattered lives, branding them criminals and pledging to imprison them for decades. Even Michael had to grudgingly admit that Ferland was an especially effective and intimidating adversary. In a state known for its corrupt politicians, the former East Greenwich police officer, detective, and sergeant was widely regarded as an honest and decent man with old-time New England values, a by-the-book cop who'd spent four years putting himself through law school while working full-time and helping his wife raise two small children. He had a reputation for following rules, so when Ferland publicly condemned the Derderians it carried a formidable feeling of truth, making him more believable than his politician boss, Attorney General Patrick Lynch.

Michael was warned to never make any contact with the prosecutors without his own lawyers present, and now it looked as if Ferland was about to speak to Michael. Hagerty also emerged from the judge's chambers and signaled to Michael it was okay for him to talk to the prosecutor.

Ferland sat next to Michael and after a pause asked, "What's it going to take to settle this?"

What's it going to take? The preamble of a used car salesman.

Michael's mind raced, making it impossible to speak. In that instant he realized a change had occurred. Ferland was talking to *him*—just one guy to another guy, the way people really did business in Rhode Island. He listened as Ferland explained why it would be best for everyone to avoid a surely brutal trial, including the victims' families, and both sides should try to come to terms. Michael felt paralyzed, unable to respond or resurrect his old deal-making instincts. That brash younger self, the entrepreneur who negotiated and argued with the best of them, was long gone, a casualty of the nightclub's flames. All Michael could do was mumble something in the affirmative, and Ferland left.

For a moment Michael wondered what had just happened, if it was some ploy, or a figment of his imagination.

Weeks later at the Kent County courthouse near the fire scene, jury selection began, and Michael sat through two days of the process. He watched as questionnaires from five hundred potential jurors were completed and copies sent to California for analysis by Michael's jury consultant, Howard Varinsky, the world-renowned expert who had aided in the high-profile prosecutions of Timothy McVeigh, Martha Stewart, and Michael Jackson, and helped defend Bernhard Goetz, Imelda Marcos, and Dr. Jack Kevorkian.

As Michael absorbed the proceedings, his attorney Hagerty met with Ferland. The prosecutor had scaled back on earlier plea bargain demands that both brothers spend a decade behind bars. The encounter with Michael in court was genuine. Ferland negotiated Hagerty's "buy one, set one free" deal, and the details were scribbled out by Ferland in his own handwriting on the only scrap paper they could find—a piece of cardboard, part of a box that held copies of the jury questionnaires.

The Derderians' vow to never plead guilty to crimes they did not commit would be kept, and instead they could plead nolo contendere, where a defendant agrees not to contest the charges. Nolo contendere was not quite the same as a straight guilty plea, especially in the brothers' minds, but in the end it would be a criminal conviction, in many ways the same as accepting guilt. But "buy one, set one free" was also a devil's bargain in an unusual way: the Derderians themselves would decide which brother went to prison. The short sentence would equal what Daniel Biechele received, and just like the band manager, the time would be spent in Minimum Security with daytime work release at a job outside of the prison, meaning that on those days only the nights would be spent inside.

"Jeffrey is not going to prison," Michael said when he first heard the terms.

Jeffrey, his little brother, had suffered more than anyone else in the family. He saw the horror from inside the inferno, where so many of their friends perished. Jeffrey suffered post-traumatic stress disorder, and three and a half years later he wasn't healed. No one was.

Besides, Michael had a promise to keep, one made decades earlier.

Michael was sixteen when he returned home from his part-time job running shopping carts around in the parking lot of the local Ann & Hope discount store. As he drove up to the family's house in the middle-class Governor Francis Farms neighborhood of Warwick, Michael saw his uncle Richard hanging around the front yard.

"What's up?" Michael cheerfully asked.

"Your mother's in the hospital," Richard said.

Michael said he'd go there immediately and headed back to his car. "Wait," his uncle said. Their father was on his way home and would explain everything.

When Archie arrived he took his three sons, Michael, Robert, and Jeffrey, into his bedroom and sat them down. "She didn't make it," Archie said, and began sobbing. Michael had never seen his father cry before. They all began weeping.

Through his tears Michael asked, "What do you mean?"

Their mother had died of heart failure while at a friend's home for a baby's christening. She passed away in front of Jeffrey, who was eleven years old. There was nothing the hospital could do.

"We all have to stay strong," Archie cried. "We all have to take care of each other now."

Michael promised then to look after Jeffrey, and it was his moment now to keep that pledge. No, Michael would not let his little brother go to prison.

Besides, Michael figured, he got along with everyone. He was sociable and outgoing, and that personality would serve him well behind bars. Of course, he would need to get Jeffrey and the rest of the family to agree to the plea bargain, including Kristina, his girlfriend who had become his wife despite the drama and accusations of the fire. This would impact all their lives in ways Michael could only begin to imagine.

CHAPTER 54

I N THE GALLOWS humor of newsrooms there's an expression: "On the cover of *Time* one week, doing time the next."

Jeffrey Derderian thrust himself into the spotlight as a rising local television star, and after the fire felt he'd been tried and convicted in the court of public opinion by his former journalism peers, unable to present his version of events in a media maelstrom he saw as biased. The overwhelming presumption of guilt would be difficult, if not impossible, to overcome at a trial. So when the brothers were presented with a possible plea bargain, it was something Jeffrey and Michael needed to consider.

The deal put them into yet another troubling and controversial part of America's justice system. Nearly every criminal case in the United States ends with a plea deal, but investigations and studies have raised considerable doubts about whether the process is just or accurate. An alarming number of defendants plead to offenses they know they did not commit, and that was the deal offered to the Derderians as well.

The brothers' plea involved the deadly foam. They were prepared to present evidence that they had, in fact, ordered sound foam, which was supposed to be flame retardant. The written order by Michael Derderian for the foam confirmed that, and grand jury testimony by Barry Warner and American Foam owner Aram DerManouelian could bolster that defense.

Since criminal law greatly relies on the concept of intent, it might seem nonsensical for the Derderians to plead to something they know they did not do. The brothers quickly learned that those who say they'd never plead guilty to a crime they did not commit are simply ignorant of how America's legal system works.

Journalist David Krajicek* investigated widespread concerns about such plea bargains in a story called "The Guilt Mill" for *The Crime Report*, a publication affiliated with John Jay College, AlterNet, and CBSNews.com, and supported by a grant from the Fund for Investigative Journalism. Krajicek concluded that an overburdened system forces thousands of Americans each year to accept plea bargains to crimes they did not commit, and it has been that way for generations.

Krajicek cited a groundbreaking article for the Yale Law Journal in 1992 in which Harvard Law School's William Stuntz and Robert Scott said plea bargaining "is not some adjunct to the criminal justice system; it is the criminal justice system." Since then the United States justice system has become even more overburdened, and the courts could not function without deal making, even if much of it is dubious.

Krajicek reported that in 2013, for example, law enforcers arrested more than eleven million people in America, an average of thirty-one thousand every day. Half a million of those arrests involved violent crimes, with another 1.6 million for property crimes, including burglary, larceny, and theft. There is no way for the legal system to accommodate trials for two million serious crimes per year. Traffic crimes, civil suits, divorces, and other matters add millions more cases. As a result, 97 percent of criminal cases in federal court and about 95 percent in state courts are resolved through negotiated pleas.

Survivors and people who lost loved ones in the nightclub fire expected a trial to be a search for the truth and provide "justice." Research shows that the reality of the overburdened United States criminal justice system is actually quite different. In practice, it is designed to find a conclusion.

Without truth as the central tenet, people face the resources of the government and struggle to defend themselves. Poor people or those with limited resources are especially vulnerable, and some first meet their public defenders as they go into court and are informed then that a plea bargain deal has already been made. Since the United States has the highest incarceration rate in the world, a significant number of Americans have family members and friends who have experienced

---

* Author's note: David Krajicek was my classmate at the Columbia University Graduate School of Journalism.

the criminal justice system, and as a result have developed a sense of hopelessness for their fate. Even if not guilty, they will take a plea.

Marvin Zalman of Wayne State University, a leading wrongful convictions scholar, told Krajicek, "I think that when they get convicted of relatively minor stuff where they didn't do anything wrong, they just chalk it up to a bad experience, do their time, and simply move on."

In 2013, the Sentencing Project, a nonprofit group that advocates for a fair and effective criminal justice system, reported that one in three black American males born today can expect to go to prison. "I think you see a lot of pleas by people who have had previous contact with the criminal justice system, and maybe it didn't turn out well for them," said Zalman. "Maybe they've had a brother or an uncle who was locked up. Maybe they say, 'I'm branded already so I'm screwed one way or the other. I'll take the better of two bad options.'"

That judges and prosecutors go along with such a system might seem amoral, but Krajicek reported that many aren't bothered.

"The first thing you're dealing with is cynicism," Christine Freeman, executive director of the Middle District of Alabama Federal Defender Program, told Krajicek. "Everyone who works in courthouses has a deep cynicism about the clientele they are dealing with. There is an assumption that they must be guilty of something; if they didn't do this, they probably did something else."

Even in high-profile cases, where scrutiny should not allow a bogus presumption of guilt to persist, the system has failed. In New York's Central Park Five case, one of the most widely publicized crimes of the 1980s, five young men were convicted of assaulting and raping a female jogger in the Manhattan park. The convictions were based on coerced statements, even though DNA evidence did not match the men to the rape. The defendants, four African Americans and one Hispanic, spent between six and thirteen years in prison, and in 1989 a prominent New York real estate developer, Donald Trump, took out full-page ads in four New York newspapers saying the case showed the need for reinstating the death penalty. "I am looking to punish them," Trump wrote. In 2002, however, another man confessed to the crime, and his DNA matched the rape evidence. The five falsely convicted men were eventually released and the city paid $41 million in damages.

The Derderian brothers were not minorities or destitute. In the course of two generations their grandparents and parents had elevated the family from poverty to working class and eventually the middle class. However, the cost for defending multiple trials over the course of years could be hundreds of thousands of dollars, perhaps millions, even if found innocent.

There had been a rush to judgment in their case from the night of the fire, when the local police chief told the Associated Press the Derderians would face criminal charges, even though at that point there had been no investigation. Chief Peter Brousseau later said that he came to his conclusion based on logic: the fire had to be the Derderians' fault, simply because they owned the business.

The chief was not alone in trying to predetermine the outcome of the investigation before it started. In the disaster's immediate aftermath Attorney General Patrick Lynch ordered his staff to create an analysis of other fatal fires worldwide to determine who it was possible to convict in such cases and the typical prison sentences. "I think it's a wonderful document. Was probably twenty pages long," Lynch later said. "Take the complexity that you have in front of you, and put it into an acceptable, articulable mold that you can at least put a logic to the illogical . . . And then look at every state penalty. What is the trend?" The document made the prosecution of the Derderians a fait accompli before the investigation was completed—the brothers had to be the perpetrators because business owners were the guilty parties in other cases—and the research document became the bible for Lynch's team, a guiding force and reference tool used for years.

Such a presumption of guilt is difficult to overcome, but there was also the Rhode Island factor. The attorney general's office had a history of convicting and imprisoning the innocent, even betraying someone from their own law enforcement ranks, and this fact intimidated the Derderians.

The brothers knew about the case of Jeffrey Scott Hornoff, a Warwick police officer. Hornoff had an extramarital affair with Victoria Cushman, and in 1989 her body was found in her home, brutally bludgeoned to death with a fire extinguisher. A note to Hornoff was found nearby, in which Cushman asked the officer to leave his wife for her. The note made Hornoff a suspect, and when confronted he admitted that he knew her, but did not confess to the affair.

In the eyes of investigators, this made Hornoff look guilty. Years went by with the case unsolved by Hornoff's own police department. Eventually the case was handed to the state police and Hornoff was charged with first-degree murder. Even though there was no physical evidence linking Hornoff to the killing, he was convicted and sentenced to life in prison. As an ex-cop, he was held in a special protective unit with child molesters. He appealed his conviction, but when he asked that some key evidence be tested for DNA, the evidence could not be found.

Six years later, in 2002, Cushman's sometimes boyfriend, Todd Barry, confessed to the murder. He'd reportedly waited to come forward and admit his crime until after his mother died. In 2003, after Barry pled guilty to second-degree murder, Hornoff was released from prison.

The prosecutor in the Rhode Island attorney general's office who wrongly convicted officer Hornoff was Randall White, brother of Doug White, the top news anchor at WJAR-TV 10 in Providence, and one of the same prosecutors assigned to The Station nightclub case. Rather than being fired or leaving in disgrace after the false conviction of Hornoff, White was the deputy chief of the attorney general's criminal division. It was White who interviewed Jeffrey Derderian at the scene the night of the fire, acting affably, as if they were friends.

For the Derderians, it was a powerful and frightening message: if the government would falsely convict and send an innocent cop to prison for life, their chances for fairness or justice had to be slim. The brothers felt they had little choice. They would become like most Americans in the criminal justice system and accept a plea. In their case, however, the details would lead to a terrible choice and widespread public outrage.

CHAPTER 55

THE LEGAL TWIST that would send ripples of new despair into the lives of nearly everyone touched by the fire was finalized in a dingy strip-mall donut shop.

As Jeffrey Derderian entered the Dunkin' Donuts with his wife, Linda, his eyes scanned the room and its occupants. It had become Jeffrey's instinct to identify threats wherever he went, a habit his family nicknamed "going in radar."

There were few customers in the coffee shop at Cranston's Garden City shopping plaza. During the morning rush the café would be packed with patrons fueling up for the day, but at 6 p.m. there was barely a soul.

"Small with milk and Sweet'N Low," Jeffrey told the girl behind the counter, plus a medium with cream for Linda.

He sized up three older men at a table against the wall. They didn't appear dangerous, but Jeffrey kept on the blue Old Navy baseball cap he often sported to obscure his identity. He also had one in faded red, both stained on the inside from hair gel, and sometimes wore a pair of black-rimmed eyeglasses or grew a goatee, part of a varying combination of disguises. He'd changed his demeanor too. In his old television news days he'd almost strut, bathing in the limelight of his local celebrity, but since the fire he walked with his face downward, avoiding eye contact.

The attempts to go unnoticed started when his twins were old enough to attend kindergarten several months after the fire. Jeffrey and Linda had shielded the boys from learning about the deadly blaze—and the anger and blame focused on their father and uncle. Jeffrey feared that with so much rage, constantly whipped up by the *Providence Journal* and other media, someone might hurt his children, so he altered his appearance to prevent those at the school from making the connection that the man vilified in the media was also the father of little Max and Jake.

Jeffrey was only fooling himself.

He and his brother Michael were so infamous that the mere mention of the surname *Derderian* anywhere in the state led to the question— are you related? The staff at the Cranston-Johnson Catholic Regional School knew perfectly well who Jeffrey was. Like everywhere else, the school had also been scathed by the tragedy.

One of the teacher's aides, Kathy Iannone, was the mother of Michael Iannone, a student at Rhode Island College who was one of the most severely injured victims and spent months at Massachusetts General Hospital and endured dozens of painful surgeries.

Yet Mrs. Iannone greeted Max and Jake each morning with hugs and kisses, showing them love and warmth as if they were members of her own family. She knew exactly who their father was, as did the school's principal, Paul Zona, who was a close friend of the Iannone family. No one at the school ever exhibited any ill will, and the Derderians would only learn years later that those who cared so closely for their children were among those devastated by the nightclub catastrophe.

It was one of the unreported truths of the fire that feelings toward the Derderians were more complex than their portrayal in news reports as the most hated men in the state. The brothers never faced vitriol while in public, were never attacked or berated, and often received kind words of condolence when recognized. Michael would tell the story of when he was pulled over for a driving infraction and after the state police officer confirmed this was one of the infamous Derderians he was told, "The State's screwing you over enough. I'm gonna let you go."

But on September 19, 2006, when Jeffrey walked into the Cranston Dunkin' Donuts, he didn't yet understand the public's complicated perception. Like everyone else, Jeffrey followed media accounts that portrayed him and his brother as despised villains, leading to disguises and paranoia as Jeffrey's constant companions.

After getting their coffees Linda and Jeffrey walked over to Michael and his wife Kristina, who sat at the shop's large front windows. In their view was the Victorian-era cupola of one of the oldest buildings in the state's sprawling prison complex, known locally as "the ACI," short for the Adult Correctional Institutions. The couples picked the donut shop to be out of earshot of their children. They didn't notice the prison out-side, even though they'd gathered to discuss the fact that one of the men would soon be incarcerated behind those same barbed wire fences.

"Here's where we're at," Michael said. There was no hugging, tears, or wails of despair. Later each would remember how the discussion about the possible plea bargain was so matter-of-fact. One of the brothers would go to prison, pleading to a crime he knew he did not commit, and the brothers themselves would choose which one went to jail.

Although Michael had received the deal offer, it was not his decision alone. Jeffrey and the wives objected to the idea that Michael would go to prison, but as they examined the situation from every angle, it seemed like the more logical choice. Jeffrey's boys had just turned seven, so much younger than Michael's children, and it seemed a bad idea to deprive Max and Jake of their dad at such a formative age. Still, there were other children to consider. Michael's son Alec had just turned sixteen. He too was at a critical age where he needed his father, and what about Michael's daughter Ashley, and Kristina's daughters Jennifer and Alena from her first marriage? There were so many responsibilities there as well.

For every possible path forward, there was a litany of consequences, and none of them were pleasant. "We have a bad choice and a worse choice," Kristina said. She never favored a trial, knowing it would tear everyone apart and dredge up painful memories for the victims.

Everyone agreed there was little chance of a fair trial, even though the Derderians felt the evidence should exonerate them, and they were eager to tell their side of the story. The brothers had even lined up re-nowned fire expert Dr. Robert Schroeder of Minneapolis to testify on their behalf, and he would say that when an order is placed for "sound foam" it is standard industry practice that it be flame retardant whenever the intended use is in a place of public assembly. That testimony, com-bined with the written order that said "sound foam," should vindicate them on the manslaughter charges linked to the foam.

They didn't cheat the system. If anything, The Station was the canary in the coal mine that showed how deeply flawed fire protection systems were in the United States. The nightclub had been deemed safe by the fire inspector, and the chief of police had praised the brothers for how they operated the club—Jeffrey so believed the experts that his place was safe that he was prepared to include it in a TV news story about public venue safety. After the disaster the National Fire Protection Association, which set national fire protection standards, put in place "tough new code provisions" for sprinklers and crowd management, and specifically cited the nightclub fire as the reason. This effectively showed that the Derderians had followed the rules. The problem was, the rules were deadly wrong.

Even the setting of the trial was tainted against them. Proceedings were scheduled to take place at the brand-new Kent County Courthouse, just down the road from the location of the nightclub's remains, meaning that jurors would likely drive by the fire scene each day filled with homemade memorials to the victims, a devastating visual reminder of the disaster that would stir emotions. To further stack the deck against the brothers, the jury would be drawn from that same insular community.

The Derderians had proof a jury trial would be risky. Just like the attorney general's office, they too had secretly tested the likely arguments of the prosecution and defense. The brothers had commissioned two mock trials in Baltimore, and similar to the state's results, the mock jurors would not convict the Derderians. But this was hardly comforting. Deliberations suggested the jury might be swayed by feelings, rather than facts.

And it appeared the jury pool had been effectively poisoned. Prosecutors, through the news media, had used alleged misdeeds of the Derderians to vilify them in the public's mind, painting them as scofflaws on several different fronts, such as failing to have Workers' Compensation coverage, paying employees under the table, and installing a nonconforming exit door. None of these failures caused the fire, but when combined with questions about the foam and fireworks, the brick-by-brick piling of other offenses was played up so much it felt like the club owners had to be guilty of something.

Conversely, evidence that helped the Derderians' case was downplayed by the news media, if mentioned at all.

The Derderians commissioned jury consultant Howard Varinsky to poll potential jurors from Kent County just prior to Michael's scheduled trial. Ninety-nine percent of those polled had heard about the fire, and more than two-thirds had closely followed news coverage. More than 40 percent felt justice had still not been served in the case after tour manager Daniel Biechele's plea bargain.

The survey showed that the government's misdeeds campaign had stuck. Eighty-two percent said they knew about the Workers' Compensation violations, and 61 percent were aware that Biechele had information in his laptop that allegedly condemned the brothers. Forty-seven percent were aware that Jeffrey had done a TV news report on the dangers of foam before the fire, and 46 percent knew the brothers had exaggerated the club's audience size in booking bands.

Only 16 percent had heard there was paperwork that showed the Derderians ordered sound foam. When told about the paperwork, half thought the evidence made the Derderians less responsible for the fire.

The survey also showed that 48 percent thought, "The nightclub owners are being singled out for criminal prosecution because of public pressure to do something because the fire was such a huge tragedy." And more than two-thirds thought, "Attorney General Patrick Lynch is politically motivated in prosecuting the nightclub owners."

In the end, however, that didn't matter. Fifty-two percent said they would still convict the Derderians and send them to prison.

Eighty-six percent of those polled described themselves as readers of the *Providence Journal*.

With such odds stacked against them, it would be a tough fight for the Derderians to prevail, but they still felt they should debate the idea of going to court. At the Dunkin' Donuts meeting the brothers and their wives talked about the collateral damage any trials would cause. If found guilty, Michael and Jeffrey could spend twenty years or more behind bars, with six children without their fathers, a far worse fate than if Michael alone went away voluntarily. If trials ended in hung juries, which polling suggested was possible, retrials could last years.

Michael had seen what just two days in court for jury selection was like. His daughter Ashley, now in college, insisted on attending, and they faced a circus of cameras and reporters taunting them as they walked into the courthouse. Michael's attorney Kathleen Hagerty was shoved and nearly fell. An officer was assigned to protect them.

Inside the courtroom Michael watched each of the four sessions where 125 jurors filled out questionnaires. They came from all walks of life, young and old, affluent and working class. He studied their faces—somewhere in this crowd were the men and women who would decide his fate. The legal case was no longer an abstraction, or a debate over strategy in lawyers' offices, and as the stakes became suddenly vivid, Michael fell into despair, unable to draw any conclusions from the hundreds of benign, expressionless faces.

After just two days of the preliminary proceedings the Derderians were emotionally and physically exhausted, and this was just the beginning.

As the couples sat at the donut shop their discussion turned to the others who would be hurt by the trial—the families of those killed. If the trial was painful for the Derderians, it would be agony for those who lost loved ones. The prosecutor was expected to profile every victim, people in the primes of their lives, and then compare smiling snapshots of them alive with photos of their corpses in the ruins of the nightclub. It was a technique used to represent the prosecution in the defense's mock trials, which was especially disturbing because many of the photos were not of charred unidentifiable remains: they were clearly recognizable, with some victims appearing almost unharmed and simply asleep, having succumbed to toxic smoke rather than flames.

That was the torment awaiting families of the dead, some of whom expected the trial to bring them justice and closure.

Others saw the tragedy differently. Some survivors and victims' families did not want a trial, realizing the pain it would cause, and believed the fire was an accident, not manslaughter. But these views received scant media attention, which instead focused on outspoken families who called the fire mass murder.

A trial would bring new pain to everyone. Prison time and its effects seemed trivial by comparison. The Derderians felt responsible for the suffering of the dead, the burned, and their families. If the brothers had never bought that nightclub, or never booked that band, maybe the accident never would have happened. They knew they were not criminals, in the legal sense, but an endless stream of "what ifs" never left their thoughts. There was no escaping the feelings of guilt, regardless of what any court decided.

The conversation turned to logistics. Kristina worried about raising a sixteen-year-old boy on her own. Jeffrey agreed to step in and be a de facto guardian for his nephew Alec. For more than an hour they talked out the likely scenarios they'd face when Michael lost his freedom.

Linda's mind wandered. Jeffrey would turn forty when Michael was in prison. She'd always wanted to do something special for her husband's fortieth birthday, but she'd never have any celebration without Michael—it was inconceivable.

"Are you the Derderian brothers?"

Like a phantom one of the three older men who sat across the room in the donut shop suddenly appeared at the Derderians' table, peering down at the brothers.

Jeffrey's radar hit high alert. The man was heavy-set, probably in his sixties. Blue-collar. Was he someone who'd lost a loved one? Would he attack?

Michael and Jeffrey both tentatively nodded.

"You guys got a raw deal," the man said in his thick Rhode Island accent. "You should fight this thing."

"We appreciate that very much," Jeffrey said, his shoulders relaxing. *No danger.*

"Thank you for coming over," said Michael. "It means more than you know."

The two brothers gave each other a knowing look as the man walked away. What bizarre timing. Right at the moment they were deciding to abandon the trial—the chance to finally prove their innocence—a complete stranger approached them to tell them to keep fighting. Were they making the wrong decision?

No. It was a bad choice, but the alternative was worse. The two couples continued talking, further working out the details. Michael admitted that he'd already sat in his car outside the minimum-security prison, the building where he'd do his time, and watched the inmates from afar. It didn't look so bad. And with the work release, he'd be off-site at a job much of the time. Really, he'd only be sleeping behind bars most nights. How bad could that be? Besides, Michael got along with everyone. With his personality, he'd be fine in prison.

And he had the support of his children. Earlier Michael told Ashley and Alec, in the parking lot of a University of Rhode Island football game, that he might be the one to go to prison. He explained the rationale. They listened thoughtfully and said, "We'll do it." *We.* Everyone would be in this together.

It would be hard, but they'd get through it. Michael would do the time, take the hit for the sake of everyone else. There was nothing that could heal the wounds of the fire, but at least this would prevent the ordeal from becoming even worse.

They could not have been more wrong.

CHAPTER 56

T HE SENTENCING OF the Derderian brothers at the Kent County Courthouse on September 29, 2006, started with photographs of lost loved ones projected onto a screen. There would be no forgetting what this day was about.

When news of the plea deal broke, family members were livid. With so few people indicted, the case against the Derderian brothers represented their last hope for justice. In some minds, nothing less than a conviction for murder and life behind bars was warranted.

More important to some than the punishment was the fact the plea bargain meant there would be no criminal trial. Family members, and many in the public, thought a criminal trial would shed new light on the fire's causes. Did the band have permission for fireworks or not? Did the Derderians know the foam on the walls was flammable? Was the club crowded over its legal capacity? For years the government and media made these accusations, but the allegations were never vetted because prosecutors had never been required to provide proof in court. Now no one would be put under oath, cross-examined, and required to provide evidence, one way or another. To some that meant that the truth would never be known.

Further upsetting to survivors and victims' families was Attorney General Patrick Lynch's seemingly implausible claim that the plea bargain was done behind his back and without his permission. Even though his own prosecutors had forged the deal in the most significant criminal case in his tenure, Lynch contended that he was unaware of the plea bargain ahead of time and opposed it. In a letter to victims' families, the attorney general tried to shift blame onto the judge. "Most significantly, I strongly disagree with the court's intention to sentence Jeffrey Derderian to less than jail," Lynch wrote.

The attorney general's decision to blame the judge for the plea bargain enflamed emotions and caused confusion. The terms of the plea were, in fact, written in prosecutor William Ferland's own hand—the outline of the deal was made on remnants of a cardboard box of jury questionnaires and handed to the Derderians' defense attorney Kathleen Hagerty. Lynch would later describe that paperwork as scribbles that were simply part of a back-and-forth process, and when he'd heard that the judge had been brought into the discussions and agreed to those terms, the attorney general dressed down his prosecutors, Ferland and White, for even discussing such a lenient plea—Lynch had been adamant about ten-year sentences, based on his department's analysis of similar cases.

"My guys come back and give me the message, and I said, 'That's not where it is, so I'm hoping you didn't make that.' They plead with me that maybe this should be the answer, and we had very long, difficult, painful and emotional discussions about it. And I said, 'That's not where we were. Call him back immediately, just so there's no confusion, and say we will not agree to anything like that,'" Lynch said, referring to the judge. Despite the attorney general's objections, it was too late. The "buy one, set one free" deal stuck.

Adding to the drama was the apparent decision by someone in Lynch's office to leak news of the plea bargain to WJAR-TV 10 News before informing the victims' families. The court blasted the leak as despicable, unethical, and "devoid of any consideration for the victims of this tragedy. Without question this information emanated from the attorney general's department."

The mishandling of the news and Lynch's blame game led to scorn for the attorney general. "If I were to punch Patrick Lynch, would I get more time than the Derderians?" asked Michelle Hoell, who lost her sister Tammy Mattera-Housa in the fire. "After three years, we thought this was going to be our justice, and now it isn't."

Associate Justice Francis J. Darigan Jr. of the Rhode Island Superior Court acknowledged the widespread feelings that once again the justice system had failed those killed and hurt by the fire.

"I am well aware of the tremendous dissatisfaction, anger, bitterness, and some disgust at the way this case has unfolded and at the disposition the court has indicated it is willing to accept," Judge Darigan said. "My greatest regret, my most sincere regret is that this criminal justice system cannot give you the relief you seek, cannot assuage your grief."

The judge added that having a trial would traumatize the families and the community since it would involve viewing the video and photographs from the fire that were "graphic and very difficult" and that "this court, after many years of trial practice, found to be horrifying and gruesome in their graphic detail." The sentences for the Derderians, the judge said, were based on "the crimes to which they pled" and not on "the terrible outcome." Family members of the deceased could make victim impact statements, to talk about how the loss of their loved ones affected their lives, but that testimony would not change the outcome of the case. The plea deals remained as negotiated.

Family members refused to follow the judge's instructions. This was their last day in court, televised live, and they would say what they wanted.

Susan Rezendes, sister-in-law and sister of Ben and Linda Suffoletto, the woman so badly burned that a firefighter prayed for her death, wondered aloud who, among the survivors, had violently trampled her sister and broken her watch in the stampede to save their own lives. She berated the judge and the court for the lack of a trial. "I say shame, shame on the State of Rhode Island."

Diane Mattera, who vandalized the memorial to Great White's guitarist Ty Longley at the nightclub site, scoffed at the idea that justice had been served. The loss of her daughter Tammy was a life sentence for her family. "What about the sentences they gave all of us?" the grieving mother asked, reading from a prepared statement. "Where's our deal? Where's our plea bargain?"

Jay McLaughlin, brother-in-law of victims Mike and Sandy Hoogasian, repeated the widely circulated false story that Jeffrey had saved the cash drawer the night of the fire instead of helping others escape. He said he felt intense "hatred of the sniveling little coward who hid the moneybox in the snow while people were dying in the club." With McLaughlin's outburst, Judge Darigan stopped the proceedings and took the court into recess.

Not everyone berated the judge and the Derderians. Jody King, Michael Derderian's childhood friend and brother of Tracy King, the club bouncer who rescued people from the inferno until he lost his life, agreed with the disposition of the case. "The fire was simply an accident. Like the perfect storm, all things had to come together for this to have worked the way that it did. We must never forget, and we must always remember, the lesson is, with this fire, is to not ever let it happen again. Although many more deserve the share of the blame, these plea agreements are the best thing for all parties concerned, the victims, their families, the jurors, and the witnesses who would have been forced to relive this tragedy as well as the State of Rhode Island as a whole."

Gina felt frustrated as she watched the statements. No one in the courtroom was really listening. Instead there was nonstop commotion in the rows of spectators, upset rumblings about the unfairness of the proceedings. She'd carefully written a prepared statement, but there was no way she was going to share those words now—no one would hear what she was trying to say. She took her notes, folded them, and put them away. If she got a turn to speak, she'd simply speak her mind. Perhaps, maybe then people would listen.

Gina wore a black short-sleeve top. The legal system had decided the suffering of the survivors did not matter, but she wanted everyone to see the burns on her arms. Gina would bear witness for Freddy, but he had always encouraged her stand up for herself, and she would do that, whether or not it strictly followed the rules the court prescribed for the sentencing.

People expected that from her. In many minds, Gina had become the most well-known survivor of the nightclub fire. At nearly every opportunity, she'd shared her story, as she did at the Wang Theatre. It had become her therapy, but also useful for the Station Family Fund, where she'd become a volunteer. When people heard a compelling account of the tragedy, they gave money. Gina would say she had a "big mouth," but her ability to articulately recount the devastation caused by the disaster had made her a fixture in local media, plus it thrust her into the national spotlight, with appearances on network news broadcasts and even the pages of *Rolling Stone* magazine. The attention and money was desperately needed: some of the gravely injured were scraping by, expected to live on as little as a thousand dollars a month of Social Security disability benefits, if they received any government assistance at all.

When it was her turn to take the stand, Gina was calm and respectful, although up front she told the judge how she felt about the light punishment the brothers were receiving and how the legal system had failed to provide transparency and justice.

"Your Honor, no doubt you know how disappointed I am."

No opinions about the plea bargain, she'd been instructed. Only talk about the impact of the loss of Fred. For Gina, Freddy's final moments said everything about the man.

"What I need to tell you now is my experience that night in that club and what Freddy did to save my life." Gina recounted the confrontation with the bouncer who would not let them escape through the stage door due to "club policy," and how she and Fred made it halfway through the club when panic erupted as "the crowd realized that this was real, this was a real fire. This wasn't part of the show. The ceiling was on fire. The last moments that I remember of Freddy was him putting his hand on the middle of my back and just screaming, 'Go!' and just shoving me across the room."

Gina choked up as the memories flashed back. "When I tried to turn around to find him, he was completely gone in a sea of people that were on fire. Their heads were burning. What I now call black rain coming down from the ceiling, it was melting and it was black and toxic. I made it to the front doorway and realizing I wasn't going anywhere. I was body-to-body and shoulder-to-shoulder with people. I got jostled around a little bit more, and my last thoughts were of my children standing in front of me, their faces, and I just prayed to God to let them forgive me for dying in this club, in this nightmare. Let them have a good life and let them forgive their mom for dying in this situation. And I remember hitting the hardwood floors.

"I don't know how I got out of that club that night and whoever my angel was, whoever got me out of there, I am forever grateful. I spent eleven weeks in a medically induced coma at Shriners Hospital in Boston and Mass General. I owe my life to them. They're my second group of angels. My children were told their mother wasn't going to live. I was read my last rites. I hope to God no one's children ever have to hear those words, that their parents are going to not make it because of someone's negligence. This was just a tragedy that should have never happened. There was ways to prevent this, and no one bothered to. But my children have suffered deeply and greatly with counseling. They waited and waited to see if their mom was going to live. They got very lucky I did, but not without forty-five surgeries. And hopefully they're done. I don't really know.

"What you see before you today isn't the same person that laid in that hospital bed. You could see my skull. You could see the bones in my arms. I can cover it up now pretty well I guess, because you can't really see it. You can see the scars on my arms. That's all you'll get to see, because I'm not brave enough to take off the wig that I have to wear to cover the burns on my head and the scarring on my head."

Gina spoke about trying to explain the unexplainable to her children and Fred's son Brandon. Why did this happen? A trial might have provided some answers, but now there would never be a trial. She turned to face Judge Darigan.

"Judge, you're not going to change your mind, but you have done us a great disservice by not allowing us the opportunity of a trial. We were owed that. I have waited three and a half years for this. And it's been ripped out from us.

"This is my life sentence. I have to look at myself every single day with my life sentence. I go to Freddy's grave every week and cry for the life that should have been, that I'll never get."

WHEN THE VICTIMS' families finished their statements Judge Darigan turned to the brothers. "Would the defendants like to make a statement at this time prior to sentencing?"

As Jeffrey walked to the stand he took his carefully folded two-page typed statement from the inside pocket of his charcoal-colored suit jacket. He'd spent hours crafting exactly what he would say. In his career as a television journalist he'd mastered the art of speaking without a script to hundreds of thousands of viewers, but today he planned to read word-for-word. He stared down into the pages, thanked the judge for letting him speak, then cleared his voice with a cough and stretched his jaw in an attempt to fight back emotions.

"I first want to say how very sorry I am for all the heartache resulting from this tragedy," Jeffrey started, his voice stilted, clearly reading. He apologized to the victims and their families, his eyes glued to the pages. "The grief we feel, not just here today but every day for the last three and a half years, is so overwhelming it's hard for us to put it into words."

He talked about the foam, and how he had no idea how deadly it was.

"I take responsibility for believing it was okay when in fact it fueled the fire that consumed the building in approximately three minutes. How I wish we knew then what we know today about that foam." He acknowledged that by not having a criminal trial there would be unanswered questions, but he promised to make himself available "to any agency or civil attorney representing victims of the fire and provide all information as best I can."

"Please know we never ever intended to bring harm to anyone. Through a long list of mistakes, including our own, this tragedy occurred. We're not here to blame others. We want to simply say that for our part we understand your anger, and we know that your pain never stops. We realize the business we own has caused so much heartache and loss. It has our name on it forever. That will never go away. We wanted to say so much for so long, but we were instructed that the legal process did not allow for that until today. I have always wanted to say I will live with the fact that your son . . ."

As the words came out, Jeffrey thought of his own young sons, Max and Jake, and imagined the horror if they'd gone to a party and had never come home.

". . . daughter, father, mother, husband, wife," Jeffrey sputtered through tears, "girlfriend, boyfriend are no longer here, and all the little kids who wish they had their parents back. We also live with the knowledge that so many people have been scarred, both physically and emotionally, and that torment will be with me every day of my life. As you all well know, I was there that terrible night. And the memory of that evening is something I will never forget. It's with me when I go to bed at night. It's with me when I wake up in the morning. I tried, like so many other people that night, to do all I could, but the fire moved so fast. I was scared. I wish I did a better job. I'm not asking you to feel sorry for me at all in any way, I just want you to know that the thoughts on my conscience will never be erased, just like your suffering will never go away."

As Jeffrey spoke Michael bowed his head and wept uncontrollably. He'd tried to hold it together emotionally since the fire, to be strong for the sake of his family, to stand firm against enormous pressure. Now as he watched his little brother break down, Michael was overwhelmed. He knew this moment was coming, but now that it was happening, it hit him with unexpected brute force.

"There are many days when I wish I didn't make it out of that building, because if I didn't maybe some of these families would feel better," Jeffrey said as he cried. "To those families, I'm sorry I did make it out. I know you would have liked it if I had died too. I hear the screams, the broken glass, the terror from that night in my head. The images of people fighting for their lives plays over and over in my head, leaving me to wonder what more I could have done to help that night."

He pledged to help educate others so a similar nightmare would never happen again. As he ended his statement, Jeffrey sobbed between words. "I would never ask for your forgiveness, that would be simply insulting. And no brief statement could represent all that could be said. But please know how truly sorry I am."

Like the rest of the day's proceedings, Jeffrey's statement was carried live on television. As a young journalist he had craved his time in front of the camera, loved the notoriety, and wished for more. That wish had come true, but with a terrible reversal of fortune. Instead of being the TV reporter famous for chasing bad guys down the street with his camera, Jeffrey was now officially the bad guy. Guilty. His statement in court would be the last words he'd speak on the medium he once worshipped: live television news.

Michael wiped the tears from his face with his bare hand as he approached the stand. He also read from a prepared statement, but looked up to address the room, his tone stoic, hoping every word would be heard. He grabbed the thin desk microphone, moved it toward his mouth, and held it firmly in place.

"I just want to say how deeply sorry I am for the role that I played in this tragedy and fully accept as business owners we should have relied, should *not* have relied on other people. And for that, so many families are hurting and I will always be reminded of that. I also want to say I'm sorry for not asking more questions about the deadly and toxic foam that we hung on the walls of our business. We were trying to respond to our neighbors' needs as part of the community. So many times I have looked back and in hindsight wish we had never hung that foam at all, or we never even bought that business. If I had known now what that foam was, we definitely would have done things differently. We would have never, ever knowingly put our patrons, our employees, our family and our friends at risk."

Jeffrey watched his brother from across the room, fighting back tears. Jeffrey wondered if the people in the court were listening to what was being said, or grasped the enormity of what was being explained. Are the victims' families hearing this? Are they taking it to heart?

"I was not at the club that night and cannot even begin to imagine the horror of that night," Michael said as he raised his head and made eye contact with the crowd. "I have viewed all the tapes, photographs, witness statements, and have listened firsthand to accounts of people who survived that fire. We will never forget all of our friends and employees, Steven, Andrea, Tracy, and Dina, who worked so hard for us, and who treated us like we were part of their family. They, too, like many others are innocent victims in all of this. And I realize that nothing I could ever say or do will bring back the person that you love or make your scars go away. And for that, I am sorry. I am always mindful of the more than seventy-five children who lost the love and companionship of one or both of their parents. I will also live with the fact that the passage of time will do nothing to make you feel better."

Michael, like his brother, ended with a promise: "to make sure that all the facts, not just some of them, come out, so everyone can understand what happened that night. We know that that is the least of what you're owed."

Although the brothers knew this day would end the government's prosecution, and there would never be a criminal trial, they both counted on another day in court. Soon there would be a civil case to determine financial damages, and everyone who played a role in the tragedy would be held accountable, not just the few the attorney general's office targeted. The civil case would be broader, and all the evidence would finally be put on display in court, which would hear all sides for the first time, including the brothers' versions of events. When all the facts were known, the public would see that the story presented by the prosecutors and the media, especially the *Providence Journal*, was not the whole truth. The civil trial would provide the answers that the survivors, the victims' families, and the public so sorely needed.

After a recess the court resumed the session and Judge Darigan officially passed sentence. The brothers stood side-by-side, their hands clasped together solemnly at their waists, shoulders forward and eyes staring down, as if at a memorial service. Michael received fifteen years in prison, with eleven years suspended and work release while behind bars, plus three years of probation upon his release. Jeffrey was sentenced to ten years in prison, all years suspended, and five hundred hours of community service, plus three years of probation. There were no gasps, howls of agony, or shouts of injustice from the families in the courtroom, as there were when Daniel Biechele was sentenced. Those proceedings felt like a jab on an open wound. Now the families seemed in shock, resigned. The mood that consumed the room was defeat, of being beaten down by the system yet again.

"Sheriff, you may take custody of the prisoner," the judge said as Michael was handcuffed and led away.

CHAPTER 57

For attorney max Wistow, walking around the warehouse was eerie and troubling. "Very, very depressing," he said. It was a joyless, dreadful place, but desperately needed, and the contents could one day help those hurt by The Station disaster.

Inside the Cranston storage facility was a macabre re-creation. Lawyers representing the fire's victims in civil lawsuits hired experts to take seven hundred pieces of evidence from the scene and rebuild the nightclub. Large pieces like the remnants of the drummer's alcove were there, but also "little odds and ends of things that had belonged to people," Wistow recalled. The items prompted him to remember the images from Brian Butler's Channel 12 news footage that captured the final moments of joy inside the club. "You would see video of people dancing, and drinking, and laughing, literally minutes before they were charred. It's really just horrendous," he said.

Wistow, a native New Yorker who had adopted Rhode Island as his home beginning in the early 1960s but still had traces of his native accent, awoke to the news of the tragedy on the morning after the fire. At that hour there were reports of about twenty-five dead, a number so large that Wistow's first thought was of the devastating impact on such a tiny state. As he followed the news coverage, his instincts kicked in as a longtime attorney who specialized in negligence and personal injury cases, and he worried that the fire scene needed to be preserved, since it likely held clues about exactly what went wrong. "In any kind of accident, especially a fire, you wanna know what happened, and you wanna maintain the scene in as pristine condition as possible, for the purpose of looking backwards in time, to determine what caused it. So to have people traipsing around there, and rearranging things, moving things, taking things away, makes it all the more difficult, if not impossible."

Wistow did not remain an outside observer for long. Within days people injured and families who'd lost loved ones contacted his firm. Lawyers across the state were engaged, and in time the number of plaintiffs grew into hundreds. The legal team would eventually include eight different firms, with pieces of the case preparation workload divided among them.

At the warehouse Wistow looked backward in time as he walked among the ruins. Piecing together the evidence and the case was challenging on several levels. Wistow had to take the attorney general's office to court to get a small sample of the foam from the club. Many of the plaintiffs were children who lost parents, some still in utero at the time of the tragedy, and they required legal guardians. Additionally, the case was not a class action suit. The legal team, in essence, represented hundreds of individuals, which meant court filings for all of those people.

The list of defendants was also a complicating factor. Dozens were pursued, including companies that sold or manufactured the foam, and those involved in promoting the concert. Attorneys even looked at the company that owned Great White's tour bus, since it had played a role in transporting the fireworks across state lines, an illegal act that contributed to the disaster. Every legal theory was considered and researched. The Station fire was considered the worst tragedy to hit the state since the Hurricane of 1938 killed 262 people. The nightclub disaster left hundreds of lives destroyed—physically, emotionally, or financially—by the fire, and the civil suit was seen as a way to provide them with the resources to move forward. The lawyers worked on contingency, asking for no money from victims in advance, and would only be paid a percentage, about one-third, of any monies recovered in the event of a legal victory or settlement. In the meantime, the legal team fronted the costs to mount the case, including re-creating the nightclub, and the bills added up to hundreds of thousands of dollars. The warehouse rent alone cost $2,500 a month.

Beyond the costs of pursuing the civil suit, there was a significant obstacle at the start: Rhode Island law. The legal team needed to seek permission from the state legislature to pursue all the defendants. Local laws limited the ability to hold all the defendants fully financially culpable for any role they might have had in the fire. State lawmakers could pass legislation to override those restrictions in certain circumstances. Wistow said that the state had allowed that leeway in Rhode Island's infamous banking system collapse, and he argued for the same allowance in The Station fire. "We went to the speaker of the house" and the state senate president, Wistow said. "I had a personal meeting with him, explained what the need was."

There were clear cases for civil liability against the Derderians and Great White, Wistow said, but settlements would have been limited to the amount covered by their insurance policies, about $1 million each for the club and the band. The legislature's approval cleared the way to fully pursue others who might be responsible, making it possible to obtain millions more for the fire's victims.

In Wistow's mind the Channel 12 footage was key to the civil case. Brian Butler's footage provided rare insight, but Wistow thought the photojournalist himself also created a wall. Butler "was filming, was backing out and was filming the people coming to get to the exit. And frankly, our view was that, that reporter was delaying the exit, and was probably responsible for a number of deaths," Wistow said.

WPRI-TV 12 and its corporate owner, LIN Broadcasting, were on the defensive since the fire. Jeffrey Derderian was their employee, as well as co-owner of The Station. The video had been viewed around the world, intrinsically linking Channel 12 to a moment of infamy. It was the biggest news story in the TV station's existence, and the news department was placed in the awkward position of covering itself, and some of the tough questions that needed to be asked involved the newsroom's own employees.

Channel 12 also faced withering criticism from within the journalism profession that it had crossed an ethical line by allowing Jeffrey to videotape in his own nightclub. It was blatant self-promotion, detractors argued. Station managers pointed out that the story had not actually aired, and the footage was just to be shot and used generically to cover voiceover, but these explanations were dismissed and the ethical taint lingered.

The station tried to manage both its coverage and other potential fallout by placing strict controls on what was reported on its own broadcasts. Reporters and producers had to run stories about the fire through managers, a layer of scrutiny that was not typical and created a barrier in responding to such a large, constantly breaking news story. A general feeling evolved in the newsroom that covering the fire was a land mine, and any sort of aggressive or enterprising reporting was problematic. In some minds, this meant Channel 12 News, one of the largest news organizations in Rhode Island, was effectively sidelined from uncovering anything about the tragedy that was not distributed by officials or presented at press conferences. At one point during a newscast there was a report about a remark made by Great White's lead singer that called for a graphic to read "Jack Russell Speaks." Instead of putting up a photo of the aging rocker, a picture of a Jack Russell terrier appeared next to the news anchor's head. The incident was seen as emblematic of how weak and detached from actual events the station's coverage had sunk.

The station's owners hired a high-powered attorney. Charles "Chip" Babcock had grabbed the national spotlight in the late 1990s when he successfully defended talk show host Oprah Winfrey for remarks she made about mad cow disease. A group of Texas cattlemen claimed that Winfrey violated the False Disparagement of Perishable Food Products Act when she responded to a description of the practice of feeding processed livestock to cattle by saying the idea "just stopped me cold from eating another burger." Babcock was based in Texas, but had a Rhode Island connection as a graduate of Providence's Brown University.

Babcock pushed back at the suggestion by Wistow and the civil lawsuit lawyers that Brian Butler had added to the tragedy, and instead Babcock claimed the photographer had "saved lives that night."

It was a statement that seemed at odds with the video Butler had shot.

A federal investigation by the National Institute of Standards and Technology and the United States Department of Homeland Security took more than two years to study the fire, determine its causes, and issue its findings. The Channel 12 video was key to the probe, and the footage was analyzed frame by frame. The moment the fire ignited the wall is considered the start of the incident, setting the counter at zero at that first flame for purposes of studying the video.

33 seconds before: Platform lights turned off for beginning of show

14 seconds before: Band first shown on platform

8 seconds before: Pyrotechnic display initiated

0:00:00: First flames on upper wall, left of platform

9 seconds: Flames on upper wall, right of platform.
Pyrotechnic display ends

11 seconds: Band members first notice flames

16 seconds: Flames reach ceiling to right of platform

18 seconds: Camera operator begins to evacuate

25 seconds: Flames touching ceiling on both sides of
platform

30 seconds: Band stops playing, begins to evacuate

32 seconds: Flames extend fully across ceiling above
platform

41 seconds: Fire alarm sounds and strobes begin to flash

54 seconds: Camera operator reaches exit lobby

One minute and 6 seconds: Smoke in outer exit lobby

One minute and 11 seconds: Camera operator exits building

One minute and 26 seconds: Smoke coming out of platform
exit. Flames visible inside at this location

One minute and 30 seconds: Thick black smoke from pool
room windows. Smoke appears to be at floor level inside.
Occupants egressing through windows

One minute and 42 seconds: Camera operator returns to
main exit. People piled up in doorway. Smoke pouring
out above people

Source: NIST report

The footage is continuous, indicating the camera was never turned off, and there is no notation in the federal analysis of Butler helping anyone.

But Butler said in his testimony to the grand jury that when he saw the flames crawling up the wall he immediately sensed that something was wrong. He alerted the person standing next to him. "I don't know who it was but he was in front of me and slightly to the left and he was within arms length, 'cause I, I reached over and tapped him and said look."

Butler "put the camera back behind me and I went out shoulder first," he testified, "and when I turned to leave I noticed a space about that wide, about a foot wide, and it was a little pathway through people. Immediately when I turned I saw the pathway, and I just started taking the pathway, and as I got, the two girls I remember looking at me like should we leave? Yes, time to go. The music's still playing. I went back through the little pathway and got caught in a crowd of people that were already moving toward this front door. The camera's still laying back over my shoulder and I never looked back this way. I just went this way through the crowd until I got up crushed against those people and crushed in from behind and crushed in from other angles where everybody was trying to get through the front door."

Even though it appeared in the video that Butler was doing his job as a photojournalist and recording the mayhem, he said he wasn't constantly looking through the viewfinder, and that the camera happened to capture events as he exited and alerted others to evacuate. Instead of walking backward and recording and blocking people's escape, as Wistow contended, Butler said he was "baby-stepping" out with the rest of the crowd.

As he exited the club Butler said he grabbed and discarded a table that thwarted people from leaving "and basically turned it and pulled it right out the door with me." Butler said he also kicked out a panel from the side of the building to create an opening he thought might help others escape.

If the situation was as Butler described, many of his actions happened behind the camera and not in eyeshot of the lens. For a few seconds the video is shaky near an exterior wall that fits the description of the panel Butler said he kicked out, but it is not completely clear what is happening. An analysis of the video by federal investigators concluded, "The lower portion of one of the bay windows was removed. This appeared to occur as the cameraman passes by on his way to the rear of the structure." If true that Butler was the one who kicked out the panel, it could be argued that he provided a route to safety. But lawyers contended that the video did not support Butler's version of events, and created a discrepancy over what he testified had happened versus what was seen on-screen.

The answer to the question of whether Butler saved lives, was an obstacle that killed people, or acted as a photojournalist doing his job would eventually be worth tens of millions of dollars.

CHAPTER 58

MICHAEL DERDERIAN STUDIED his latest uniform, this one yellow. His hands trembled. The color of the uniform denoted one's place in the prison hierarchy, and yellow was about as bad as it got, the color of F Mod, the worst floor of Minimum Security. This was the section set aside for the building's troubled inmates. In Michael's mind, F stood for fuck-ups.

When he and Jeffrey changed their pleas from not guilty to nolo contendere there was a plan, and Michael agreed for the sake of Jeffrey and the entire family to a relatively short prison term in exchange for finally stopping the relentless persecution and prosecution they'd faced since the fire. Michael would serve most of his time in work release. In essence, he'd only sleep nights at the prison.

Now draped in the yellow garb of failure, Michael realized those plans and negotiations with the prosecutors, the court, and the prison were a scam, a classic bait and switch. There was no work release, his incarceration was extended to what seemed like eternity, and he was pretty sure he was on the cusp of insanity. His hands would not stop shaking.

Michael replayed events in his mind, trying to dissect where things had gone wrong. Maybe there was one last chance to fix things. *No, don't try to fix things*, he scolded himself. That's how he got into so much trouble. Fixing equals disaster here. His nature as a gregarious dealmaker in the outside world, attributes everyone thought would serve him well in prison, were problematic here. He'd made so many enemies in such a short time.

Weeks earlier when they handcuffed him in court, Michael felt good. It might seem strange to see it that way, especially since the judge insisted on a public spectacle and would not allow Michael to quietly remand himself to prison. Still, Michael understood the politics. Judge Francis J. Darigan faced a vicious public backlash for accepting the deals. Outspoken survivors and victims' families believed the fire represented one hundred cases of murder and wanted the Derderians to pay with their lives.

Michael was told what to expect when he surrendered, and at first it was perfectly planned and executed, like following a script. From the cuffs in court he was led to a secure parking lot, surrounded by a SWAT team, placed in an unmarked car, and given police escorts in front and back for the drive to the prison. No one wanted to risk an assassination attempt. At the prison's Intake Center he was fingerprinted, photographed, and strip-searched. At every step he wondered if he would be harassed. For years he'd been depicted in the media as a callous killer, but even during the intrusive cavity search, there was just the one person in the room and his privacy was respected, as much as it could be in a situation like that. *This is going to work as planned*, Michael thought at the time, to his great relief.

After changing into the uniform of the Intake Center, a blue sweat suit with matching slippers, Michael was placed in isolation in the psych ward for the weekend—a small, soundless, and windowless cell with white walls and a gray floor, furnished with a stainless steel combination sink and toilet, without a seat, and a metal-framed bed with a thin mattress, no pillow, sheets, television, or radio. A guard sat on the other side of a glass door and watched. Michael asked for something to read and was told he would not be allowed anything until Monday's move to Minimum Security. For three days he would stare at those walls and ceiling.

This was fine with Michael. His mind raced with so much to unpack from the past weeks and months. It wouldn't be so bad to be alone with his thoughts for a few days. The meals were something to get used to, though. In the psych ward he was not allowed utensils or anything that might cause harm, and everything was served in a brown paper bag and eaten with bare hands, whether it was a cold pancake or government surplus bologna.

His attorney Kathleen Hagerty visited Saturday morning, and Saturday night Michael was allowed a visit from his kids. If not for that, he wouldn't have known the time. By Monday morning he was eager to move in with the other inmates. In the days after the plea bargain was forged and he knew he'd be incarcerated, Michael studied the Minimum Security facility from his car outside the gates and met former prisoners, so he could understand what to expect once inside.

As he lined up with other newbies to be processed and change into a new uniform, this one tan, Michael was ready to get things moving so he could serve his time and get it over with. He'd be out on work release by Wednesday, back in the normal world.

Despite his preparation, Minimum Security wasn't as expected. The place was a free-for-all, and inmates seemed to come and go as they pleased. The building was a former hospital, and each floor was its own module of inmates, called a Mod, designated with the letters A through F. A Mod was the most desirable because inmates there had the most privileges, and it was the floor that housed those with good enough behavior to be allowed out of prison for work release. Michael had not done anything to achieve this special status, but as part of the plea the judge ordered prison officials to immediately place Michael in work release, so he was assigned to A Mod. A guard escorted him to a bottom bunk in a room for twelve men.

"That's yours," the guard said.

An inmate explained how things worked. Michael would have to scrounge up his own pillow, bedding, and other necessities. If he wanted soap, toothpaste, shampoo, et cetera, he'd purchase those supplies from the commissary with money from an account set up by his family. As he got settled, many of his roommates watched *The Price Is Right*, and Michael noted the peculiar television set encased in thick clear plastic, exposing all the electronics so nothing could be hidden inside. Down the hall was an open shower room where men washed together, with no privacy, and a row of toilets tightly spaced together with no dividers, so intimately close that men's knees might touch as they sat next to each other.

Michael could deal with that, he told himself, but the overall vibe of the place already got under his skin. It looked more like a dormitory than a prison. There were no bars, just normal rooms without doors, some with as many as twenty men or as few as two. Despite a façade of normality, A Mod was a surging sea of nonstop obnoxious chatter and antics, reminding him of an *Animal House* college fraternity. There was no escaping it, even at night, and Michael found himself sleep deprived and on edge. It wasn't that anyone had given him trouble, even though the inmates watched the news and knew he was the most infamous new convict to join them. "Hey, Mike," was a fairly constant refrain, acknowledgment that, yes, this was the dude they'd all seen on television, the one from the nightclub fire, the one the media said was the most hated man in Rhode Island, if not the most despised man in America.

Everyone in prison knew about the fire, and the only other person ever imprisoned for the tragedy was just a few doors away. On his first day inside Michael saw Daniel Biechele, Great White's tour manager. Biechele had a place of honor in A Mod, a coveted room for only two inmates, and was treated with deference and respect, plus allowed out each day on work release. Inmates seemed to agree with the perception that Biechele was the working-class patsy who'd taken the fall when others were just as culpable. In addition to accepting guilt for the deaths, the tour manager tried to heal wounds by writing personal letters of apology to each of the victims' families, customizing the notes with details about the lost loved ones, such as their favorite sports team. Some families destroyed Biechele's letters without reading them, infuriated that he would dare to make contact—they saw the letters as an inappropriate effort by the man to make himself feel better for what he'd done. But news of Biechele's letters got out to the news media and the public, and others saw the notes as well intentioned, perhaps even honorable.

When Michael and Biechele made eye contact that first day they silently acknowledged each other with a nod. Michael, however, did not share the benign feelings others had about Biechele. This was the guy who irresponsibly set off fifteen-foot fireballs in a club with twelve-foot ceilings, something any idiot would know not to do, and that stupidity had killed one hundred people and doomed countless others to lifetimes of pain. Admired? What is to be admired about any of that? Michael also despised Biechele for how he lied and claimed that the band had permission to set off the explosives, saying that Michael explicitly gave approval. It wasn't true, like it wasn't true at all the other venues where Great White set off fireworks without permission, but Biechele's allegation helped the state build its case and was widely reported by the news media as fact. Michael wasn't about to forgive Biechele for any of that, and he saw no reason for them to become friends behind bars. Still, Michael noticed how Biechele lived like a relative king in A Mod, with his semiprivate room and days spent outside the prison. Perhaps that was a sign that Michael too would fare well.

Within hours of his arrival in Minimum Security Michael was summoned to see the person in charge of work release. The job arranged and approved weeks ahead of Michael's incarceration was inappropriate. Michael was incredulous—his entire plan for surviving prison depended on that job. The reason for the denial was not clear, so Michael pushed back to strike a new deal, as he always did running businesses. "What does that mean? How do we fix it? What do you need to have happen?" Michael asked.

The decision was final. Michael had to arrange a new job if he wanted to be in the program. He'd been surprised to learn weeks earlier that in many cases prisoners arranged their own work release employment, and that it was not something the corrections department managed directly with businesses. Prisoners were not paid ten cents an hour or some other ridiculously low amount, as was often depicted on television, but a normal wage—the more money the better, since the state collected a percentage of the income for administering the program. Employers of some inmates were also responsible for transportation. Participating in the work release program required a special effort by companies, so Michael knew his job disapproval was a significant setback. Unable to accept this or strike a new deal, he decided instead to see if he could force the prison to his will. He contacted his attorney Hagerty, the former prosecutor, who complained to prison officials that they were interfering with a judge's order.

After the complaint Michael was summoned to a captain's office and told that snitching to an attorney on the outside was not appreciated. That's not how it works around here. Who the hell do you think you are?

Michael told Hagerty about the new confrontation, and by Wednesday, after a new round of heated phone calls and complaints, found himself in the office of an associate warden. Michael walked into the meeting as if it were a business negotiation between rivals of equal footing. He did not address the prison officials as sir or ma'am, and tried to charm and finagle his way back into the work release job. Now there were answers for the denial: the location was too close to his home, and they were worried he'd leave during the day.

"If I go home, I've actually escaped from prison, right?" Michael scoffed. Why would he do a stupid thing like that? He was the one who had agreed to this incarceration.

Later back at A Mod, Michael went to visit the managers of the work release program, and was confronted by a guard. Why had Michael left the section without getting permission first? Michael objected, making the argument that everyone in A Mod seemed to come and go as they pleased.

"I'm booking you," the guard said.

Michael had been in Minimum Security a few days, but knew a booking was an infraction for violating a rule, like receiving a ticket for bad behavior, and had potentially devastating consequences, including revocation of work release privileges. One violation meant his entire plan for surviving prison was scuttled, and he could end up in segregation, one of the punishment units. Michael reached out again to his attorney Hagerty, and there was another scene, this time involving guards, captains, and the warden. The guard who issued the violation to Michael was overruled, and the booking was downgraded to a reprimand. Michael prevailed, but made enemies in the process.

With the help of his family, a new work release job was found, this time at an auto body repair shop not far from the prison. It wasn't the plan, and Michael remained aggravated, but even greater trouble brewed on A Mod. Since the confrontation with the guard, Michael felt scrutinized, as if everyone was waiting for him to violate another prison rule he didn't know. When he first arrived in prison he sensed curiosity as the state's most notorious new criminal, but now he felt he was no longer welcome.

On his second day on work release two officers from the prison walked into the auto body shop.

"We've got to take you back to the prison," one told Michael. "There's been a threat on your life."

Back at Minimum Security, during a meeting with an official from the prison's Special Investigations Unit, Michael was asked about the death threat. Although he didn't know anything, he speculated and offered the name of someone associated with the fire case who might want to cause some harm. Later Michael told another inmate what happened. "You don't tell them that here," the inmate explained. "You just ratted yourself." If there was no evidence of an actual death threat before, now there was a real name on the record, and that would scuttle the work release job.

When that happened Michael again called Hagerty, who again complained. Increasingly upset, Michael confronted a guard about the problems with work release and joked about whether it would be a violation if his wife brought him soup while at work. The guard then reported that he suspected Michael received food from his wife while on work release.

Michael received a booking for that suspected violation, and his work release was revoked. With his plan for prison survival in ruins, more confrontations with guards and prison officials followed, and in one week he was booked about a dozen times, and received punishments that added up to hundreds of days in segregation. That put him in F Mod and a yellow uniform, amid a madhouse of fifty men, many screaming all day and night. Segregation, Michael learned, meant he was kept apart from the general population and had severely limited privileges, but unlike in the movies, it did not mean he was kept alone in a dark windowless cell. Instead there was no escaping the relentless mayhem. It was worse than ever, but Michael didn't have the energy for rage. He sat in a daze when he wasn't weeping, his hands wouldn't stop shaking, and his mind was pushed to its breaking point.

Michael no longer differentiated between reality and delusion. Despondent and irrational, he was taken to the infirmary, where he was visited by his attorney Hagerty. Michael pointed to the air vents above his head and told Hagerty the prison was trying to poison him via invisible fumes.

Instead of psychiatric treatment, Michael received more bookings for erratic behavior, enough violations to have him removed from the building and transferred to Medium Security, an imposing penitentiary on the ACI complex's grounds surrounded by fences and barbed wire. All that Michael had been promised about his incarceration was gone, and he was in a real prison, one with murderers, rapists, pedophiles, and career criminals. His uniform was orange.

He was placed in a segregation cell to serve his punishment. Michael took note of how different Medium Security was from Minimum. For starters, he was in a cell by himself or just one other inmate, rather than surrounded by fifty out-of-control guys. The guards were different too, treating prisoners in a professional, even courteous way. By comparison, Minimum Security felt like a zoo, with Michael as endangered prey, but in Medium there was a level of normalcy. His punishment was eventually reduced to about fifty days in segregation, due to improved behavior, and Michael was allowed to read and have conversations—his mind began to rebuild from the breakdown.

But when Michael was moved out of segregation and sent to a regular cell in Medium Security with the general population, it seemed like the prison had once again conspired for him to fail, or worse.

"Holy shit," his new cellmate said when Michael entered and the door was shut behind him. "Wow. I can't believe you're here. Unbelievable."

Michael could see the man was astonished and rattled, and he looked like a force to be reckoned with. At five feet eight inches tall and two hundred pounds of prison yard weight-lifting muscle, the late-thirties cellmate was physically intimidating, with a mustache, shaved head, white skin, and tattoos. *Built like a brick shithouse*, Michael thought.

"Dude, what's up?" Michael said, trying to be friendly. He scanned the room. It was sparsely furnished with yellow walls, a bunk bed, a toilet-sink combination, and a desk with a chair, all metal and bolted to the cement floor. On the wall was a small photo of a man that looked as if it had been clipped from a newspaper obituary.

"My best friend died in that fire," the man said. The small photo on the wall was of the best friend.

Michael panicked. Had the prison set him up? First he'd been lumped in with Biechele, the man who ruined his life, and now he was in a cell with a guy who lost his best friend in the nightclub fire. This couldn't happen by accident, and Michael wondered if this was where he'd die, or at least be severely beaten.

The cellmate did not think it coincidence either. Rather than a prison conspiracy, however, the man marveled at what he believed was divine intervention. That Michael had been placed in the same room was a message from the afterlife from his best friend, now looking down from heaven and manipulating events back on earth like a marionette with puppet strings. "My friend must have put you here for a reason," the inmate told Michael. "Maybe I needed to have you here."

Michael was stunned. The cellmate's name was Kevin, and he seemed to be having a spiritual epiphany. The message from the dead best friend, Kevin said, meant he was not only destined to meet Michael, the man condemned for killing his friend, but there had to be a mission with the message. Kevin had been in and out of prisons for much of his adult life, and he knew how to survive. If his best friend had somehow matched the two men in that cell, it was because the friend wanted Kevin to share that skill with Michael. "I'm going to take care of you," Kevin said.

He taught Michael how to stay healthy and fit behind bars, another step in Michael's recovery from his mental collapse. Michael was also allowed visitors, and his wife Kristina made sure he had someone at the prison every day.

Michael worked in the kitchen, where he made friends and eventually figured out the prison system. Confrontation and outside lawyers were not the way things worked here, and just like anywhere else in Rhode Island, it was about connections and quid pro quo. *One hand washes the other.* He earned days off his sentence by working the system and complying, not complaining.

His punishment was to be separated from the outside world, but it found him nonetheless. In the prison yard he was approached by an intimidating figure, a brawny black man nearly six and a half feet tall, who towered over Michael's five foot four. "Listen, I know who you are," the man said.

Finally, Michael thought, *this is when I'm taken down.*

The man told Michael he'd grown up in South Providence, in the same impoverished neighborhood as the Derderian family's grocery, and Michael's father Archie had treated the man's family with kindness when he was a boy. The family was so poor that by the end of the month there was often no money for food on the table, but Archie would extend credit to his mother and others in the neighborhood, allowing them to stock up on groceries and pay later. At a time when his family was not extended credit by anyone else, Archie did, and the man had not forgotten that act of compassion.

"There was a time my mother needed milk or something, and your father took care of my mother," the man told Michael. "You let me know if you need anything." Michael would hear the same story from other prisoners, and even from a guard. They admired Archie, and now they would look out for Michael's well-being in prison.

When asked about Michael's treatment in prison, corrections officials declined to be interviewed or allow access to records. "Disciplinary records are not considered Public Information and as such we do not disclose that information," said J. R. Ventura, spokesperson for the State of Rhode Island Department of Corrections, in an email.

CHAPTER 59

NEARLY FOUR YEARS after the fire, Attorney General Patrick Lynch released evidence his prosecutors had gathered in the investigation. When the criminal cases ended in plea bargains, Lynch promised the government would be transparent about its findings. On February 1, 2007, Lynch's office made public more than ten thousand pages of documents, including witness statements and transcripts of previously secret grand jury testimony. There were also videos of the burning building and its charred remains. The disclosures were the first of several.

At first the attorney general's office declined to release the contents of the laptop belonging to Great White's tour manager Dan Biechele. "We fully intend to go through the contents of the laptop and release everything we can possibly release," a spokesman told the *Providence Journal*. "We wish we could include the Biechele laptop information with this, but it's not possible."

Later some of the computer's contents were released, redacted, and the *Journal* reported that Biechele's spreadsheet said "PYRO yes" at The Station. But the story did not include the spreadsheets from the laptop involving other clubs, and how Biechele's notes conflicted with what actually happened with pyrotechnics at those venues, a fact that would have raised doubts about the credibility of the tour manager's records.

The information release happened after Lynch was excoriated for his handling of the case, especially his claim that his prosecutors made the deal with the Derderians without the attorney general's knowledge or permission. To many that seemed absurd, since the case was so high-profile, and the controversy damaged Lynch's political standing. Releasing evidence could fight widespread, if unsubstantiated, feelings that the government was engaged in a cover-up of its botched management of the criminal proceedings.

At the time of the plea bargains, all sides, including the judge, reasoned that the deals spared the survivors and victims' families from hearing and seeing the grisly details. With the release of the documents and evidence, Lynch made much of that disturbing information public anyway.

"I understand that the release of case information—and particularly today's information, which describes and depicts the events of Feb. 20, 2003, in vivid detail—could well be very traumatic and painful, and I want the victims' families and the survivors to know how much I regret any further sorrow this causes them," Lynch said in a statement.

The release of the documents came after considerable legal battles. The *Providence Journal*, joined by other media organizations, asked Lynch to fulfill his post–plea bargain transparency pledge, and petitioned for the release of information from the case, and the attorney general's office had to argue in Superior Court to make public the secret grand jury transcripts. Opponents argued that upcoming civil lawsuit trials would provide a more appropriate venue for the disclosures. The Derderians' lawyers favored releasing the transcripts, but other defense attorneys balked at the idea and accused Lynch of playing politics with the legal system.

"The attorney general's current petition can be characterized as nothing more than an unprecedented course of conduct that is politically expedient to quell public criticism of the office's handling of this case," said a statement from the Rhode Island Association of Criminal Defense Lawyers.

If Lynch thought the document releases would quash the public's concerns over his managing of the case, he was mistaken.

The transcripts revealed Lynch's prosecutors did not use the grand jury as an investigative probe to determine what happened in the fire. Instead, prosecutors appeared to have only one goal in mind: target the Derderians, and to a lesser extent, Great White's tour manager Dan Biechele. Jurors were also steered away from indicting the band's leader, singer Jack Russell, a decision that seemed incredible to the brothers' defense attorney, Kathleen Hagerty. She understood that Russell held an ignition button to set off a second set of fireworks later in the show, and in Hagerty's mind as a former prosecutor, that should have made him at least a co-conspirator.

The documents also revealed that any public officials who might be held responsible for any role in the disaster were shielded. Prosecutors told jurors they could not indict officials, including Denis Larocque, the fire marshal who had repeatedly inspected the nightclub and deemed it safe. Larocque had failed to take notice or test the foam on the club's walls, even after the Derderians testified before West Warwick's town council that they had installed the foam to address noise complaints. In many minds, Larocque had failed to do his job, but prosecutors told the grand jury this was not a crime—he had immunity from criminal prosecution, unless there was evidence of bad faith or malice.

The transcripts showed that jurors pushed back at this idea.

"Whether you agree with it, whether you disagree with it, it's the law of the State of Rhode Island and the law that we must follow," prosecutor Michael Stone told the grand jury.

One grand juror then asked for a definition of "bad faith."

"I think our legal interpretation of *bad faith* would be that the person would have to be, you know, acting and knowing that there's something wrong and ignoring it for some particular purpose and the *maliciously* would be equal to an evil intent almost as in, you know, the maliciousness you need for committing any crime," said Stone. "You really have to find, and there would have to be evidence to show, that the person either knew there was something wrong and ignored it purposely or perhaps was doing it for other reasons, maybe for pecuniary gain or something like that, but as far as acting in good faith and without malice, they're exempt from civil or criminal liability."

"Why have a fire marshal?" the juror asked. "If the fire marshal did nothing, not responsible for anything, why have a fire marshal? There's no use in having a fire marshal."

Prosecutor William Ferland jumped into the discussion. "Sir, you would have to ask the General Assembly that," referring to the state's legislative branch.

A conversation about semantics followed, and the discussion concluded that "malice" meant "evil intent." The idea of "bad faith" led the grand juror to present Ferland with a hypothetical. "Can you give us an example of bad faith? Let me ask you a question. If someone works for the Department of Labor & Training and their job is to go out and see if a list of companies have Workers' Compensation, and they turn in a report that says, yeah, okay ABC Company, I checked them, they got Workers' Comp, when, in fact, they don't have Workers' Comp and the employee was really just not doing their job, would that be considered bad faith or just lousy workmanship?"

"You are asking me to qualify or give you the quality of that act, which I can't do, because that would be my subjective interpretation of that," Ferland responded.

Another grand juror asked prosecutors why the government had laws that protected fire marshals from being held responsible or liable for their work.

"It would be pure speculation on our part to say what the rationale is," said Ferland. "One thing to consider though is that many of these fire inspectors . . . are volunteer firefighters and they perform these duties on behalf of fire districts, local fire districts in a volunteer capacity, so one thing that the General Assembly could have had in mind—and this is mere speculation—is that you're not going to find many people coming out and volunteering their time to conduct such inspections if they know they are going to be liable for negligently performing those tasks."

Larocque was not a volunteer, but a full-time fire marshal paid $49,000 a year at the time of the disaster.

Such details aside, Ferland's explanation for the lack of accountability in the deadliest single building fire in the United States in modern times was illuminating: people would not take government jobs if there was a chance they'd be punished for not doing their work.

Critics would take issue with this interpretation of the law, and a cynical whisper campaign went even further: as a Democrat, Lynch needed the support of unions to be elected, and could not risk running afoul of the powerful firefighters union by targeting a fire marshal.

In the end the once secret grand jury transcripts revealed that prosecutors instructed jurors that they could only indict the Derderians and Biechele. Not Great White's Jack Russell as the leader of the band who planned fireworks for his shows, not fire marshal Denis Larocque for failing to protect the public, and not those who provided the club with flammable foam, instead of the "sound foam" that was ordered.

The trove of documents did not include transcripts of grand jury testimony from Michael or Jeffrey Derderian. They did not testify or present their evidence or version of events to the jurors, since investigators had already publicly stated that they would be indicted. Grand jurors never heard the brothers' side of the story, so that was not included in the information release.

Once again, the survivors and victims' families were denied a full telling of what happened.

Patrick Lynch's office seemed to anticipate that the revelations from the grand jury transcripts would raise new questions about the attorney general's stewardship of the case, so a press release was included with the document disclosures:

"I would also remind the public that although a grand jury has broad powers, it is impaneled for a very narrow purpose: to review the adequacy of evidence, and then, based on the existing laws of the State—not the laws that somebody might wish could be applied to a case—to decide whether or not to indict a suspect. A prosecutor who fails to keep a grand jury focused on its purpose is misusing and even abusing his powers."

It was a spin that seemed to fall flat. Lynch had once been a rising star of the Rhode Island Democratic Party, where his family had pulled strings for generations. He was the Lynch political dynasty's best hope for governor. Instead, Lynch's political fortunes were badly damaged after the nightclub fire, and when he ran for governor in 2014 he dropped out of his own party's primary. Later Lynch went into private practice as an attorney and specialized in advising corporate clients in how to guard against zealous attorney generals, and he worked with e-cigarette maker Juul, which was accused of fostering a deadly national health crisis by promoting vaping, especially to children.

Years later, when asked to reflect on the fire, Lynch remained focused on the Derderian brothers, claiming that the nightclub's noncompliant stage door caused up to 80 percent of the deaths, despite a two-year scientific federal investigation that concluded this was not true, and the Brian Butler Channel 12 video that showed the door wide open. Lynch also said it was unfair to blame fire officials for failing to notice and test the deadly foam during inspections. "The Derderians couldn't have cared less about the people and cared more about their purse at the same time," Lynch said. "They could have bought soundproof, fire-resistant foam, and they instead got, like, packaging foam that you'd ship wine in."

But about the brothers Lynch also said, "There are evil people out there. These aren't bad people. They just made bad decisions, and a lot of it was bad luck."

IT WAS *PROVIDENCE Journal* executive editor Joel Rawson's determination and focus on facts that helped make the documents from the fire public. Under his leadership the newspaper fought to bring the information to light, and with the newspaper business in decline from changes in the media landscape, fewer papers were expending the resources to take on such battles.

About a year later Rawson retired after spending twelve years at the paper's helm, and at age sixty-four he retreated to his home in Rhode Island's countryside. There he was able to spend more time pursuing his lifelong pastime, flying.

There was nothing like the sensation of being up in the air. Rawson was a pilot in the Vietnam War, but these days he flew small planes. One day, a lesson from The Station fire hit home.

"I bought an airplane," Rawson said, a four-seater. "Needed to reupholster it. Said, 'Okay, take the seat that's in there. You have to take the seats out. You take them to the upholstery guy.' I said, 'Burn the foam on that seat.' Boom! Up it went."

The explosion made an impression on the former editor. When Rawson was a spy plane pilot in the Vietnam War he lived in fear of being burned alive while flying missions. Laws, and common sense, had long required that foam in airplanes be flame retardant. Yet in his own plane that was not the case, the seats contained highly flammable foam, like the kind that killed so many at The Station.

"Aviation has regulations on the kind of foam you can put in an airplane. You don't want to be sitting on a seat that's gonna go up like five gallons of gasoline," said Rawson. "So we put in the regulated foam that doesn't burn."

CHAPTER 60

EXPECTATIONS WERE EXTRAORDINARY for the civil lawsuit trial. Money from a court victory was desperately needed for survivors and victims' families, but many also saw the proceedings as a way to finally receive justice in a case where they felt betrayed by the government. In the civil case, witnesses would be under oath, with evidence vetted in court for the first time, and people would learn what really happened at The Station.

Michael and Jeffrey Derderian felt this way. When they pleaded nolo contendere they forfeited their day to defend themselves in court, so at their sentencing the brothers pledged to reveal what they knew in the civil proceedings. They had the evidence to counter the claims of prosecutors, partial truths that were eagerly fed to the public by the *Providence Journal* and other media, but no one had heard the Derderians' side.

But the Derderians, the survivors, and the victims' families had underestimated the role of a key piece of evidence that had been prominent since the first moments of the disaster: the Channel 12 videotape shot by Brian Butler.

WPRI-TV 12 and Butler's attorney, Charles "Chip" Babcock, claimed the photojournalist had "saved lives that night." Butler testified before the grand jury that he had flung his camera over his shoulder and evacuated with the crowd, helping others, and that the camera just happened to record the quickly spreading fire.

Max Wistow and his colleagues from the civil lawsuit team, however, argued that Butler got in the way of people escaping and cost lives because he was actively videotaping and walking backward. Butler himself is not seen in the footage, so his actions weren't captured on video in those crucial first minutes.

The recording, however, did not end there.

Butler's camera never stopped rolling. Several minutes after the fire started, Butler returned to his news vehicle and set the camera on the ground, but did not shut it off, and called his newsroom to report what had occurred.

"Butler set his still-running camera on the ground next to his TV station truck," John Barylick, a lead attorney in the civil case and colleague of Max Wistow, wrote years later in his book *Killer Show*, "where it captured audio of his breathless cell phone call to station management: 'You need a live truck down here right now! There are multiple, multiple deaths in this thing. You've got to get people down here. I'm fine. I got out, and I was one of the first people to get out of this place, but I saw what happened. I have it all on tape from inside.'"

The camera was recording continuously, as it had been since the first sparks, so Butler had not reviewed the footage when he called his newsroom. Butler testified the camera was flung over his back, and that he did not watch events unfold through the viewfinder. If that were true, the attorneys could argue, Butler would have no idea what, if anything, had been recorded. Yet in the call he allegedly said, "I have it all on tape from inside."

It was a revelation that became a turning point in the civil lawsuit.

"At the time of his phone call, Butler had not even stopped, much less reviewed, his tape," Barylick detailed in *Killer Show*. "I argued at settlement mediation that his cell phone call was not the statement of someone who 'did not see what was occurring' behind him, or someone who 'did not look into the camera viewfinder again to film a shot' until he was outside. Rather, his call was the excited utterance of someone who had held his ground inside the club to get the shot. How did Butler know he had 'gotten it all on tape from inside' if he never looked through his viewfinder?"

Eyewitnesses also contradicted Butler's story. "He was definitely filming. We were looking right at him. I heard people telling him to get the hell out of the way, because he was blocking one side of the door," said Todd King, the survivor who went on to lead the Station Family Fund.

Butler would later explain that the truth was more complex than the spin of civil lawsuit attorneys. It was accurate that he saw some of the events unfold through the viewfinder, like when the band started playing and the fireworks exploded, but when the flames started he took his eye away from the camera to see the situation with his own sight. As he "baby-stepped" out the front door the camera was over his shoulder or against his chest as the crowd pushed up against him. *Don't stop rolling, don't get stuck in the crowd,* he remembered saying to himself repeatedly. Butler had been in a pushy crowd situation weeks earlier on a story, and that feeling rushed back. He also felt he needed to remain professional, since judging eyes were always on him as a TV news photographer. *Set a proper example,* he said to himself. "I never looked back to see how it was framed," Butler said, referring to the moments when he was not looking through the viewfinder. While leaving the building, he said he removed a table blocking the exit and kicked out a wall panel to help others escape, then he resumed the role of photojournalist and recorded from outside, capturing the growing inferno, the void of people escaping through the open stage door, and the pile of screaming victims jammed in the front doorway—a scene that would haunt all who saw it, but in the split seconds that Butler captured the image, it did not completely register what he'd recorded. "Oh my God, what did I just see? And it turns all to hell," he later said. Only moments had passed, but as the horror of the disaster started to become apparent—"I heard the smashing glass. I heard the screams"—Butler began to unravel. *Just do your job!* he scolded himself.

It was true he recorded some of the footage looking through the viewfinder as a photojournalist, but that was not the whole story. In the fire's aftermath Butler was condemned by some survivors and victims' families as someone who only cared about getting the story while people died in front of his eyes.

Even without reviewing the tape, Butler knew when he called the TV station that he'd recorded the beginning of the disaster from inside. But the civil lawsuit attorneys saw contradictions in the photojournalist's testimony that could be used to raise credibility questions. The tape did not prove that Butler caused deaths, but questions about the recording made it difficult for Channel 12 to have the case easily dismissed.

"The insurer for Brian Butler and his employer had to realize those defendants were probably not going to get out of the case on summary judgment. And, if summary judgment were denied, the price to settle would go up significantly," Barylick explained. "In light of this, the insurer eventually agreed to settle all claims against Butler and his employer for $30 million. By no means did Butler admit liability. But his settlement was the first chink in the Station defendants' collective armor."

With WPRI-TV 12 settling for such a significant amount, the remaining defendants fell like a house of cards. No one wanted to continue to bear the cost to fight the lawsuit, or to be the sole defendant at a risky jury trial.

By May 2010 the civil case ended with the news that money was finally headed to those hurt by the fire. It had been eighty-seven months since the disaster. Sixty-five defendants—representing those with virtually any connection to the concert or the nightclub and its construction or operation—and their insurance companies settled for a total of $176 million. Foam manufacturers settled for more than $30 million. Anheuser-Busch and its local distributor, McLaughlin & Moran, settled for $21 million. Clear Channel Broadcasting, which owned the radio station that promoted the concert and employed the deejay, Mike "Dr. Metal" Gonsalves, who died in the fire, settled for $22 million. The state of Rhode Island and the town of West Warwick settled for $10 million each.

Denis Larocque, the West Warwick fire inspector who declared the nightclub safe and failed to notice or test the deadly foam as required by the fire code, was not fired by the town. Instead the fire department gave him a raise and Larocque retired early on a disability claim.

Triton Realty, which owned the nightclub building, paid $5 million, and High Tech Special Effects and Luna Tech, the companies that supplied and manufactured the gerbs, settled for $6 million.

Neighbor Barry Warner's employer, American Foam, which sold the highly flammable packing foam to the Derderians to place on the nightclub's walls, even though the brothers ordered "sound foam," settled for $6.3 million. American Foam's insurer paid $5 million of that settlement, and $1.3 million came from the estate of Aram DerManouelian, the company's former president who had died in 2006. At the time of his passing DerManouelian's estate was reportedly valued at $18 million.

Beyond the settlement, American Foam also changed its practices after the fire to include a prominent warning on receipts: "WARNING. POLYURETHANE FOAM IS FLAMMABLE. Do not expose polyurethane foam to radiant heat, open flames, space heaters, burning operations, cigarettes, welding operations, naked lights, matches, electric sparks, or other ignition sources."

The civil case was on behalf of 305 plaintiffs, people harmed or killed at the fire. Duke University School of Law professor Francis E. McGovern, an expert in such matters, determined how the funds were divided using a complex formula that took into account factors like the extent of injuries, the impact of a parent's loss on their children, and victims' earning potential. Survivors who were badly injured tended to receive more than families who lost a loved one. Checks went out to about 550 recipients, since some of the deceased had multiple beneficiaries, with sums ranging from $3,000 to $7 million.

The civil lawsuit legal team, which spent more than a million dollars preparing its case, received $59 million.

Critics would point out that the lawyers collected more money from the nightclub disaster than any of the fire's victims. Some thought the attorneys should have donated their time, or greatly reduced their fees, since thousands of others, including those with very limited means, had given money or resources during the crisis. But lawyers pointed out that the percentage they kept for themselves was in line with industry standards, and had they not prevailed, few victims would have seen any significant compensation.

Even with the settlements, some victims did not get all the money they were allotted. In the seven years it took for the lawsuits to be resolved, some plaintiffs essentially sold their stakes in the lawsuit, leaving them with little once the case was resolved.

"Some people couldn't wait for the outcome," said Wistow. "I'm not blaming them. They just couldn't. They needed money and effectively sold part of their cases." These advance payments on the expected settlements were in the form of loans. "They charge a fantastic rate of interest, varying with the case, but what otherwise would be a usurious rate. We did have a couple of people who insisted on doing it. We fought with them, 'Don't do it.' Wrote them letters. 'Don't do it.' Then finally when the case settles the bulk of the money goes not to them but to the company that had given money to them in the first place."

When monies were distributed it was difficult for some recipients, many from modest working-class backgrounds, to manage amounts of cash so large, and the money was hastily spent, squandering the cushion and support the lawsuit intended to provide. Fearful this might happen with people unaccustomed to dealing with such a windfall, Wistow urged clients to take structured settlements that would disburse the money in regular payments over time, rather than a tempting lump sum. Some refused, and ran through the money quickly.

Even some who received structure settlements sold those annuities for quick cash, ending up with a fraction of what they would have received. "People are people. They have their frailties. We try to do the best we can to protect them, but these are adults. Short of having them committed or putting them under conservatorship, we can't tell them what to do," Wistow said.

Those frailties, for many, involved alcohol and drug abuse in the wake of the tragedy. Brian Loftus and Dave Fravala, who had gone outside to smoke a joint before the fire started and lost ten friends, spent years trying to escape the trauma of that night. "After it was drinking all the time, then it was do a little bit of cocaine and then that turned into smoking crack all the time. We were out of control for a few years," said Fravala. Loftus used his settlement from the civil case for a drug rehabilitation program.

But having the settlement allowed questions about the fire to remain.

Without a public civil trial to put evidence and different sides on display, some felt they'd once again been denied justice and the chance to learn the truth. Michael and Jeffrey Derderian, who had counted on the civil case to present their version of events, never got to share their side in court. The only public telling of the nightclub tragedy would be from the government and media.

"All of these years later, because we never had the opportunity to go to trial with anybody with criminal proceedings, we never had the opportunity to figure out what really went on that night. There's still a lot of unanswered questions about what went wrong that could've been avoided," said Michael Ricardi, the Nichols College student deejay who escaped the flames but lost his friend Jim Gahan that night.

Attorney General Patrick Lynch said what people really sought was closure, and in all his years prosecuting deadly crimes, he'd learned that this was not possible for victims' families—after a case concluded "they go home to a house with a bedroom where their child used to be. And then they go to a gravesite. And it's at that moment they know that he ain't coming back. There's nothing changing it, like the scar on your face," Lynch said. "Closure does not happen."

Attorney Wistow said that people misunderstood the capabilities and limitations of the legal system. Police, lawyers, judges, investigators, and officers of the court have specific jobs to perform, and those roles don't always match the public's expectations.

"People are frustrated. I guess the reason is people don't realize that the lawyers in the criminal case and lawyers in the civil case have these functions, which are not necessarily to put on a play or a documentary of *this is the history of what happened*. Everybody is trying to prove certain things," said Wistow.

People think the legal system is a search for the truth. It is not.

"It's a search for a result."

MEMORIAM

CHAPTER 61

G LOOMY SKIES THREATENED a pall on the day. All morning as work crews raced to finish the stage, arrange chairs, and get the professional-grade sound system absolutely perfect, darkened clouds hovered. Gina Russo looked up into the gray. Not this day.

For Gina, the dedication of the Station Fire Memorial on May 21, 2017, more than fourteen years after that horrific night, was a celebration of the lives lost. These were partiers. Rockers. People out for a good time, enjoying the escape of live rock music. There had already been years of tears, suffering, and fury. Victims like her fiancé Freddy lived life to its fullest, and that would not be lost today.

Rather than a grim tombstone at the site of the nightclub, the memorial was a living tribute: a garden, one designed to become more vibrant and lush as years passed. The ceremony to finally introduce the memorial to the world would be equally full of vitality.

Guests arrived, many wearing T-shirts emblazoned with logos of their favorite bands, revealing arms sleeved with ink. Many of those tattoos remembered loved ones lost in the fire, a personal and permanent tribute. As attendees took their first glimpses of the memorial, a sound system fired up with recorded music, hits the departed would have enjoyed, including AC/DC's "Shoot to Thrill," "Dirty Deeds Done Dirt Cheap," and "Big Balls." Then the rhythm and blues band Steve Smith and the Nakeds, a local favorite since the 1970s, took the stage. "For the first time we're bringing music back to this hallowed ground," one of the band members said before belting out songs like the Rolling Stones' "Miss You," backed up by two saxophones, a trombone, trumpet, two guitars, and a keyboard.

The memorial grove seemed designed for performances. At its focal point was an open-air chapel raised on a knoll, creating a natural amphitheater. In front of the chapel for the dedication were a podium, seating for invited dignitaries, and space for performances. Bricked pathways flowed down from the chapel mound to adjoin large circular memorials scattered around the garden. Surrounding each circle were markers designed to look like concert speakers, the kind typically found at the edge of a stage. The speaker memorials were engraved with the name of a victim, their birthdate, and image. In the center of each circle was a round granite bench for rest and reflection. The benches also had a musical theme, topped with the relief of a 45 rpm record adaptor.

The memorial devastated those seeing the engraved images of their loved ones' faces for the first time, and despite the upbeat soundtrack of the live band, many succumbed to tears. Some, while sobbing, couldn't prevent themselves from instinctively tapping their feet while Steve Smith and the Nakeds did their rendition of "Hot Fun in the Summertime."

The scope of the memorial was larger than anyone first imagined, requiring fundraising of $2 million, plus hundreds of thousands more of in-kind donations of labor and supplies. Plans to transform the nightclub site into a permanent remembrance started soon after the fire, but efforts were thwarted by the bitterness that divided those hurt by the tragedy into different groups. Families of those who perished felt strongly that they alone should create a memorial, and with the rage many felt toward survivors—that they were somehow responsible for the deaths—survivors were excluded from helping. That divisiveness had never relented, even fourteen years later.

The main obstacle for creating the memorial was the land. It remained owned by Raymond Villanova, and until there was an agreement to transfer ownership to the memorial's nonprofit group, planning and fundraising could not move forward. Outspoken victims' families resented Villanova, believing he should have known his building was a deathtrap, and should have donated the land immediately for a memorial. There was talk of taking the property forcibly using questionable legal tactics, like eminent domain. This aggression led to a stalemate, and by 2011 a memorial was still no closer to being built.

After the civil lawsuit settlements were disbursed, and her work on the Station Family Fund ended, Gina and fellow fund board member Victoria Potvin Eagan, an uninjured survivor, went to the Station Fire Memorial Foundation and offered their assistance. They'd helped raise millions for the emergency fund, and Gina shared her experience with the power of storytelling—that the public listened and donated after hearing personal accounts. It took several attempts, and some board members angrily resisted, but eventually the group agreed to change its bylaws to allow help from Gina and other survivors.

Some victims' family members, however, kept attacking Villanova, owner of the nightclub site. On the Dan Yorke show, a local radio program, Gina offered a friendlier approach. "I said, our hope is that he will eventually trust us enough, and we can either buy the land from him, we can figure something out, and we can build a proper memorial," Gina later said. Days later Villanova agreed to donate the land.

Since then it was a dash to plan the memorial and raise the funds, with Gina promoted to lead the foundation. She hired a professional fundraiser, and got some of the biggest names in the state to serve on her board, including former governor Donald Carcieri. The homemade memorials that covered the lot were removed, preserved, and eventually placed in a vault under the garden. Gina quickly realized that managing the many emotions involved would be as challenging as the construction project, and because the bitter divisions between some victims' families and survivors never truly went away, she was taunted and harassed, especially online, for nearly every decision.

Others also turned their backs on the memorial—it was just too painful. Freddy's uncle Rene Valcourt vowed to never set foot at the nightclub site. "No, I can't go over there," Rene said. He also never visited his nephew's grave. Gina understood. How many times had she closed her eyes and wished the past fourteen years never happened?

As the two o'clock start of the ceremony edged closer, more than a thousand attendees filled the garden, its parking lot, and adjacent Cowesett Avenue. The street, normally one of the area's busier roads, was closed for the dedication. A color guard and bagpipers marched in from the street, followed by uniformed firefighters, some carrying shiny axes. The gray clouds suddenly parted, as if on cue, as the service began. People in the crowd whispered to one another, taking note of the abrupt change from dreary to sunny, accompanied by a light comforting breeze.

Gina smiled. She wondered if the beautiful rays of sunshine were a message from Freddy and the other lost loved ones. *Maybe it's their blessing.*

Veteran local television news anchor Gene Valicenti of WJAR-TV 10 took to the podium and welcomed everyone. "This is such a unique little state," he said, "and only we really know what happened here and can maybe tell the story."

As the anchorman spoke, Gina knew there was no "maybe" when it came to telling the story at the memorial. Built into the back of the chapel, under the open-air nave, was the Station Memorial Story Wall, a display of ninety-seven panels, each square telling a piece of the tragedy. Written by Tom Viall, a local volunteer long involved with the design of a memorial, it was a chronological telling of the threads that led to the nightclub fire, such as the dates when Great White became a band and when the Derderian brothers purchased the business. Had just one of these events never occurred, everyone would be alive.

The timeline reached further into the past, noting the Cocoanut Grove nightclub fire in Boston on November 28, 1942, that killed 492 people, a horror that should have led to strict safety requirements like sprinklers in public spaces, but did not.

The timeline traced the moments as Great White's fireworks blasted off, and counted second-by-second the aftermath, an exact retelling made possible because of the footage by Channel 12's Brian Butler. Then the Story Wall progressed to the investigations and finger pointing, the plea bargains and settlements. Pledges to reform the fire safety system in the wake of the disaster were noted, but so were similar deadly fires that occurred, including in Brazil in 2013 where 242 people were killed at the Kiss nightclub when the band Gurizada Fandangueira illegally set off pyrotechnics inside and ignited foam on the walls, and the Ghost Ship warehouse fire in Oakland, California, where thirty-six people died in 2016 during a concert in a dangerous building the city failed to properly inspect.

Also on the Story Wall was the headcount, determined after years of conversations by those present at the inferno: when the fire started there were 355 people inside the nightclub, "245 men and 110 women." The number was below the 404 legal capacity for patrons set by the town of West Warwick, and far less than the 462 that the *Providence Journal* said were present.

After a litany of politicians praised Gina for making the memorial a reality, she stepped up to the microphone, resplendent in a radiant dark teal dress under a short-sleeved white jacket, her arms bare, revealing her scars. A shoulder-length dark brown wig with bangs covered her head, and she donned clear-framed glasses, even though she had no intention of reading word-for-word from a script. She'd always just spoken her mind, and once again she'd talk from the heart.

Around her neck she wore Freddy's cross. Whenever she saw the cross Gina wondered: What if they'd gone back home that night to get that necklace when Freddy noticed it missing? They probably would have arrived back just after Great White started its act. *After the fireworks started.* Freddy would not have died that night, and her whole world would be different.

Gina looked at the enormous crowd. This was her world now. For good and bad, make that lots of bad, fate had brought her to this moment. Even though she'd spoken to so many large audiences in recent years, today felt somehow different.

Her eyes focused on two young men in the audience, her sons Alex and Nick.

"You know, well . . . been a long fourteen years, I can tell you that," Gina said, her voice soft at first. "There are so many people here out in this crowd, but I have to start with my family and my two sons, Alex and Nick. You are my everything. You're my reason for life. Thank you for sticking by me."

There was Steve, too, her husband. They'd married exactly one year after that first date, when she bluntly described her injuries from the fire and he said, "So what. I'm going bald too." She'd healed enough by then to let love back into her life, surprising herself that she was capable after her heart had been broken, first with a bad marriage, and then Freddy's death. Steve walked into her life at the right moment, another salve on her wounds.

Gina scanned the grove and noted the local schoolchildren, one hundred standing next to the memorial speakers. In a few moments the kids would each raise a red rose as the name of the victim on their assigned speaker was read. Gina said she had a message for those children.

"A tragedy happened on this site, but you can rise above anything. That no matter how hard life becomes, think about it, stop, breathe, and just rise above it. Because I promise you, life is really, really good. I learned that fourteen years ago, when I thought I'd never survive this with all the injuries and all the pain," she said. "The fire could have sunk me and I didn't let it."

Gina felt a sensation of release. That's how this speech was different. There was a finality she'd not experienced before. There was no rage in her voice, no hatred for those who caused her so much agony—the ones who killed Freddy. Anger was her constant companion for so many years. She nursed it, and in some ways it provided the edge to survive, even though such poisonous thoughts came with their own terrible cost.

Somehow she'd finally made peace. Creating this place of harmony on the location of so much suffering helped her heal. She'd made a better place for others, and now, perhaps, found one for herself.

"For the families, you deserve this, I hope you feel we've honored your loved ones. We did everything possible, and I know our angels are absolutely shining down on us today," Gina said, looking at the brilliantly sunny skies. "They absolutely are."

GREAT WHITE'S JACK Russell tried to make a donation to the memorial fund, but it was rejected. He scheduled a benefit concert near Los Angeles, but when organizers of the memorial discovered the plan they publicly announced their opposition—many victims' families blamed the lead singer for the fireworks that killed their loved ones.

Russell's fans responded to the snub by posting on blogs that the people who opposed accepting the money should have "been the first to die in the fire."

It was the latest bungled attempt at reconciliation by Russell. It was not the last.

In recent years Russell had also worked with filmmaker David Bellino on a documentary called *The Guest List*. The original conceit was for Bellino to shadow Russell as he sought redemption and forgiveness for the nightclub fire. The penultimate scene was to be a contrived meeting between the aging rocker and one of the worst-injured survivors, and with cameras rolling that burn victim would absolve Russell of any guilty feelings for his role in America's deadliest rock concert.

Gina Russo said she was approached twice over several years to co-star as the burn victim who grants forgiveness. She declined. She did not forgive Russell, and felt Russell had never sincerely apologized for his role in the fire.

Filmmaker Bellino had better luck with Joe Kinan, who was severely disfigured by the fire and received a hand transplant. Bellino was granted permission to document Kinan's inspiring life as a burn survivor for the documentary, including his wedding day, but Kinan said he refused to be in the same room as Russell for the staged forgiveness scene.

Russell, meanwhile, kept touring. He'd become sober, declared bankruptcy multiple times, lived on an aging boat in a marina in Redondo Beach, California, and scratched together a living with gigs at small- to medium-sized clubs, including the Stone Pony in Asbury Park, New Jersey—the same nightclub that publicly vilified Russell and his band for setting off fireworks there without permission days before the Rhode Island fire.

At his shows Russell's face looked wrinkled and weathered, and his belly protruded, but on some nights he could still hit the high notes.

Russell said he had no financial interest in the documentary, but he wasn't above the idea of making money for himself from the nightclub disaster. After he scheduled an in-depth interview to talk about the fire for this book, Russell wanted to know how much he'd be paid. When the answer was zero, he canceled the formal interview.

Dan Biechele, Russell's tour manager who pleaded guilty for installing and igniting the illegal fireworks and went to prison, left the rock touring business and stayed out of the spotlight. He moved to Florida after serving twenty-two months of his prison sentence and went to work in a flooring store.

BRIAN BUTLER, THE Channel 12 photographer who shot the video of the fire, did not attend the dedication, and had only seen the memorial while driving past. He had always thought of himself as a "survivor, not a victim" of the fire, but he was never allowed in the ranks with those who escaped the inferno, and some tarred him as uncaring for videotaping while people died.

"You look back at what you did and didn't do," he said. "*If* is the biggest word in the English language."

Butler remained haunted by the tragedy and wept when remembering that night. He "thanked God for every minute" he has had with his family after not perishing. He said a fire official once told him the nightclub footage has become an important—possibly life-saving—warning about the deadly dangers of fire.

"We don't shoot video, we shoot history," Butler said about his profession. "You never know when history is going to jump up and bite you on the ass."

IN THE PARKING lot of the memorial, back a hundred feet from the stage of dignitaries, Phil Barr stood with his family. His wife Kara and parents Philip and Barbara were by his side, and baby daughter Brooke, just nine months old, sat on Phil's shoulders, her eyes wide open in amazement.

They'd driven down that morning from their 1881 home in historic Concord, Massachusetts. Like Gina, Phil volunteered on the memorial committee and helped Gina raise the funds to build the garden. Dealing with money and business was something Phil was accustomed to in his professional life, working in the world of start-ups, so he knew what Gina had gone through to make this day happen. He was so proud of her. They met in dark times over Christmas presents for Gina's boys, and now she was feted by nearly every dignitary in the state.

As one of the youngest fire survivors, Phil realized that someday he would be among the final witnesses able to recount what happened. "I'm going to be one of the last people carrying the torch for this in forty, fifty, sixty years," he said. On this day Phil was thirty-five.

As he felt Brooke on his shoulders, he wondered if this would become a place of meaning for her. Phil wouldn't tell her about the fire for many years. He cherished her innocence.

Despite the dedication service's cheerful rock music soundtrack, Phil and his family wept. The emotions overpowered, and there was no way to remain his buttoned-down self. As baby Brooke straddled his shoulders, representing life, hope, and potential, Phil knew that her very existence hinged on those few seconds when he somehow summoned the strength to get out of that inferno.

Between the tears, he felt immense gratitude. He scanned the garden and was thankful—thankful that no one had carved one of those engraved speaker memorials with his name and image.

THE TABLE WAS set for four in Jeffrey and Linda Derderian's tidy dining room in their modest Cranston Colonial, with plates of takeout from a local Italian restaurant, including eggplant and chicken parmesan.

"It's baked, not fried," Linda said. There was no pasta.

In the years following the fire, Jeffrey had become obsessed about his health. He'd always been trim and well-kept during his days on television, but many years after his last live report on local TV news he was in the best shape of his life, the result of a daily gym routine and strict diet of lean proteins and whole foods. Jeffrey worked for a health and nutrition product company, a job he took with longtime close family friends in the wake of the tragedy that morphed into a new career, but it wasn't his profession that drove him to be fit. He stayed healthy for his family. In the crushing aftermath of the disaster—when so many succumbed to despair, demons, and drugs—Jeffrey found the strength to endure whenever he thought of Linda and their twin sons, Max and Jake. Jeffrey and Linda's efforts to give their boys a normal childhood and shield them from the devastation of the fire until they were old enough to understand had worked. Max and Jake grew up to be accomplished young men, one an athlete and one a dancer while in college.

Jeffrey had survived because of them, and for them, but good health was not a birthright. He'd seen his mother die from heart disease, and cardiac problems claimed his father Archie and his middle brother Robert in recent years. So with laser focus Jeffrey ate healthily and exercised. He wanted to be around for an active role in his family's future.

It was the same motivation that long ago convinced him to leave Channel 7 in Boston, move back to smaller-market television in Rhode Island, and invest in a side business to support his family. That venture had been The Station.

Michael Derderian sat at the far end of the dinner table, alone. His marriage to Kristina, which endured the blistering government and media persecution and Michael's thirty-three months in prison, did not endure.

Due to his conflicts at the prison, Michael was not incarcerated for just the eighteen months some had expected, and ended up spending nearly a year longer behind bars than Great White's tour manager Dan Biechele. Upon his release Michael was skeptical when told how long it would take to fully acclimate back into society after prison—a month of adjustment for every month spent behind bars. That's ridiculous, he thought, but it was true. It took time for him to feel as comfortable with the world as he was before his incarceration, and the experience altered him in a way that would never allow him to feel completely normal.

Somehow, though, he was as close as ever with his son Alec and daughter Ashley. Their constant visits and calls while Michael was jailed tethered him back to the normal world, making prison bearable. He was so proud of them—Ashley was now a labor room nurse, and Alec followed Michael's career path into the financial services business.

After his release Michael tried to become the entrepreneur he was before the fire, at first dabbling with small projects, like selling water heaters. He bought and renovated a small house near the airport. Eventually he worked his way back into financial services, and kept his mind sharp by keeping up with trends in the stock market and other investments.

Kristina was there for Michael's journey back into free society, just like when she stood by him at the time of the disaster. Sharp and organized, Kristina managed the overwhelming number of legal documents, maintaining a communion with the details that created a powerful insight—she knew the brothers could never get a fair trial and was an important voice in the decision to take the bedeviling "buy one, set one free" plea bargain. "We have a bad choice and a worse choice," she had said.

Then came prison and release. Michael and Kristina's marriage had been through the crucible, and when life eventually became mundane, there seemed little in common. A counselor told Michael the split was "inevitable."

The fourth place at the dinner table was for someone the brothers once pledged they'd never welcome into their lives.

A journalist.

Jeffrey had once craved to be a famous television reporter, and the infamy of the fire had indeed made him a household name, yet seeing his profession from the other side left him disgusted. But the nightclub disaster never completely left the headlines and remained the deadliest single building fire in modern American history, and the nation's deadliest rock concert—even a gunman's massacre at a concert in Las Vegas in 2017 had nearly half as many victims as The Station.

Without trials, criminal or civil, the Derderians never publicly gave their version of events, so most of the known details were from the government and media. In that telling of events, the brothers were unrepentant villains who'd avoided being fully punished. Remarkably, despite this drumbeat, many Rhode Islanders seemed to feel differently. Fifteen years later the Derderians still maintained that neither they nor their families were ever mistreated, threatened, or assaulted, even when emotions were at their highest.

The public somehow understood there was more to the story—more than the government had shared. So the lynch mob envisioned by the press—encouraged by stunts like publishing the brothers' home addresses in the newspaper—never materialized. The Derderians stayed in Rhode Island and never ran away. They didn't have to.

The only time the brothers felt their families directly threatened came on the eve of the fire's tenth anniversary in 2013, when Tracy Breton, a reporter for the *Providence Journal*, asked the Derderians to grant their first interviews. The request went to the brothers' attorney, Kathleen Hagerty, who thought of it as an innocuous "where are they now?" anniversary story. But in the request Breton mentioned Michael's and Jeffrey's children in a way that Jeffrey, as a former journalist, interpreted as suggesting that Breton might write about the children, who had nothing to do with the disaster and who were never the focus of news coverage, if the brothers refused the *Journal's* interview request.

Breton would later deny that she employed such a tactic to pressure the Derderians into an interview, and called the allegation "ridiculous."

"Anyone who knows me and my reporting techniques knows I would never try to extort an interview from anybody," Breton wrote in an email.

Whatever the intentions, Jeffrey was upset—he had used many strategies to entice subjects into interviews when he was a reporter, but they never involved someone's children. The brothers stood firm and declined the interview request, and no story about the children was published, but the incident further cemented the Derderians' disgust for the press, and especially the *Providence Journal*.

Since 2012, however, the Derderians had started to open up and begun to tell their version of events to another journalist. They'd promised at their sentencing to reveal all during the civil case, but that never happened with the settlement, so this would be the way for them to finally tell their story. Over the course of several years they submitted to countless hours of interviews, reliving the details over and over, answering every question. In time they provided previously unseen materials that had been produced for their defense, including documents that offered a different depiction of events than those offered by the government, attorneys, and the media.

At the dining room table in Cranston over the healthy Italian fare, they were asked for the umpteenth time to review details for what would become a book about The Station fire. Picking at old wounds was painful and frustrating, but the brothers determined that it was time for them to be heard.

It would not bring anyone back. It would not end suffering. It would not change their guilt—they had always felt responsible. If they had not bought that nightclub, if they had not booked that band—the "what ifs" never went away.

But they knew the story was more than just the tale of victims and villains that had been depicted.

The Derderians were not naïve. Some would never believe anything they said, and nothing would change those minds. The *Journal*, of course, would probably attack them, and speaking out after so many years would surely lead to speculation:

Did they want absolution? Impossible. They couldn't even give that to themselves.

Was this a scheme to make money? They did not and would not receive any compensation for telling their story.

Maybe, though, by providing new pieces for the first time they could help those who still searched for answers.

And for everyone else, the Derderians thought, it would be a lesson about how the system really works.

IN MEMORY OF

Louis S. Alves, 33, Lincoln, RI

Kevin P. Anderson, 37, Warwick, RI

Stacie Jude Angers, 29, Worcester, MA

Christopher G. Arruda, 30, Coventry, RI

Eugene Michael Avilez, 21, Burlington, MA

Tina Marie Ayer, 33, Warwick, RI

Karla Jean Bagtaz, 41, Stoughton, MA

Mary Helen Baker, 32, Fall River, MA

Thomas A. Barnett, 38, West Greenwich, RI

Laureen M. DeSantis Beauchaine, 35, West Warwick, RI

Steven Thomas Blom, 40, Cranston, RI

William Christopher Bonardi III, 36, Smithfield, RI

Richard A. Cabral Jr., 37, Attleboro, MA

Kristine M. Carbone, 38, Taunton, MA

William W. Cartwright, 42, Pawtucket, RI

Edward Bradley Corbett III, 31, West Warwick, RI

Michael E. Cordier, 31, North Kingstown, RI

Alfred Carmano Crisostomi, 38, Warwick, RI

Robert J. Croteau, 31, Fall River, MA

Lisa M. D'Andrea, 42, Barrington, RI

Matthew P. Darby, 36, Coventry, RI

Dina Ann DeMaio, 30, West Warwick, RI

Albert Anthony DiBonaventura, 18, North Dighton, MA

Christina Ann DiRienzo, 37, Plymouth, MA

Kevin J. Dunn, 37, Attleboro, MA

Lori K. Durante, 40, West Warwick, RI

Edward Everett Ervanian, 29, Cranston, RI

Thomas J. Fleming, 30, Worcester, MA

Rachael K. Florio-DePietro, 31, Coventry, RI

Mark Adam Fontaine, 22, Johnston, RI

Daniel John Frederickson, 37, Coventry, RI

Michael A. Fresolo, 32, Millbury, MA

James C. Gahan IV, 21, Falmouth, MA

Melvin A. Gerfin Jr., 46, Groton, CT

Laura L. Paterno Gillett, 32, Pembroke, MA

Charline Elaine Gingras-Fick, 35, Central Falls, RI

Michael J. Gonsalves, 40, Warwick, RI

James F. Gooden Jr., 37, Cranston, RI

Derek J. Gray, 22, Dracut, MA

Scott "Skott" C. Greene, 35, Warwick, RI

Scott Griffith, 41, West Warwick, RI

Pamela Ann Gruttadauria, 33, Johnston, RI

Bonnie L. Hamelin, 27, Warwick, RI

Jude Henault, 37, Lisbon, CT

Andrew R. Hoban, 22, North Kingstown, RI

Abbie L. Hoisington, 28, Cranston, RI

Michael B. Hoogasian, 31, Cranston, RI

Sandy Hoogasian, 27, Cranston, RI

Carlton L. Howorth III, 39, Norton, MA

Eric James Hyer, 32, Scituate, RI

Derek Brian Johnson, 32, West Warwick, RI

Lisa Jean Kelly, 27, Swansea, MA

Tracy F. King, 39, Warwick, RI

Michael Joseph Kulz, 30, Warwick, RI

Keith R. Lapierre, 29, Worcester, MA

Dale Latulippe, 46, Carver, MA

Stephen M. Libera, 21, North Kingstown, RI

John Michael Longiaru, 23, Johnston, RI

Ty Longley, 31, Northridge, CA

Andrea Louise Jacavone Mancini, 28, Johnston, RI

Keith A. Mancini, 34, Cranston, RI

Steven Mancini, 39, Johnston, RI

Judith I. Manzo, 37, North Providence, RI

Thomas Frank Marion Jr., 27, Westport, MA

Jeffrey W. Martin, 33, Melrose, MA

Tammy Mattera-Housa, 29, Warwick, RI

Kristen Leigh McQuarrie, 37, Ledyard, CT

Thomas P. Medeiros, 40, Coventry, RI

Samuel J. Miceli Jr., 37, Lisbon, CT

Donna M. Mitchell, 29, Fall River, MA

Leigh Ann Moreau, 21, Providence, RI

Ryan M. Morin, 31, Allston, MA

Jason R. Morton, 38, West Greenwich, RI

Elizabeth Ellen Mosczynski, 33, Millbury, MA

Katherine M. O'Donnell, 26, Seekonk, MA

Nicholas Philip O'Neill, 18, Pawtucket, RI

Matthew James Pickett, 33, Bellingham, MA

Carlos Louis Pimentel Sr., 38, West Warwick, RI

Christopher Prouty, 34, Pawtucket, RI

Jeffrey Scott Rader, 32, Danville, CA

Theresa Lynn Serpa Rakoski, 30, Taunton, MA

Robert L. Reisner III, 29, Coventry, RI

Walter Rich, 40, Attleboro, MA

Donald Roderiques, 46, Mashpee, MA

Tracey Romanoff, 33, Coventry, RI

Joseph E. Rossi, 35, Pawtucket, RI

Bridget Marie Sanetti, 25, Coventry, RI

Rebecca Elinor Shaw, 24, Warwick, RI

Mitchell C. Shubert, 39, Newberry, FL

Dennis Joseph Smith, 36, Pawtucket, RI

Victor Lowell Stark, 39, Mashpee, MA

Benjamin Joseph Suffoletto Jr., 43, Chepachet, RI

Linda Dee Suffoletto, 43, Chepachet, RI

Shawn Patrick Sweet, 28, Pembroke, MA

Jason R. Sylvester, 25, Coventry, RI

Sarah Jane Telgarsky, 37, Plainfield, CT

Kelly Lynn Vieira, 40, West Warwick, RI

Kevin R. Washburn, 30, Franklin, MA

Everett Thomas Woodmansee III, 30, Charlestown, RI

Robert Daniel Young, 29, Taunton, MA

AFTERWORD

I'd always thought of Jeffrey Derderian as confident, cocky even. But as he sat beside me in the passenger seat of a rented sedan, Jeffrey was anxious and upset. A flash of anger swept over his face as he felt betrayed—by me.

"I'm not going back there," he said, wounded. "I won't go there."

There was the site of The Station nightclub where one hundred people lost their lives when the rock band Great White ignited fireworks and turned the low-slung roadhouse into an inferno.

After Jeffrey left the fire scene, splattered in blood, not his own, he never returned to the club and vowed he never would. His feelings about the site had caused a gnawing inner turmoil. Jeffrey did not want to relive the horrors of that night, but he also longed to pay his respects to the dead. Still, he knew his presence there would upset so many grieving loved ones. He couldn't risk that.

As we sat in the rental car more than a decade later he wondered if I intended to drive him there against his will anyway, a stunt a journalist might contrive to see what would happen if Jeffrey was forced to confront his past.

We'd spent the day reconstructing events that led up to the fire, the last "normal" day of Jeffrey's life. I was deep into the research for this book, but Jeffrey had never spoken in detail about that night. Not to investigators, not to his brother Michael, and not to his wife Linda. Jeffrey even held back when he sought help from a counselor who treated him for post-traumatic stress disorder. Jeffrey couldn't trust the counselor, and besides, many of his memories were blacked out, as if his brain said: you don't want to know these things.

We'd gotten to this day after several years of talking about the fire in bits and pieces. Jeffrey and I had worked together in television news in Providence twenty years earlier. I was his boss, and he was one of my reporters. I'd long ago moved to work in California, six and a half years before the fire, and Jeffrey took a job at a top station in Boston. My family still lived in Rhode Island, so I'd be back at least once a year and would sometimes connect with my former news colleagues, and occasionally I'd see Jeffrey. During one of these visits I was surprised and skeptical when he invited me to see a small nightclub he'd purchased with his brother Michael. Television news was notoriously demanding, and Jeffrey was at the apex of his game in that profession, so I couldn't understand how he was also in the nightclub business.

During that visit in 2000 I was even less impressed in person. I immediately recognized The Station as a former Papa Brillo's restaurant, a defunct regional Italian chain. I noted that the carpet and furnishings were worn, and the air was stale with cigarette smoke and beer. It was a typical blue-collar dive, the type my working-class relatives frequented. If not for my journeyman's work in journalism, I might be on one of those haggard stools.

Jeffrey was excited about his new venture, and with the old dynamic of our lingering boss/employee relationship, I peppered him with questions about the nightclub business. I was impressed with how much he knew, even though he'd just started. Yes, it was challenging to continue working in Boston television and take this on, he admitted, but for the sake of his young twin sons he felt that he needed ways to support his family that didn't completely rely on the unstable world of TV news.

I didn't give the nightclub another thought until three years later when from California I watched nonstop coverage of the disaster unfold on CNN. I still had colleagues working in Rhode Island media, so I was able to learn that Jeffrey had survived. I was astonished to see the tragedy had been captured on video, something exceedingly rare in those days before smartphone cameras.

The sensation of that footage soon took an unthinkable turn as authorities declared that dozens had perished. Then the local police chief made an announcement: Jeffrey would face criminal charges.

I'd watched the video of Great White setting off fireworks that started the blaze. Jeffrey didn't light those flames, and yet while the ruins still smoldered—before an investigation—the government decided he would take the fall. Having previously covered the news in Rhode Island for the better part of a decade, I knew how corrupt the government was, from the lowest-level civil servants to the highest offices in the land. My career in journalism had taken off after I developed an investigative series in Rhode Island called "You Paid for It" that exposed government malfeasance, and after leaving the station I became a consultant to television stations across the nation who wanted to do the same type of reporting.

Police proclaiming guilt before an investigation seemed a textbook definition of corruption. I wondered if Jeffrey was targeted because he was one of the reporters on those "You Paid for It" stories that excoriated and embarrassed so many officials, the same government that now held his fate in their hands.

All I could do, however, was wonder. I didn't cover daily news anymore, so I watched from afar. The death toll hit one hundred, unimaginable suffering for a state so small. The government said Jeffrey and his brother Michael had cut corners and run the club in a reckless, dangerous way that ultimately caused so many deaths. Jeffrey's colleagues in the news media turned on him nearly as quickly as the government, with one telling me, "Well, you know how *those* people are," referring to the fact that the Derderians were of Armenian heritage and stereotyped as greedy.

Plea bargains and settlements followed. There were no trials, criminal or civil, so evidence was never vetted or challenged in open court. The public mostly heard only the government's version of events—a government with a long track record of corruption. That's a troubling lack of transparency for the deaths of one hundred people.

As the story faded from daily news headlines, it remained in my thoughts. The reported facts never added up, and when I spoke to people in Rhode Island it seemed that nearly everyone had lingering doubts about whether they'd been told the whole truth. I reconnected with Jeffrey in 2011 and began asking questions. I didn't know if there was more to be reported on the fire, and I had no expectation of writing a book, but I learned that the Derderian brothers had never publicly shared their version of events. Many journalists had tried to get them to talk, including some of the biggest names in the national news media, but Michael and Jeffrey felt the media was complicit in a rush to judgment, had reported on them unfairly and inaccurately, and made it impossible for them to get an impartial trial.

I hoped that Jeffrey and Michael would talk to me and give me access to the evidence they'd amassed for their defense. I thought the fact that Jeffrey and I once worked together, albeit decades ago, would be in my favor. But Jeffrey had worked with dozens, if not hundreds, of other journalists during his career, and he had not spoken to any of them. Complicating matters was our time together at Channel 6, when I was Jeffrey's boss and somewhat infamous for being intense and demanding. Mistakes, especially by reporters, were not tolerated on my watch, and there were some whose careers ended during my tenure. Jeffrey certainly knew how I felt about paying attention to details, and the fire had labeled him as one of the worst screw-ups in history, so he would get no break when it came to accountability. There are much nicer and kinder people in the world of journalism than me.

But I had one significant advantage over my peers when approaching the Derderian brothers: I never covered the story when it happened. I had left Rhode Island to work elsewhere years before the fire. The only reporting I did on the tragedy happened one year later when Jeffrey forwarded to me a statement from the brothers that noted the anniversary. The Derderians had grown to despise the news media so much that they issued the statement by email to me, a journalist in California not affiliated with any news organization, to break the news to the Associated Press.

That was the only "reporting" I'd done on the tragedy, so I had a relatively clean slate and fresh eyes, in addition to a certain level of familiarity because I knew Jeffrey, or at least thought I did. Still, there were many conversations before Jeffrey introduced me to his brother Michael. Later the brothers and their families agreed to their first interviews. In time I was granted access to information and documents never made public before. Over the course of years I kept asking questions and returned to Rhode Island to cull through records and conduct additional interviews. Then I read documents that seemed to contradict and undermine the state's entire rationale for pursuing criminal charges in the case.

"Who has seen these besides me?" I asked.

"We got them from the attorney general's office," Michael Derderian said, explaining that the documents were given to the defense before scheduled trials as part of discovery—trials that never happened.

I requested all the files related to the case from the attorney general's office and was given 170 gigabytes of data that seemed designed to overwhelm, rather than inform—many of the files could not be opened without advanced technical expertise. Then when I spoke to the two veteran local journalists about inconsistencies in the fire investigation I was warned, "It sounds like you're planning to write something. You better not."

These were signs that the nagging doubts I'd had all those years ago were warranted. My reporting progressed to other sources and interviews, resulting in additional insight about the tragedy that had not been reported. The Derderians were not the only ones who had remained silent. Barry Warner, another of the so-called villains, gave me his first candid and lengthy interview, with no questions off limits, and offered additional details never reported about one of the central causes of the fire. Brian Butler, the videographer who captured the tragedy on camera, had never been interviewed at length by a journalist until this book. Attorney general Patrick Lynch and West Warwick police chief Peter Brousseau also did interviews, offering new information. I interviewed *Today* anchor Matt Lauer in the aftermath of his firing by NBC News, at a time when he otherwise was not doing on-the-record interviews with journalists, but he put no restrictions on our discussion and remembered details about his encounter with the Derderians that led to a more accurate portrayal of events.

One of the quandaries of reporting about the nightclub disaster is that while nearly everyone I encountered felt they had not been told the entire story about the fire, many of those same people do not want to hear from key figures in the tragedy. For some, anything the Derderians say will be condemned, simply because they spoke. Many survivors and victims' families want the brothers to remain silent for their rest of their lives, and they bitterly resent any attempt by the Derderians to tell their side of the story. In 2010 Michael and Jeffrey were booked to appear at a safety seminar in Pennsylvania and speak publicly for the first time about what happened at their club, but once news of their appearance became public the fallout led to concerns that the event would be disrupted or cause an upset, so the brothers were forced to cancel.

Barry Warner, Patrick Lynch, and Brian Butler are also disliked by a fair number of people, and it will bring no joy to some that they too have been given the opportunity to speak in this book. For others, any interview with Matt Lauer could be seen as an affront that somehow normalizes him, post scandal.

These reactions are understandable. Anger and grief are processed in so many different ways. Fire survivor Gina Russo, who knows too much about rage, often said to me that we should never judge people for how they process grief. And while many might still be outraged by Attorney General Lynch for his handling of the criminal case, he shared one of the undeniable truths of this tragedy: there is no closure.

So there will be people who will be upset that the Derderians and others are depicted in this book, including many of the same people who have long demanded to get all sides of this terrible story. How can they object to getting something they say they want? People and their emotions are complex.

Journalism, however, is not so complicated. Basic journalism requires making an effort to include all sides of a story. This sometimes means being accused of giving controversial subjects a platform. One of my goals with this book was to make sure the main subjects were each depicted as human beings, and to try to capture their points of view, but this should not be interpreted to mean that I endorse everything they've done, said, or believe.

As a person in the news business, I'm compelled, no doubt to a flaw, to focus on new information. The word "news" is three-quarters composed of the word "new." New information in this book could raise doubts about whether justice was served, and if adequate steps have been taken to prevent similar disasters.

But the most important part of this tragedy was not new or news at all: one hundred people perished and hundreds more were hurt in the fire, with ripple effects that impacted thousands. Every soul deserved to have his or her story told. The confines of a book don't allow me to tell them all, so I've selected a few to represent the many. If I did not speak to someone in the course of reporting this book, it was not due to lack of interest or compassion.

It is worth noting that the Derderian brothers had two conditions for telling their side for the first time. First, they wanted it known that they will make no money from this book or any subsequent treatment. They won't, and neither will anyone else in these pages. Great White's lead singer Jack Russell asked me for money in exchange for speaking. After I told him he would receive none, he canceled our formal interview.

Second, the brothers wanted it clear that they're not telling their side of the story to receive pity, sympathy, or be exonerated. Had there been trials, they would have shared their side in court, rather than with a reporter.

The reporter/subject relationship can be intense. Nearly every interview I conducted led to tears. That so many people shared their most intimate thoughts indicates how deeply they felt this story needed to be told. I'm grateful for their trust.

That brings me back to Jeffrey's anxiousness the day in that rental car when he thought I might betray his trust and drive him to the scene of the fire, even though he'd told me that he'd never been back there and would never return.

I needed Jeffrey to remember. We'd spoken for hours in many interviews, but when we'd get to that terrible night, he'd withdraw. It was blocked, he said.

I'd heard stories, mostly rumors, about what Jeffrey did that night. Some involved heroics, but others recounted despicable behavior that would later be part of a campaign to demonize him. It was documented that Jeffrey was splattered in blood, but it wasn't his own. He was uninjured, physically. Even though the police declared Jeffrey a criminal suspect the night of the fire, investigators failed to gather the basic physical evidence of his clothing, so there was never testing done to determine the source of the blood.

Getting Jeffrey to recount details of that night was key to trying to determine exactly what he'd done when disaster struck. I'd consulted with a psychotherapist about how to get repressed memories to emerge. He warned me that memories were suppressed by the subconscious for good reasons, and that direct provocation, like taking him to the scene of the fire, even if Jeffrey wanted to go, could be harmful. I could, however, do prompts and details might emerge on their own, if his mind was ready.

With his consent we retraced Jeffrey's steps from earlier on that fateful day. It was his fifth day at his new job, and the first few story assignments had fallen through. He was dispatched to cover breaking news, the robbery of a bodega in crime-ridden South Providence, near the former location of a small grocery store Jeffrey's family once owned, where his father Archie and brother Robert were shot and wounded many years earlier. What would later turn out to be the worst day of Jeffrey's life started close to the spot where both his father and brother were nearly murdered.

From there we drove to WPRI-TV Channel 12 in East Providence and parked in the street just outside the television station's tall security fence. Jeffrey's mind went back to that moment, in the newsroom. Then he recalled going home to his house in suburban Cranston, and how he changed out of his television news uniform, a suit, and into his night-club uniform, a blue denim shirt with the club logo embroidered on the front. It was the same shirt that would be splattered in blood.

"I'm not going back there," he said. "I won't go there."

I assured him we would not drive to the scene of the fire.

But as we sat in the car he began describing explosions, screams, and desperate people stacked atop each other trying to escape. It happened so fast, he said, yet each second inside the mayhem lasted an eternity—*does that make sense?* As thick smoke submerged the nightclub into complete darkness, followed by an inferno and gruesome chaos, the same words kept playing over and over in his head.

Then, finally, he remembered those words.

This isn't good.

ACKNOWLEDGMENTS

There's no way I could attempt to tell the tragedy of The Station nightclub fire by myself.

This book would not be possible without the reporting of journalists at the time of the inferno. Television news coverage was especially important in capturing vivid accounts from survivors and rescue workers at the scene. I'm indebted to those who did this challenging work. Some reporters remain traumatized by what they witnessed—yet another ripple effect of the disaster.

Citizen journalists were also incredibly helpful, although many can't be credited by name because they're anonymous. In 2003 the Internet was not the instant repository of constantly streaming information that it has become. Television news, for example, was not always archived and easily accessible after it aired, and some newspapers restrict access to their coverage from that time by charging exorbitant per-story fees.

But strong feelings that this tragedy should not be forgotten have led to an online uprising. Unedited raw footage of key moments, including court proceedings, press conferences, and even Brian Butler's infamous video are all viewable online, uploaded by digital vigilantes. Sometimes the copyright holders of the footage will demand that the videos be removed, but then the clips surface elsewhere. Print stories that otherwise would be difficult to find buried in inaccessible archives are also copied and pasted onto defiant message boards.

There's clearly a passionate desire by these anonymous posters to make sure the facts of this disaster are witnessed, often unedited and not subject to the news media's filter. This material was incredibly valuable.

Librarians are the nation's unsung heroes as the keepers of information for all, and key details of this story would have been lost without access to unalterable materials, like microfilm.

Before embarking on my own project I read every book I could find that touched on this case, many of them from small presses or self published. One I found especially interesting was *Killer Show* by John Barylick, a top lawyer in the fire's civil proceedings. I've attempted to include a summarized retelling of the civil suit as part of the broader story, and I've quoted Mr. Barylick as much as I could, but for those who want to know more about the legal machinations that led to such a huge settlement, *Killer Show* is recommended reading.

I'm fortunate to be part of a supportive community of journalists and authors. The Castro Writers' Cooperative workspace in San Francisco and co-founder Shana Mahaffey have provided ears for chewing, a quiet retreat, and an incubator for this project.

My dear friend and newspaper colleague Jill Agostino was the first to kick the tires on the full manuscript. Her expertise and passion have made me a better writer for more than a decade, and she worked her magic yet again.

Feedback from early readers was also an important part of my process, and this book greatly benefited from their views. They include Mary Jo Fortuna, Mark Fortuna, Jesse Lampf, Alex Olshonsky, and Dawn Whipp.

Attorneys for both the prosecution and defense were often helpful and generous with their time and expertise. They include William Ferland, Randall White, Tom Briody, and Kathleen Hagerty.

Therapist James Wright advised me on how to interview people who suffer from post-traumatic stress disorder without further hurting them. M. Charles Bakst, the revered *Providence Journal* political columnist, provided timely wisdom.

Thank you to publisher Thomas Dunne and editor Stephen S. Power for their enduring belief in this project, and their patience. Both of my parents, Helen and Owen James, passed away while I wrote this book, and it is dedicated to them. Tom and Stephen gave me as much time as I needed to step back from my work at these times of family crisis, and that compassion made this a better book. A reckless driver killed my mother and police and prosecutors mishandled the investigation and criminal case. I found myself dealing with some of the same issues and feelings that victims' families faced in the nightclub fire. I'd always felt deep sympathy for the fire's victims and their loved ones, but the experience with my mother's killing made me relate to The Station tragedy in a more intimate way.

Also at Thomas Dunne Books and St. Martin's Press, thank you to William Vogan for keeping me on task, and to Bill Warhop and Jennifer Fernandez for their astute copyedits. Henry Kaufman's legal review was sharp and savvy. Thank you to Anna deVries for stepping in to shepherd this project when the pandemic struck.

I am so grateful to have Michael Carlisle, the extraordinary literary agent, in my corner. More than simply an advocate, his careful thoughts shaped and cajoled this project to bring it to reality. He's my champion and now a cherished friend.

I would not have connected with Michael without the support of Julia Flynn Siler and Frances Dinkelspiel, two accomplished journalists and authors whom I have long adored, both professionally and personally.

Two people from my days in television news in Providence opened doors that made this book possible. Former anchor and news executive Dave Layman, one of the first to hire me at the beginning of my journalism career, provided introductions and provocative discussions.

Former anchor Pamela Watts, one of my first colleagues in TV, has been there at each step, from initial ruminations through publication. Several of the subjects in this book probably would not have spoken to me if not for Pamela's urging. She's one of Rhode Island's most beloved personalities, and I've always marveled to be part of her universe.

When you work on a project over the course of nearly ten years, you often find yourself sussing out the details with those around you, and that must be maddening—for them. In journalism there's an old saying that "no one wants to see how the sausage is made." My husband, Jerry Cain, has endured years of passionate discourse and debates, and yet he has remained a constant source of support. This book could not have been written without his encouragement and love.

SOURCE MATERIAL, REFERENCES, AND SELECT BIBLIOGRAPHY

Most of the sources of information in this book are attributed or cited directly within the story. Below is more information about those, plus a listing of additional sources considered in the writing of this book, categorized by chapter in the order they appear. These citations reference materials that were primary story elements or secondary sources that helped confirm or add details to the statements of interview subjects.

FEBRUARY 20, 2003, 11:07 P.M.

"The Ins and Outs of Breath Holding: Simple Demonstrations of Complex Respiratory Physiology," *Advances in Physiology Education*, September 2015; plus consensus from Quora responses to the question.

"Do You Read Fast Enough to Be Successful?" by Brett Nelson, *Forbes*, June 4, 2012.

"The Star-Spangled Banner: A Traditional Version," April 15, 2011, Clifton Ware, tenor. YouTube: https://youtu.be/kijnCp-4n64.

Report by National Institute of Standards and Technology (NIST) and National Construction Safety Team (NCST) Act, June 30, 2005, page 232.

NIST Re-creation of "The Station Night Club fire" without sprinklers. June 7, 2009, via YouTube. https://youtu.be/IxiOXZ55hbc.

Interview with Jeffrey Derderian.

Grand jury testimony of Kevin Beese, August 20, 2003, page 93.

Grand jury testimony of John Arpin, April 24, 2003, page 35.

Grand jury testimony of Raul Vargas, October 29, 2003, page 20.

Videotape of Brian Butler, WPRI-TV 12, February 20, 2003.

CHAPTER 1

Interview with Gina Russo.

HipDates.com website confirmed by Internet Archive Wayback Machine.

Interviews with Rene Valcourt, Eileen Valcourt, the younger Rene Valcourt, and Brian Valcourt.

CHAPTER 2

Interviews with Jeffrey Derderian, Michael Derderian, Linda Derderian, and Kristina Derderian.

Firsthand observations of television news market and trends, and Derderian employment from author, who worked at WLNE-TV from 1988 to 1996.

The Night the Music Ended: The Station Nightclub: March 2000–February 2003, by Marilyn Bellemore, Merry Blacksmith Press, 2012.

Station Nightclub Insurance Inspection Report 2001.

Interview with Pamela Watts.

"The Station's Manager Stunned by 'Witch-hunt,'" by Paul Edward Parker, *Providence Journal*, March 3, 2003.

"The Station Nightclub Fire" raw footage, including pre-performance generic b-roll shots, videotaped by Brian Butler, WPRI-TV, February 20, 2003. YouTube: https://youtu.be /1wWktCkulV0.

Interview with Brian Butler.

CHAPTER 3

Interview with Phil Barr.

Interview with Evan Clabots.

"Williams Wraps Up Third-Straight Men's Swimming & Diving Title," Wesleyan Sports Information, February 27, 2005.

CHAPTER 4

Interviews with Linda Derderian and Jeffrey Derderian.

"Fire Ruins Home but Family OK," Rhode Island newspaper clip.

CHAPTER 5

Interview with Gina Russo.

Video by Brian Butler, WPRI-TV, confirms location of Crisostomi and Russo near stage.

Location interior description confirmed by NIST report, plus interviews with Jeffrey Derderian and Michael Derderian.

CHAPTER 6

Interviews with Phil Barr and Evan Clabots.

Extinguisher headed toward flames confirmed by Jeffrey Derderian and multiple eyewitness accounts in grand jury testimony.

Video by Brian Butler, WPRI-TV, confirms alarm, smoke, and other details. February 20, 2003.

Cross-referenced with NIST investigation to confirm timing of events.

CHAPTER 7

Interview with Gina Russo.

Video by Brian Butler, WPRI-TV, confirms details.

Multiple grand jury witness accounts confirm stampede and frenzy.

Additional details confirmed by Jeffrey Derderian, in interview.

NIST investigation confirms smoke, fire, and death details.

Crisostomi physical attributes confirmed by relatives and photographs.

CHAPTER 8

Interview with Jeffrey Derderian.

Grand jury testimony of Charlene Prudomme, June 8, 2003, page 26.

Video by Brian Butler, WPRI-TV, confirms presence of Daniel Biechele.

Interview with Michael Derderian.

"Survival Stories: Analyzing Witness Statements to Create a New Look at the Station Nightclub Fire," by Fred Durso Jr., National Fire Protection Association, *NFPA Journal*, January/February 2011.

CHAPTER 9

Interview with Phil Barr.

Timing of firefighters' arrival confirmed by Brian Butler WPRI-TV videotape and dispatch reports.

CHAPTER 10

Interviews with Brian Loftus and Dave Fravala.

Jessica Studley information confirmed by police investigation interview conducted and recorded on August 23, 2004.

Joe Barber interview with Connie Chung on CNN, conducted February 24, 2003. Via broadcast transcript: http://www.cnn.com/TRANSCRIPTS/0302/24/cct.00.html.

"95 Die as Fire Engulfs Nightclub in 3 Minutes," by David Rennie, *The Telegraph*, February 22, 2003.

"Christopher Arruda, Coventry, R.I." by Mark Pothier, *Boston Globe*, 2003.

CHAPTER 11

"Triangle Shirtwaist Factory Fire," History.com, December 2, 2009.

"The Triangle Shirtwaist Fire—March 25, 1911; A Tragedy That Echoes Still," by Tamar Lewin, *New York Times*, March 23, 1986 (with original archive coverage).

"The Station Documentary—Part 3," directed by David Bettencourt, funding from Tyco Fire Products. April 2013. YouTube: https://www.youtube.com/watch?v=asHW7tw2rAk.

"In Memoriam: Victims of the Station Nightclub Fire," by Shaun Towne, WPRI-TV, May 19, 2017.

"Linda Dee Suffoletto," *Providence Journal*, March 20, 2003.

Susan Rezendes victim impact statement. WPRI-TV, September 29, 2006. YouTube: https://youtu.be/wfnEVIgC4ho.

"Hospitalized Victim of Great White Club Fire Dies," by Joe DAngelo, MTV News, February 28, 2003.

"Blaze Left Orphans with Uncertain Future," by Patricia Wen, *Boston Globe*, February 15, 2004.

CHAPTER 12

Interviews with Phil Barr and Evan Clabots.

CHAPTER 13

Interview with Barry Warner.

Grand jury testimony of Barry Warner, June 4, 2003.

The Night the Music Ended: The Station Nightclub: March 2000–February 2003, by Marilyn Bellemore, Merry Blacksmith Press, 2012.

"Deception, Missteps Sparked a Tragedy," by Stephen Kurkjian, Stephanie Ebbert, and Thomas Farragher, *Boston Globe*, February 14, 2013.

"The Station Nightclub Disaster—Shattered Dreams—Family Fights, Violence and Fire Mark the History of the Station Nightclub Site," by Zachary R. Mider, *Providence Journal*, July 13, 2003.

Grand jury testimony of Howard Julian, April 4, 2003.

Interviews with Michael and Jeffrey Derderian.

Chief Peter Brousseau memo dated May 12, 2000, original obtained by the *Providence Journal*.

Grand jury testimony of Aram DerManouelian, president of American Foam, June 4, 2003.

Video by Brian Butler, WPRI-TV, confirms fire details and victims in shocked state.

CHAPTER 14

Interviews with Linda Derderian, Jeffrey Derderian, and Michael Derderian.

"West Warwick Station Fire Part 1," video shot by Greg Best, February 20, 2003. YouTube: https://youtu.be/TwdEXZmK9lk.

Interview with Greg Best.

CHAPTER 15

"Dateline NBC," NBC News, correspondent Stone Phillips, producers Steve Cheng and Bob Gilmartin, February 2003. YouTube: https://youtu.be/TwdEXZmK9lk.

Grand jury testimony of Raul Vargas, October 29, 2003.

"The Station Nightclub Disaster—Firefighters Can't Stop Hearing the Screams," *Providence Journal*, by Amanda Milkovits, February 23, 2003.

CHAPTER 16

Interview with Gina Russo, based on her memories and health records.

"Shriners Hospitals Waive Age Limit For Rhode Island Nightclub Fire Victims," hospital press release, February 2003.

CHAPTER 17

Interview with Phil Barr.

CHAPTER 18

Interview with Rhode Island governor Donald Carcieri.

Florida's Hutchinson Island visitor's guide.

"Carcieri for Governor" campaign literature, circa 2002.

CHAPTER 19

"Saving Burn Victims," by Douglas Hand, *New York Times*, September 15, 1985.

Interview with Gina Russo, based on memories and medical records.

From the Ashes, Surviving the Station Nightclub Fire, by Gina Russo and Paul Lonardo, Infinity Publishing, 2012.

CHAPTER 20

Interview with Rhode Island governor Donald Carcieri.

Video by Brian Butler, WPRI-TV, February 20, 2003.

Killer Show: The Station Nightclub Fire, America's Deadliest Rock Concert, by John Barylick, ForeEdge, 2015.

Interview with Brian Butler.

Interview with Jeffrey Derderian.

"Remains from 14 Victims from EgyptAir Crash Identified," United Press International, March 7, 2000.

"Death in the Nightclubs: The Overview; Finger-Pointing in Club Fire and Task of Naming the Dead," by Sarah Kershaw and Lydia Polgreen, *New York Times*, February 23, 2003.

"Station Nightclub Disaster—State Releases Names of 21 More Victims," by Mark Arsenault, *Providence Journal*, February 27, 2003.

CHAPTER 21

Interviews with Michael Derderian, Kathleen Hagerty, and Kristina Derderian.

"R.I. Nightclub Blaze Kills at Least 96," Associated Press and FoxNews.com, February 22, 2003.

CHAPTER 22

"Roger Williams: Founding Providence," National Park Service.

State of Rhode Island, RI.gov, history portal.

"Rhode Island to Vote on Name Change," by Alex Nunes, National Public Radio, *All Things Considered*, October 27, 2010.

Rhode Island Name Change Amendment, Question 1 (November 2, 2010), Ballotpedia results: No 77.9%, Yes 22.1%.

Rhode Island: Roger Williams National Memorial, National Park Service.

"Samuel Slater: American Hero or British Traitor?" by Neil Heath, BBC News, September 22, 2011.

"Newport Mansions: See How the Elite Lived During Newport's Gilded Age," *Newport Discovery Guide*, 2018.

"Rhode Island State House," visitor's guide.

"Birth of the Mob," National Museum of Organized Crime and Law Enforcement.

Notes from Kathleen M. Hagerty, former Rhode Island special assistant attorney general.

"Is Rhode Island the Most Corrupt State?" by Nancy Cook, *Newsweek*, March 10, 2010.

Institutional Rhode Island news and government knowledge by author, due to work as journalist and news executive in the market from 1988 to 1996.

"Rhode Island's Image: Down in the Dumps," by Christopher B. Daly, *Washington Post*, December 24, 1995.

"Personal Trials Grow in Rhode Island Bank Crisis," *New York Times*, February 25, 1991.

"Buddy Cianci, Flamboyant and Roguish Mayor Who Rebuilt Providence, Dies at 74," by Adam Bernstein, *Washington Post*, January 28, 2016.

"Buddy Cianci Enjoys Life Without 'the Squirrel,'" interview by Andrew Goldman, *New York Times*, June 21, 2013.

"Providence—An Eventful Night for Cianci—The Former Mayor 'Sort of Fell Back' During a Portrait Unveiling at City Hall, but Was Later Well Enough to Attend Dinner in His Honor," by Donita Naylor, *Providence Journal*, November 20, 2015.

"Cianci Memorials—City Hall, Federal Hill Goodbyes—People Pay Their Respects to Former Mayor for 2nd Day at His Wake and in the Neighborhood He Knew So Well," by Alisha A. Pina, *Providence Journal*, February 8, 2016.

"RI News," by Tom Mooney, John Hill, and Jacqueline Tempera, *Providence Journal*, February 9, 2016.

"The Mayor Who Never Stopped Finally Did," by Mark Patinkin, *Providence Journal*, February 9, 2016.

CHAPTER 23

Interviews with Rene Valcourt, Eileen Valcourt, Brian Valcourt, and the younger Rene Valcourt.

Videotape of Brian Butler, WPRI-TV, February 20, 2003.

CHAPTER 24

Interview with Jody King.

Late Show with David Letterman, CBS, "1993—Stupid Human Tricks with Tracy King." YouTube: https://youtu.be/7GiTJUtq7aY.

"Tracy King—East Greenwich, R.I.," by Emily Sweeney, *Boston Globe*, 2003.

"No Relief from Night of Horror," by staff reporters, *Cranston Herald*, February 25, 2003.

"Compassion's King: Rising from the Ashes of the Station Nightclub Fire," by Leslie Schultz, *New Paris Press*, Sunday, December 1, 2013.

"Tracy F. King, 39; a Master at Balancing," *Providence Journal*, March 20, 2003.

"Station Fire, 15 Years Later: He Lost His Brother but Didn't Blame Derderians," by Amanda Milkovits, *Providence Journal*, February 18, 2018.

Interview with Gina Russo.

CHAPTER 25

Interviews with Michael Derderian, Jeff Derderian, Linda Derderian, and Kathleen Hagerty.

West Warwick police chief Peter Brousseau letter to Town Clerk, dated January 15, 2003.

Videotape and transcript of Derderian press conference, February 22, 2003.

"Death in the Nightclubs: The Overview; Finger-Pointing in Club Fire and Task of Naming the Dead," by Sarah Kershaw and Lydia Polgreen, *New York Times*, February 23, 2003.

"Death Toll Rises in Rhode Island Nightclub Fire," by Pam Belluck, *New York Times*, February 21, 2003.

"Fire in a Nightclub: The Trigger; Fireworks Like Those Used Are a Common Part of Events," by Andy Newman, *New York Times*, February 22, 2003.

"A Special Report—The Station Nightclub Disaster—96 Die in Nightclub Fire; Families Hunt for Missing," by Jennifer Levitz and Zachary R. Mider, *Providence Journal*, February 22, 2003.

Interview with Rhode Island attorney general Patrick Lynch.

"About the Office" duties description for Rhode Island attorney general, state government official website.

Videotape, "Press Conference Station Nightclub Fire Patrick Lynch, Attorney General Rhode Island," WJAR-TV. YouTube: https://youtu.be/RRmRd-bCvPg.

Written statements from the fire scene of Jeffrey Derderian, February 21, 2003, obtained from Rhode Island attorney general via records request.

West Warwick police detective George Winman report, filed 9:01 a.m., February 21, 2003, altered on July 9, 2003, without included explanation of changes.

Comments attached to news stories, posting and from various message boards related to the fire.

CHAPTER 26

"2.10.13: 'It Went Up Like a Match. Everything Went Black,'" by Karen Lee Ziner, *Providence Journal*, February 10, 2013.

"Great White's Frontman Has Struggled with Fire's Legacy," by Milton J. Valencia and Mark Arsenault, *Boston Globe*, February 17, 2013.

"Great White's Jack Russell Is a Hair-Metal Survivor," by Jason Roche, *LA Weekly*, June 5, 2014.

"Once Bitten . . . Twice the Bands? The Jack Russell Story—as Told by Jack," by Ted "Hollywood" Heckman, *Thunder Roads Ohio*, 2018.

Recording Academy website confirmation of nomination.

"Great White—Once Bitten Twice Shy (Official Video)." YouTube: https://youtu.be/Bz61YQWZuYU.

"Station Club Survivor Pens Book as Tribute to Late Friend," by Richard Duckett, *Worcester Telegram & Gazette*, August 29, 2015.

"12 Years Later: Unanswered Questions Remain About Station Fire," by Patrick Sargent, GoLocalProv, February 20, 2015.

Just A Thought Away: A True Story of Friendship, Tragedy, And The Will to Carry On, as Told by a Station Nightclub Survivor, by Michael Ricardi, CreateSpace Independent Publishing Platform, 2015.

"Fire in a Nightclub Overview; 96 Dead in Fire Ignited by Band at Rhode Island Club," by Pam Belluck, *New York Times,* February 22, 2003.

"Jack Russell Great White's Side of the Story with Sally Steele," March 25, 2012. YouTube: https://youtu.be/5sHdKLplFW0.

"Ceremonies Welcome New Locations for ARC, WNRC," Nichols College website, April 22, 2013.

CHAPTER 27

Interview with Joel Rawson.

Videotape of Brian Butler, WPRI-TV, February 20, 2003.

"2.10.13: 'It Went Up Like a Match. Everything Went Black,'" by Karen Lee Ziner, *Providence Journal,* February 10, 2013.

Interview with Karen Ziner.

"Belo in $1.5 Billion Deal For Providence Journal Co.," by Iver Peterson, *New York Times,* September 27, 1996.

Institutional knowledge of author of television business from work as corporate news media consultant at JBA, Inc., beginning 1997.

CHAPTER 28

Report by National Institute of Standards and Technology (NIST) and National Construction Safety Team (NCST) Act, June 30, 2005, page 81.

"Fire in a Nightclub: The Trigger; Fireworks Like Those Used Are a Common Part of Events," by Andy Newman, *New York Times,* February 22, 2003.

Report by National Institute of Standards and Technology (NIST) and National Construction Safety Team (NCST) Act, June 30, 2005. Appendix F, page 151.

"Series of Errors Sealed Crowd's Fate," by Stephen Kurkjian, Stephanie Ebbert, and Thomas Farragher, *Boston Globe,* February 15, 2013.

Great White tour manager Daniel Biechele interview with prosecutors, March 3, 2003, page 84.

Letters to Biechele from fireworks companies obtained by lawyers for the Derderian brothers.

Grand jury testimony of Scott Vieira, March 26, 2003, page 86.

"The Station Nightclub Disaster—The Station's Manager Stunned by 'Witch-hunt,'" by Paul Edward Parker, *Providence Journal,* March 1, 2003.

Grand jury testimony of Julie Mellini, March 17, 2003.

"The Station Nightclub Disaster—Stage Manager: Pyrotechnics Not Unusual at Club," by Paul Edward Parker and Liz Anderson, *Providence Journal,* February 26, 2003.

Grand jury testimony of David Stone, April 4, 2003.

"The Station Nightclub Disaster—Station Documents Revealed—Fire Inspector Says He Focused on Illegal Door, Not on Foam," by Paul Edward Parker, Tracy Breton, and Edward Fitzpatrick, *Providence Journal*, November 30, 2006.

"The Station Disaster—'His Being Distracted Cost . . . Lives,'" by Edward Fitzpatrick, *Providence Journal*, December 1, 2006.

CHAPTER 29

Interview with Donald Carcieri.

Interview with Joel Rawson.

"The Station Nightclub Disaster—Officials Inspect over 500 Facilities in Statewide Spree," by Mark Arsenault and Tom Mooney, *Providence Journal*, March 14, 2003.

"Obituaries published Feb. 26," *Sun Chronicle*, February 26, 2003.

CHAPTER 30

Interviews with Rene Valcourt, Eileen Valcourt, Brian Valcourt, the younger Rene Valcourt, and Gina Russo.

"Alfred Carmino Crisostomi," Find A Grave, website.

Interment.net—Cemetery Records Online.

CHAPTER 31

"The Fire After," by Lynne Duke, *Washington Post*, March 8, 2003.

"Fire in a Nightclub: The Town; An Emptiness Made Crueler By Closeness," by Dan Barry and Sarah Kershaw, *New York Times*, February 22, 2003.

"Death in the Nightclubs: The Overview; Finger-Pointing in Club Fire and Task of Naming the Dead," by Sarah Kershaw and Lydia Polgreen, *New York Times*, February 23, 2003.

"Death Toll Rises in Rhode Island Nightclub Fire," by Pam Belluck, *New York Times*, February 21, 2003.

Interviews with Jeffrey Derderian and Michael Derderian.

"Rhode Island Fire: Scrutiny of Club Owners Too Tame," by Bob Steele, Poynter Institute, February 22, 2003.

"R.I. TV Station Faces Ethics Questions," by David Bauder, Associated Press Television Writer, Tuesday, February 25, 2003.

"A Special Report—The Station Nightclub Disaster—A Long History, but Few Problems," by Scott Mayerowitz, February 22, 2003.

"Where The Journal News Went Wrong in Publishing Names, Addresses of Gun Owners," by Al Tompkins, Poynter Institute, December 27, 2012.

"Restriction on Publishing Officials' Home Addresses Blocked on First Amendment Grounds," by Eugene Volokh, The Volokh Conspiracy, *Washington Post*, February 28, 2017.

CHAPTER 32

Videotape of Brian Butler, WPRI-TV, February 20, 2003.

"Foam on Club's Walls Was Decorative Packaging," by Paul von Zielbauer, *New York Times*, March 1, 2003.

"Flashover and Backdraft: A Primer," by Thomas Stone, *Fire Engineering*, March 1, 2005.

"Fire Hazards Of Polyurethane Foam," Klausbruckner and Associates, November 3, 2014.

Report by National Institute of Standards and Technology (NIST) and National Construction Safety Team (NCST) Act, June 30, 2005.

"Reporter's Guide: All About Fire," National Fire Protection Association.

Interview with Bureau of Alcohol, Tobacco, Firearms and Explosives expert.

"Bin Laden Didn't Expect New York Towers to Fall," by Toby Harnden, *The Telegraph*, December 10, 2001.

"Devastation in Three Minutes; 96 Dead, 190 Hurt in R.I. Concert Fire," by Eric Lenkowitz, *New York Post*, February 22, 2003

Killer Show: The Station Nightclub Fire, America's Deadliest Rock Concert, by John Barylick, ForeEdge, 2015, page 208.

"Effects of Toxic Gases Emitted by Burning Electrical Insulation," Electrical Contractor, April 2000.

"OSHA Hazard Information Bulletins Fire Hazard of Polyurethane and Other Organic Foam Insulation Aboard Ships and in Construction," United States Department of Labor, May 10, 1989.

Grand jury testimony of Howard Julian, April 4, 2003.

"Band Literally Burns Up the Fine Line," by Ellen Nigon, *The Journal*, February 24, 2003.

CHAPTER 33

Interviews with Phil Barr and Evan Clabots.

Emails from Barr Family to Bates College community, featured in "Junior Injured in Rhode Island Fire Recovering at Home," by Bates News, 2003.

CHAPTER 34

"Foam on Club's Walls Was Decorative Packaging," by Paul von Zielbauer, *New York Times*, March 1, 2003.

"Burn Incidence and Treatment in the United States: 2016," American Burn Association.

"History of Burns: The Past, Present and the Future," by Kwang Chear Lee, Kavita Joory, and Naiem S. Moiemen, *Burns & Trauma*, October 25, 2014.

Interview with Joe Kinan.

"The Survivor: Joe Kinan," Massachusetts General Hospital, 2012.

"How Joe Kinan Found Love After Nearly Dying in The Station Nightclub," by Nicole Weisensee Egan, *People* magazine, October 20, 2014.

"Survivor of Rhode Island Station Nightclub Fire Rebuilds His Life 14 Years Later," by Jason Duaine Hahn, *People* magazine, August 10, 2017.

"Joy After Tragedy," by Nicole Weisensee Egan, *People* magazine via Phoenix Society, October 27, 2014.

"Joe Kinan's Hand Transplant Helps Him and Donor's Family Move Forward," by Tracy Breton, *Providence Journal*, February 17, 2013.

CHAPTER 35

Interview with Gina Russo.

CHAPTER 36

Interviews with Joel Rawson, Mark Arsenault, and Donald Carcieri.

"Up in Flames," *60 Minutes II*, correspondent Scott Pelley, producers Janet Klein, Paul Gallagher, and Shawn Efran, March 2003.

"After Burn," *Dateline*, NBC, correspondent Victoria Corderi, producer Lindsey K. Schwartz, 2003.

"Losing the Beat: The Ability of Out-of-Town Papers to Offer Better Early Coverage of The Station Fire Shows How the Providence Journal Has Become a Less Surefooted Institution," by Ian Donnis, *Providence Phoenix*, May 3, 2003.

"The Station: Two brothers and a legacy of death," by W. Zachary Malinowski, *Providence Journal*, April 20, 2003 (Note: this story did not exist in the newspaper's digital archives. It was located and confirmed via microfilm images stored by the Rhode Island Public Library system).

Analysis of *Providence Journal* digital archives and microfilm image captures of printed newspapers, 2003 (Note: microfilm revealed a slightly higher number of stories featuring the Derderians, due to missing articles in the newspaper's digital archives).

"A Special Report—The Station Nightclub Disaster—A Long History, but Few Problems," by Scott Mayerowitz, February 22, 2003.

Videotape, "Press Conference Station Nightclub Fire Patrick Lynch, Attorney General Rhode Island," WJAR-TV. YouTube: https://youtu.be/RRmRd-bCvPg.

"Understanding 9/11: A Television News Archive," archive.org.

"Joseph A. Bevilacqua Dies at 70; Rhode Island Judge Linked to Mob," Associated Press, June 22, 1989.

"Rhode Island Supreme Court Chief Justice Joseph Bevilacqua Resigned," United Press International, May 28, 1986.

"Staff of Providence Journal-Bulletin for Thorough Reporting That Disclosed Pervasive Corruption Within the Rhode Island Court System. The 1994 Pulitzer Prize Winner in Investigative Reporting," Pulitzer.org.

CHAPTER 37

Interview with Gina Russo.

"Months Past Club Fire, a Struggle to Go On," by Lydia Polgreen, *New York Times*, May 4, 2003.

CHAPTER 38

"Special 175th Anniversary Section—Part Two-1950 to 1959-(1954)-103 Perish in Bennington Blast," *Providence Journal*, July 21, 2004.

"Fire and Life Safety Educator—Historic Fires, Injury Prevention, and Community Risk Reduction," by Marsha P. Giesler, Delmar Cengage Learning; 1st ed., August 5, 2010.

"The Worst Fires In US History," World Atlas.

"Devastating Photos of the Deadliest Nightclub Disaster in History," by Laura Martisiute, All That's Interesting, August 15, 2017.

"Deadliest U.S. Nightclub Fire Influences Safety Codes, Burn Care," CBS News, November 28, 2017.

"Wiring Was at Fault in Supper Club Fire Jury Finds in Retrial," Associated Press, July 16, 1985.

"5 Things to Know: Beverly Hills Supper Club Fire," *Dayton Daily News*, May 26, 2017.

"U.S. Civilian Fire Deaths 1977 to 2017," by Erin Duffin, Statista, April 29, 2019.

"MGM Hotel in Las Vegas Is Reopened," by Robert Lindsey, *New York Times*, July 31, 1981.

"25 Years to Life for the Arsonist at Happy Land," by Alessandra Stanley, *New York Times*, September 20, 1991.

"Burn Injury Fact Sheet," American Burn Association.

"The Danger of Criminalizing Construction Accidents," by Brad Gerstman, *Crain's New York Business*, July 20, 2016.

"Boeing 737 Max: What's Happened After the 2 Deadly Crashes," by David Gelles, *New York Times*, October 23, 2019.

"FAA Knew Boeing's 737 MAX Was Risky but Allowed Flights," by Andrew Pasztor and Andrew Tangel, *Wall Street Journal*, December 12, 2019.

"Eve and the Serpent: A Rational Choice to Err," by Sidney Dekker, *Journal of Religion and Health*, 2007.

"Sidney Dekker: Safety with Dignity," website, sidneydekker.com.

"R.I. Nightclub Blaze Kills at Least 96," Associated Press and FoxNews.com, February 22, 2003.

Interview with West Warwick police chief Peter Brousseau.

Interview with Attorney General Patrick Lynch.

"Rhode Island Nightclub Fire," Computational Modeling of Nonadaptive Crowd Behaviors for Egress Analysis, 2004–2005 and 2005–2006, CIFE Seed Project Civil and Environmental Engineering, Stanford University, Principal Investigators: Professor Kincho H. Law, Professor Jean-Claude Latombe, and Dr. Ken Dauber. Research Students: Xiaoshan Pan, Peng Gao.

"In California, Fires So Fast Hesitation Proved Lethal," by Thomas Fuller and Richard Pérez-Peña, *New York Times*, October 13, 2017.

CHAPTER 39

"The Station Fire: One Year Later—Facing Government Apathy, the Survivors of the Rhode Island Club Disaster Struggle to Regain Their Lives," by Peter Wilkinson, *Rolling Stone*, March 4, 2004.

"Months Past Club Fire, a Struggle to Go On," by Lydia Polgreen, *New York Times*, May 4, 2003.

"6 Firefighters Killed in Worcester Fire 18 Years Ago Remembered," by Jessica Michalski, *Western Mass News*, WGGB/WSHM, December 3, 2017.

"Federal Search and Rescue Aid Approved for Worcester Fire," Federal Emergency Management Agency press release 3148-01, December 6, 1999.

"Lincoln Chafee May Be Hillary's Biggest Problem," by Peter Beinart, *The Atlantic*, June 4, 2015.

Interview with Phil Barr.

"About Station Family Fund," causes.com.

Interview with Jonathan Bell.

"5 Years After a Nightclub Fire, Survivors Struggle to Remake Their Lives," by Abby Goodnough, *New York Times*, February 17, 2008.

Interview with Todd King.

"Fundraising for Boston Victims Tops $26 Million," by Melanie Hicken, CNN, April 25, 2013.

"Great White Court Docs: Part II: The Declaration of Obi Steinman," Classic Rock Revisited website.

"Band in Horrific Nightclub Fire Kicks Off Tour in Sterling," The Denver Channel.

"Station Fund to Focus Now on Long-Term Needs," *Providence Journal*, September 30, 2004.

"The Station Nightclub Disaster-Station Fire Survivors Launch Fund to Fill Gap in Relief Efforts," by Jennifer Levitz, *Providence Journal*, May 12, 2003.

"Great White Keeps Going, Five Years After Deadly Inferno," by Erick Tucker, *Orange County Register*, February 20, 2008.

"Great White Alters Benefit Tour Dates," by Randy Lewis, *Los Angeles Times*, July 3, 2003.

"Great White Singer Loses Lawsuit Against Former Manager," Blabbermouth.net, June 15, 2005.

CHAPTER 40

Interview with Barry Warner.

"Rhode Island Nightclub Trial Told There Was No Warning About Foam's Dangers," by Eric Tucker, *Insurance Journal*, November 9, 2005.

Grand jury testimony of Aram DerManouelian, president of American Foam, June 4, 2003.

Grand jury testimony of Barry Warner, June 4, 2003.

"The Station Nightclub Disaster—Complaint Prompted Installation," by Tom Mooney and Paul Edward Parker, *Providence Journal*, March 1, 2003.

Interviews with Jeffrey Derderian and Michael Derderian.

State v. Biechele, K1-03-653a (r.I.super. 2005), Case No. K1-03-653A (Sup. Ct. R.I. 2005) Superior Court of Rhode Island, filed December 5, 2005.

"Lynch: No Station Evidence Concealed," by Scott MacKay, *Providence Journal*, November 22, 2005.

Email from prosecutor William Ferland.

Summary of Supreme Court of Rhode Island ruling 1998: Rhode Island joins a minority of states and federal courts in adhering to the traditional view of grand juries, which does not require the prosecutor to present exculpatory evidence to the grand jury. Sara Sun Beale et al., *Grand Jury Law and Practice* 4:17, at 4-84 (2d ed. 2002).

CHAPTER 41

Interview with Phil Barr.

CHAPTER 42

Interview with Gina Russo.

Diary excerpts from *From the Ashes, Surviving the Station Nightclub Fire*, by Gina Russo and Paul Lonardo, Infinity Publishing, 2012.

CHAPTER 43

"Grand Jury Probes Deadly Club Fire," United Press International, February 26, 2003.

Grand jury testimony of Eric Powers, February 2003.

"Flash Pots," June 18, 2012, video. YouTube: https://youtu.be/HOtt5_zEKdw.

Grand jury testimony of Keith Azverde, May 7 2003, page 10.

Grand jury testimony of Thomas Phelps, July 14, 2003.

Grand jury testimony of Frank Davidson, April 22, 2003.

Interviews with Brian Loftus and Dave Fravala.

Grand jury testimony of Scott Vieira, March 26, 2003.

CHAPTER 44

Interview with Phil Barr.

CHAPTER 45

Interview with Joel Rawson.

"412 People Inside Club on Night of Station Fire: A Journal Investigation Puts the Number of People Inside at the Time of the Fire Above the Governor's Estimate and Above the Limits Set by the West Warwick Fire Department," by Paul Edward Parker, *Providence Journal*, September 21, 2003.

Video by Brian Butler, WPRI-TV, February 20, 2003.

Contract for Great White concert, Tapestry Artists.

Written statement of Jeffrey Derderian, submitted to police, February 21, 2003.

Grand jury testimony of Anthony Bettencourt, June 9, 2003.

From the Ashes, Surviving the Station Nightclub Fire, by Gina Russo and Paul Lonardo, Infinity Publishing, 2012, page 27.

"The Station Nightclub Disaster—The Station's Manager Stunned by 'Witch-hunt,'" by Paul Edward Parker, *Providence Journal*, March 1, 2003.

"The Station Nightclub Disaster—Stage manager: Pyrotechnics Not Unusual at Club," by Paul Edward Parker and Liz Anderson, *Providence Journal*, February 26, 2003.

Interviews with several longtime club patrons.

"The Station Nightclub Disaster—TV Newsman, Club Owner, Racked by Sobs," by Michael Corkery, *Providence Journal*, February 23, 2003.

Interview with Donald Carcieri.

Interview with Mark Arsenault.

Complete list of those the *Journal* directly interviewed, versus information from other sources, via the Internet Archive, https://web.archive.org/web /20071206151902/http://www.projo.com:80/extra/2003/stationfire/list/20071203 _listof462.htm.

"Jury Testimony in Club Fire to Be Public," by Eric Tucker, Associated Press, Thursday, December 21, 2006.

Grand jury testimony of Dennis [*sic*] Larocque, June 25, 2003.

"For Many Station Survivors and Relatives of Dead, Fire Inspector Larocque Culpable for

Not Spotting Flammable Insulation," by Tom Mooney, *Providence Journal*, February 19, 2013.

Interviews with Michael Derderian and Jeffrey Derderian.

"Rhode Island Nightclub Fire," Computational Modeling of Nonadaptive Crowd Behaviors for Egress Analysis, 2004–2005 and 2005–2006, CIFE Seed Project Civil and Environmental Engineering, Stanford University, Principal Investigators: Professor Kincho H. Law, Professor Jean-Claude Latombe, and Dr. Ken Dauber. Research Students: Xiaoshan Pan, Peng Gao.

"The Station Fire: Timeline of a Tragedy," by Paul Edward Parker, *Providence Journal*, February 6, 2013.

Interview with Max Wistow.

Interviews with Brian Loftus and Dave Fravala.

Interview with Evan Clabots.

"Tally of Patrons at Station Night of Fire Climbs by 3 to 430," *Providence Journal*, October 5, 2003.

"The Station—February 20, 2003—Inside the Fire," *Providence Journal*, February 20, 2004.

"Tally of a Tragedy: 462 Were in The Station on Night of Fire," by Paul Edward Parker, *Providence Journal*, December 3, 2007.

Interview with Greg Best.

Confirmed by police investigation of October 22, 2003—"Stephens, Robert" document in Witnesses (2) file of 4th document release.

"West Warwick Station Fire Part 1," video shot by Greg Best, February 20, 2003. YouTube: https://youtu.be/TwdEXZmK9lk.

Erroneous reporting of Bob Stephens being "missing" and later "found" is not included in the *Providence Journal*'s digital archives. The incident was confirmed by accessing microfilm copies of the newspaper, which are essentially photos of the printed paper that cannot be easily altered.

"Survivors Shine Lights to Remember Station Nightclub Fire Victims," by Sarah Doiron, WPRI-TV, February 21, 2018.

Online forum examples: FindaDeath.com, The Death Hag Forum.

"The Station Nightclub Disaster—Station Documents Revealed—Fire Inspector Says He Focused on Illegal Door, Not on Foam," by Paul Edward Parker, Tracy Breton, and Edward Fitzpatrick, *Providence Journal*, November 30, 2006.

"Great White Fined for Fire," by Josh Grossberg, E-News online, August 21, 2003.

"The Station Nightclub Disaster-U.S. fines Derderians, band on safety issues," by Lynn Arditi, *Providence Journal*, August 21, 2003.

Report by National Institute of Standards and Technology (NIST) and National Construction Safety Team (NCST) Act, June 30, 2005, pages 157–158.

CHAPTER 46

"Owners, Tour Manager Indicted in R.I. Club Fire; 2 Counts for Each of 100 Deaths," by Stephen Kurkjian and Jonathan Saltzman, *Boston Globe*, December 10, 2003.

Interviews with Gina Russo, Patrick Lynch, and Jonathan Bell.

"The Station Fire: Timeline of a Tragedy," by Paul Edward Parker, *Providence Journal*, February 6, 2013.

"Music Tribute to Lost Love Will Seed Legacy to Pupils," by Jessica Heslam, *Boston Herald*, December 7, 2004.

"Up in Flames," *60 Minutes II*, correspondent Scott Pelley, producers Janet Klein, Paul Gallagher, and Shawn Efran, March 2003.

"The Station Nightclub Fire," National Fire Protection Association.

"The Station Nightclub Disaster—Not Enough, Families Say," by Tom Mooney, *Providence Journal*, December 10, 2003.

CHAPTER 47

Interviews with Michael Derderian and Jeffrey Derderian.

Author's institutional knowledge of the Rhode Island news market from his work there as a news executive from 1988 to 1996.

Nielsen Ratings/Historic/Network Television by Season/2000s, TVIV.org.

CSI: Miami, "Tinder Box," original airdate May 5, 2003, CSIFiles.com.

"'CSI' Episode Too Hot for R.I.," by Zap2, *Chicago Tribune*, May 5, 2003.

"Meet the Derderians—Small-Business Men Aren't All Good Guys," by James Medoff, *Providence Journal*, May 2, 2003.

"Getting Out Alive," WHDH-TV, February 18, 2001.

"TV Journalist Who Owned Club a Familiar Face in R.I.," by Mike Dorning, *Chicago Tribune*, February 24, 2003.

"The Station Nightclub Disaster—Nightclub Had No Workers' Comp, Records Show," by Neil Downing, *Providence Journal*, February 28, 2003.

"Court Records Show Club Was Caught Up in Contentious Divorce," by Jennifer Peter, Associated Press, February 27, 2003.

Letter of June 9, 2000, from Michael Derderian to American Foam Corp, obtained from legal records.

Interview with Barry Warner.

"WPRI Reporter's Link to Club Stirs Ethical Questions," by Mark Jurkowitz, *Boston Globe*, February 14, 2013.

"Maybe It's Not So Obvious," by Deborah Potter, *American Journalism Review*, June 2003.

Interview with Brian Butler.

"The Fire After," by Lynne Duke, *Washington Post*, March 8, 2003.

"Where Lightning Struck: 10 Best Acts of the Year in R.I.," by Vaughn Watson, *Providence Journal*, December 26, 2002.

"The Station Nightclub Disaster: Workers' Comp Scofflaws Now Paying the Price," by Lynn Arditi, *Providence Journal*, May 19, 2003.

"Campaigns Didn't Insure Their Workers," by Lynn Arditi, *Providence Journal*, May 24, 2003.

"Events Since the Feb. 20 Blaze at The Station Nightclub," Associated Press, December 10, 2003.

"VH1 to Air 'Aftermath: The Station Fire Five Years Later,'" Blabbermouth.net, February 15, 2008.

Interview request letter from NBC News to Derderians, 2003.

Interview with Matt Lauer.

Interview with Todd King.

"'Aftermath' Does More Than Revisit a Tragedy," by Joanna Weiss, *Boston Globe*, March 22, 2008.

"5 Years After a Nightclub Fire, Survivors Struggle to Remake Their Lives," by Abby Goodnough, *New York Times*, February 17, 2008.

"How Matt Lauer Helped Book Bon Jovi, Springsteen, Aerosmith for Friday's Hurricane Sandy Telethon," by Andrew Hampp, *Billboard*, November 2, 2012.

"Hurricane Sandy Telethon Raises Nearly $23 Million," by Robyn Ross, *TV Guide*, November 4, 2012.

"Matt Lauer Offers Apology (With a Caveat)," by Michael M. Grynbaum, *New York Times*, November 30, 2017.

CHAPTER 48

Interview with Phil Barr.

"Bates Swimmer Phil Barr, Survivor of the Station Fire, Is Named NCAA Sportsmanship Award Winner," Bates Athletics website, August 5, 2005.

CHAPTER 49

Interviews with Joel Rawson and Mark Arsenault.

Email correspondence with Tom Heslin.

Official entry form from 2004 confirms *Journal* could have entered same coverage in two categories.

"2004 Pulitzer Prizes Journalism," Pulitzer.org.

"The Pulitzers That Got Away," by Roy J. Harris Jr., Poynter Institute, April 6, 2004.

CHAPTER 50

Interview with Gina Russo.

Details confirmed by event program, provided by Spaulding Hospital.

From the Ashes, Surviving the Station Nightclub Fire, by Gina Russo and Paul Lonardo, Infinity Publishing, 2012.

"Mother Admits She Removed Great White Guitarist's Crosses from The Station Site," Blabbermouth.net, September 17, 2003.

Interview with Dan Winston.

"Exter in Serious Condition With Fractured Skull," by Jim Connelly, USCHO, March 7, 2003.

"An NFL All Pro Recovers from a Stroke to Get Back on the Field," Spauldingrehab.org.

"From Super Bowl to Stroke—and Back Again Strokes Usually Happen to Old Men—Not Young Guys, Like NFL Star Tedy Bruschi," by Maddie Meyer and Tedy Bruschi, *Men's Health*, June 10, 2014.

CHAPTER 51

"Dan Biechele Speaks Pre-Sentencing Statement Great White Tour Manager Station Nightclub Fire RI," WJAR-TV, May 10, 2006. YouTube: https://youtu.be/kVvm1qUOh-Y.

"Manager Sentenced for Rhode Island Nightclub Fire," by Pam Belluck and Maria Newmanway, *New York Times*, May 10, 2006.

Documents obtained by the Derderian defense team.

Author's institutional knowledge of local government and news media, due to work as journalist and news executive in the market from 1988 to 1996.

State v. Biechele, K1-03-653a (r.I.super. 2005), Case No. K1-03-653A (Sup. Ct. R.I. 2005) Superior Court of Rhode Island, filed December 5, 2005.

"Station fire figure seeks no jail time," by Paul Edward Parker, Tracy Breton and Steve Peoples, *Providence Journal*, May 5, 2006.

Daniel Biechele interview with prosecutors, March 3, 2003.

"The Station's manager stunned by 'witch-hunt,'" by Paul Edward Parker, *Providence Journal*, March 3, 2003.

Daniel Biechele handwritten statement to the West Warwick Police Department, February 21, 2003, 7:13 a.m.

"Daniel Biechele Sentencing Great White Tour Manager RI Station Nightclub Fire," WJAR-TV, May 10, 2006. YouTube: https://youtu.be/7FRf6-PU66g.

"Fury, Tears and 4-Year Term in Deadly Blaze," by Elizabeth Mehren, May 11, 2006.

CHAPTER 52

Interview with Phil Barr.

Videotape of St. Louis ceremony of National Sportsmanship Awards by the Citizenship Through Sports Alliance, June 10, 2006.

Past Musial Award Recipients, 1999–2006, musialawards.com.

CHAPTER 53

Interviews with Michael Derderian, Kathleen Hagerty, and Patrick Lynch.

Email from prosecutor William Ferland confirmed details of mock trial by attorney general's office.

Grand jury testimony of Scott Vieira, March 26, 2003, page 92.

Grand jury testimony of John Arpin, April 24, 2003, pages 16, 60.

"The Station Nightclub Disaster—A Day the Heavens Cried—Fire Death Toll Climbs to 98," by Paul Edward Parker, *Providence Journal*, March 3, 2003.

"Club Fire Claims 98th Victim," United Press International, March 3, 2003.

"R.I. Club Fire Probe Resumes," United Press International, March 4, 2003.

Report of Howard Varinsky, prepared for Derderian defense.

Image of cardboard with Ferland handwriting of Derderian plea bargain deal.

CHAPTER 54

Interviews with Michael Derderian, Jeffrey Derderian, and Kathleen Hagerty.

"The Guilt Mill" by David Krajicek, *Crime Report*.

"Plea Bargaining as Contract," by R. E. Scott and W. J. Stuntz, *Yale Law Journal*, 1992.

"Go to Trial: Crash the Justice System," by Michelle Alexander, March 10, 2012.

United States incarceration rate: 716 per 100,000 residents in 2013. Roy Walmsley, World Prison Population List (tenth edition), International Centre for Prison Studies, November 21, 2013.

The Sentencing Project, sentencingproject.org.

"Trump Will Not Apologize for Calling for Death Penalty Over Central Park Five," by Jan Ransom, *New York Times*, June 18, 2019.

Interview with West Warwick police chief Peter Brousseau.

Interview with Attorney General Patrick Lynch.

"'Killer' Free After Another Confesses—Convict Whose Only Crime Was Adultery Served Six Years," *Lawrence Journal-World*, November 23, 2002.

Jeffrey Scott Hornoff, National Registry of Exonerations, University of California Irvine Newkirk Center for Science & Technology, University of Michigan Law School & Michigan State University College of Law, June 2012.

"Well-known R.I. Prosecutor Randall White Closes His Last Case," by Katie Mulvaney, *Providence Journal*, December 22, 2014.

CHAPTER 55

Interviews with Michael Derderian, Jeffrey Derderian, Linda Derderian, and Kristina Derderian.

Site visit to Dunkin' Donuts shop, place of Derderian meeting on September 19, 2006.

"Rhode Island College—'Aspire to Be Good People,'" by Jennifer Jordan, *Providence Journal*, May 22, 2005.

"The Station Nightclub Fire," National Fire Protection Association.

Documents from the Derderian defense team.

Report of Howard Varinsky, prepared for Derderian defense.

Mock trials confirmed by prosecutor Ferland and defense attorney Hagerty.

"The Station Nightclub Disaster—Derderians Will Plead; Station Fire Trial Ends—One Brother Gets Jail, The Other Probation," by Tracy Breton and Paul Edward Parker, *Providence Journal*, September 21, 2006.

CHAPTER 56

Interviews with Michael Derderian, Jeffrey Derderian, Linda Derderian, Kristina Derderian, and Kathleen Hagerty.

"The Station Nightclub Disaster-'I Wanted to See a Trial'—Survey Finds Most Disagree with Plea Deal," by Paul Edward Parker, *Providence Journal*, September 29, 2006.

"Plea Deal in R.I. Nightclub Fire Angers Victims' Families," Associated Press, Thursday, September 21, 2006.

"Victims' Families Outraged at Pleas in Deadly Nightclub Fire," Associated Press, September 21, 2006.

"Attorney General Says He Opposes R.I. Nightclub Fire Plea Deal," Associated Press, September 22, 2006.

"Sentencing in Deadly Nightclub Fire Only Adds to Anguish of Victims and Kin," by Pam Belluck, *New York Times*, September 30, 2006.

Susan Rezendes victim impact statement. WPRI-TV, September 29, 2006. YouTube: https://youtu.be/wfnEVIgC4ho.

Diane Mattera victim impact statement. WPRI-TV, September 29, 2006. YouTube: https://youtu.be/G7yIUYx9TLE.

Jay McLaughlin victim impact statement. WPRI-TV, September 29, 2006. YouTube: https://youtu.be/ucJXy1p5JIU.

Jody King victim impact statement. WPRI-TV, September 29, 2006. YouTube: https://youtu.be/GBQkHI7dtH0.

"5 Years After a Nightclub Fire, Survivors Struggle to Remake Their Lives," by Abby Goodnough, *New York Times*, February 17, 2008.

Gina Russo victim impact statement. WPRI-TV, September 29, 2006. YouTube: https://youtu.be/bhKYf2TYmmo.

"Sentencing Statements RI Station Nightclub Fire Michael and Jeffrey Derderian, Owners," WJAR-TV, September 29, 2006. YouTube: https://youtu.be/-sZdUa7_jtI.

"Sentencing of Club Owners Station Nightclub Fire Rhode Island," WJAR-TV, September 29, 2006. YouTube: https://youtu.be/vxGgNwLue80.

CHAPTER 57

Interview with Max Wistow.

"Station Fire-Motion Filed to Destroy Fire Evidence," by Tracy Breton, *Providence Journal*, July 31, 2010.

"Hurricane of '38 Wrought Unparalleled Destruction, Death on Unprepared R.I.," by Thomas J. Morgan, *Providence Journal*, September 20, 2013.

"Station nightclub Disaster—Settlement Marks Final Chapter in Fire Tragedy," by Tracy Breton, *Providence Journal*, May 19, 2010.

"The Station Nightclub Disaster—Derderians Make Settlement Offer," by Tracy Breton, *Providence Journal*, September 4, 2008.

"Oprah Accused of Whipping Up Anti-Beef 'Lynch Mob,'" CNN.com, January 21, 1998.

"Tentative Settlement Is Reached with TV Station in Fatal Nightclub Fire," Associated Press, February 3, 2008.

Report by National Institute of Standards and Technology (NIST) and National Construction Safety Team (NCST) Act, June 30, 2005.

Videotape by Brian Butler, WPRI-TV, February 20, 2003.

Interview with Brian Butler.

Grand jury testimony of Brian Butler, June 9, 2003, pages 26–29.

CHAPTER 58

Interviews with Michael Derderian and Kathleen Hagerty.

"Bereaved Families Receive Letters from Man Convicted in Nightclub Inferno," Associated Press, June 3, 2006.

Email from J. R. Ventura, Chief of Information & Public Relations Officer for the State of Rhode Island Department of Corrections.

CHAPTER 59

"The Station Nightclub Disaster—Videos, Testimony Offer Detailed Look at Tragedy," by Paul Edward Parker and Mark Arsenault, *Providence Journal*, February 2, 2007.

"More Evidence Due from Station Probe," by Paul Edward Parker, *Providence Journal*, October 13, 2007.

Documents from the Derderian defense team.

"Station Nightclub Disaster—Settlement Marks Final Chapter in Fire Tragedy," by Tracy Breton, *Providence Journal*, May 19, 2010.

"The Station Disaster—Fate of Secret Transcripts Before Judge," by Paul Edward Parker, *Providence Journal*, December 13, 2006.

"The Station Nightclub Disaster—Fire Marshal Shielded—Grand Jurors Told R.I. Law Makes Civil Officials Immune From Liability," by Tracy Breton, *Providence Journal*, February 2, 2007.

Notes from defense attorney and former state prosecutor Kathleen M. Hagerty.

"Station Nightclub Fire: How Attorney General Patrick Lynch Shielded the Guiltiest Party," by Monique Chartier, Anchor Rising, February 19, 2009.

Great White tour manager Daniel Biechele interview with prosecutors, March 3, 2003, page 71, confirmed that Russell was involved with the planning of fireworks at shows and had an igniter to set off additional fireworks at the end of the show.

"Patrick Lynch Leaves Race for Rhode Island Governor," Associated Press, February 27, 2014.

Interview with Patrick Lynch.

Report by National Institute of Standards and Technology (NIST) and National Construction Safety Team (NCST) Act, June 30, 2005.

Interview with Bureau of Alcohol, Tobacco, Firearms and Explosives expert.

Interview with Joel Rawson.

"Rawson's Rule: Write, Fly, Write Some More," by Mark Patinkin, *Providence Journal*, May 4, 2008.

CHAPTER 60

Interviews with Michael Derderian, Jeffrey Derderian, Max Wistow, and Brian Butler.

Videotape by Brian Butler, WPRI-TV 12, February 20, 2003.

Killer Show: The Station Nightclub Fire, America's Deadliest Rock Concert, by John Barylick, ForeEdge, 2015.

Grand jury testimony of Brian Butler, June 9, 2003.

"Station Nightclub Disaster—Settlement Marks Final Chapter in Fire Tragedy," by Tracy Breton, *Providence Journal*, May 19, 2010.

"U.S. Foam Makers Settle in Deadly Rhode Island Fire," Reuters, May 12, 2008.

"Anheuser-Busch, Beer Co. to Pay $21M in Club Fire," by Eric Tucker, *Kansas City Star*, May 23, 2008.

"New Settlement in 2003 Nightclub Fire," by Katie Zezima, *New York Times*, February 14, 2008.

"R.I., Town Reach $20 Million Deal in Club Fire—Money Will Be Distributed to Families of the 100 Killed in 2003 Nightclub Fire," Associated Press, August 8, 2008.

"Questions Still Linger Over Fire Inspector's Role," by Michael Rezendes, *Boston Globe*, February 17, 2013.

"Foam Company Offers $6.3 Million to R.I. Nightclub Fire Families," *Insurance Journal*, June 30, 2008.

Supreme Court of Rhode Island. IN RE: Estate of Aram DerManouelian, No. 2011–195–Appeal. Decided: June 29, 2012.

Records of Derderian defense team.

"Years in Litigation, Millions in Settlement but Never a Trial," by Tracy Breton, *Providence Journal*, February 12, 2013.

Interviews with Brian Loftus and Dave Fravala.

"12 Years Later: Unanswered Questions Remain About Station Fire," by Patrick Sargent, GoLocalProv, February 20, 2015.

Interview with Patrick Lynch.

CHAPTER 61

Firsthand observations, recording, and photographs at memorial dedication.

Interviews with Gina Russo and Jody King.

"Owner of Site of Tragic Station Nightclub Fire That Killed 100 People Donates Land for a Permanent Memorial," Associated Press, September 28, 2012.

Videotape of Brian Butler, WPRI-TV, February 20, 2003.

"Station Memorial Rejects Money from Great White Lead Singer," by Dee DeQuattro, WLNE-TV, January 18, 2013.

The Guest List, documentary website, theguestlistfilm.com.

Interview with David Bellino.

Conversation with Jack Russell.

Jack Russell bankruptcy court records.

Attended Jack Russell performance, "Frontiers Rock: LA Guns, Warrant, Jack Russell's Great White, Riverdogs," The Canyon Agoura Hills, Agoura Hills, CA, Saturday, December 2, 2017.

Interview with Joe Kinan.

"The Station Fire—After Prison, Biechele Rebuilding Life in Fla.," by Karen Lee Ziner, *Providence Journal*, February 12, 2013.

Interview with Brian Butler.

Interview with Phil Barr.

Interviews with Michael Derderian, Jeffrey Derderian, and Linda Derderian.

Notes from defense attorney Kathleen M. Hagerty.

Interview, email, and voicemail with Tracy Breton.

INDEX